Reader's Guide
to
SAMUEL BECKETT

Reader's Guide
to
SAMUEL BECKETT

Dr. Matt Bacak

CENTRUM PRESS
NEW DELHI-110002 (INDIA)

CENTRUM PRESS
H.O.: 4360/4, Ansari Road, Daryaganj,
New Delhi-110 002 (India)
Ph.: 23278000, 23261597

B.O.: No. 1015, Ist Main Road, BSK IIIrd Stage
IIIrd Phase, IIIrd Block,
Bangalore - 560 085 (India)
Tel.: 080-41723429
Visit us at: www.centrumpress.com

Reader's Guide to Samuel Beckett

First Edition, 2009

ISBN 978-93-80106-81-6

PRINTED IN INDIA

Printed at Balaji Offset, Delhi.

Contents

Preface

Samuel Beckett, born on Good Friday, April 13, 1906, near Dublin, Ireland was raised in a middle class, Protestant home, the son of a quantity surveyor and a nurse, he was sent off at the age of 14 to attend the same school which Oscar Wilde had attended. Looking back on his childhood, he once remarked, "I had little talent for happiness." Beckett was consistent in his loneliness. The unhappy boy soon grew into an unhappy young man, often so depressed that he stayed in bed until mid afternoon. He was difficult to engage in any lengthy conversation—it took hours and lots of drinks to warm him up—but the women could not resist him.

The lonely young poet, however, would not allow anyone to penetrate his solitude. He once remarked, after rejecting advances from James Joyce's daughter, that he was dead and had no feelings that were human. In 1928, Samuel Beckett moved to Paris, and the city quickly won his heart. Shortly after he arrived, a mutual friend introduced him to James Joyce, and Beckett quickly became an apostle of the older writer. At the age of 23, he wrote an essay in defense of Joyce's magnum opus against the public's lazy demand for easy comprehensibility.

A year later, he won his first literary prize—10 pounds for a poem entitled "Whoroscope" which dealt with the philosopher Descartes meditating on the subject of time and the transiency of life. After writing a study of Proust, however, Beckett came to the conclusion that habit and routine were the "cancer of time", so he gave up his post at Trinity College and set out on a nomadic journey across Europe. Beckett made his way through Ireland, France, England, and Germany, all the while writing poems and stories and doing odd jobs to get by. In the course of his journies, he no doubt came into contact with many tramps and wanderers, and these aquaintances would later translate into some of his finest characters.

Whenever he happened to pass through Paris, he would call on Joyce, and they would have long visits, although it was rumored that they mostly sit in silence, both suffused with sadness. Beckett finally settled down in Paris in 1937. Shortly thereafter, he was stabbed in the street by a man who had approached him asking for money. He would learn later, in the hospital, that he had a perforated lung. After his recovery, he went to visit his assailant in prison. When asked why he had attacked Beckett, the prisoner replied "Je ne sais pas, Monsieur", a phrase hauntingly reminiscent of some of the lost and confused souls that would populate the writer's later works.

Beckett secured his position as a master dramatist on April 3, 1957 when his second masterpiece, *Endgame,* premiered (in French) at the Royal Court Theatre in London. Although English was his native language, all of Beckett's major works were originally written in French—a curious phenomenon since Beckett's mother tongue was the accepted international language of the twentieth century. Apparently, however, he wanted the discipline and economy of expression that an acquired language would force upon on him. Beckett was the first of the absurdists to win international fame. His works have been translated into over twenty languages. In 1969 he was awarded the Nobel Prize for Literature. He continued to write until his death in 1989, but the task grew more and more difficult with each work until, in the end, he said that each word seemed to him "an unnecessary stain on silence and nothingness."

Chapter 1

Introduction

"He wanders among misty bogs turned surreal, he talks to the wee folk of his own bad dreams, he files reports on introspected black visions with a kind of blarney eloquence. Like an actress cradling a doll for her stage baby, his language keens and croons about tales that are not quite there." Melvin Maddocks is talking about Samuel Beckett, a literary legend of the twentieth century.

"It is neither night nor morning. A man must find himself without the support of groups, or labels, or slogans," writes R. D. Smith. And Beckett, by removing his characters from nearly all recognizable contexts, Smith continues, is "engaged in finding or saving" himself. Martin Esslin writes: "What is the essence of the experience of being? asks Beckett. And so he begins to strip away the inessentials. What is the meaning of the phrase 'I am myself'? he asks . . . and is then compelled to try to distinguish between the merely accidental characteristics that make up an individual and the essence of his self." A *Time* reviewer noted: "Some chronicle men on their way up; others tackle men on their way down.

Samuel Beckett stalks after men on their way out." Such is the tone of most discussions of Beckett's work. But no single reviewer could communicate the unique power of Beckett's writing, his use of "a language in which the emptiness of conventional speech is charged with new emotion." "While [his] lesser colleagues work in rhetoric," writes Smith, Beckett produces poetry.

"Well," says Harold Pinter, "I'll buy his goods, hook, line, and sinker, because he leaves no stone unturned and no maggot lonely. He brings forth a body of beauty. His work is beautiful." Leo Bersani, somewhat less politely, writes: "I know of no writer who has come closer than Beckett in his novels to translating the rhythms of defecation into sentence structure." Along with the work of Eugene Ionesco, Jean Genet, and Harold Pinter, Beckett's stark plays are said to compose the "Theatre of the Absurd." But to so label Beckett's work is to disqualify one of his own first premises—that, since no human activity has any intrinsic meaning, it is pointless to ascribe traditional or categorical significance to the existence of an object or the performance of a deed.

George Wellwarth discusses Beckett's concept of a protean reality: "What all these things—the sameness of human beings and their actions, the vanity of human ambition, the uselessness of thought—amount to is a pessimism deeper than any that has ever been put into words before. Throughout Beckett's work we can find evidence of his conviction that everything is hopeless, meaningless, purposeless, and, above all, agonizing to endure.

Beckett's people are leveled off and merged into each other by being all more or less physically disabled—as if this were really the common condition on earth. . . . Beckett is a prophet of negation and sterility. He holds out no hope to humanity, only a picture of unrelieved blackness; and those who profess to see in Beckett signs of a Christian approach or signs of compassion are simply refusing to see what is there." Perhaps Beckett himself stated his dilemma most succinctly in *L'Innommable:* "Dans ma vie, puisqu'il faut l'appeler ainsi, il y eut trois choses, l'impossibilite de parler, l'impossibilite de me taire, et la solitude." ("One must speak; man cannot possibly communicate with his fellows, but the alternative—silence—is irreconcilable with human existence.")

Smith and Esslin, however, insist that Beckett did not intend to express unqualified despair, but that, by stripping significance from the world, he showed us the one way to achieve redemption (although any salvation, according to Beckett's essentially deterministic philosophy, is necessarily only a respite). Smith writes: "Beckett's characters remain at their darkest moments anguished human beings: Beckett, when intellectually at his most pitiless, feels and suffers with them." Esslin states that Beckett's message "is anything but gloomy or despairing." He writes: "On the contrary: the starkness of [his] reminders of the evanescence of life and the certainty of death, [his] uncompromising rejection of any easy solution or cheap illusion of comfort ultimately has a liberating effect; such is the nature of man that in the very act of facing up to the reality of his condition his dignity is enhanced; we are only defeated by things by which we are taken unawares; what we know and have faced up to we can master."

Alec Reid also believes that Beckett's message must be interpreted optimistically. "Beckett's world," he writes, "is one of darkness, of disembodied voices, of ignorance, impotence, and anguish. But even as he insists that he knows nothing, can know nothing, Beckett reminds us of an astronaut, a human surrounded by nothing, walking on nothing.

Our spacemen are no cause for despair; no more are Mr. Beckett's explorations." But then, according to *Time* magazine, "Beckett's champions argue that his threnodies in dusky twilight represent the existential metaphor of the human condition, that the thin but unwavering voices of his forlorn characters speak the ultimate statement of affirmation, if only because the merest attempt at communication is itself affirmation."

But in case the reader of Beckett criticism should come to regard this question as the black and white one of "despair" versus "optimism," Richard N. Coe adds new terms to the argument: "To class Beckett himself as the simple incarnation of 'despair' is a drastic oversimplification. To begin with, the concept of 'despair' implies the existence of a related concept 'hope,' and 'hope' implies a certain predictable continuity in time—which continuity Beckett would seriously question.

'Despair,' with all its inherent moral overtones, is a term which is wholly inadequate to describe Beckett's attitude towards the human condition; nor is this condition, in the most current sense of the definition, 'absurd.' It is literally and logically impossible. And in this central concept of 'impossibility,' his thought has most of its origins—as does also his art."

Although John Gassner was not happy with the scholarly complexity of the critical response to Beckett's work (he wrote: "To a parvenu intelligentsia, it would seem that a work of art exists not for its own sake but only for the possibilities of interpreting it"), some critics believe that Beckett's theater is most meaningful when considered within the context of a recognizable literary tradition.

Kenneth Allsop writes: "His harsh, desolate, denuded style is entirely and unmistakably his own, but his literary 'form,' the stream-of-consciousness device which most young British writers wouldn't dream of using nowadays for fear of being thought quaint, derives from his years [working with] . . . James Joyce. That is only a partial explanation. He is in a monolithic way the last of the Left Bank Mohicans of the Twenties; the others of the *avant-garde* died or deserted or prospered, but Beckett was a loyal expatriate." Esslin, J. D. O'Hara, and John Fletcher prefer to align Beckett with the philosophers. "Although Beckett himself [was] not aware of any such influence," Esslin writes, "his writings might be described as a literary exposition of Sartre's Existentialism."

O'Hara sees his work as exponential to the philosophy of Descartes: "In Beckett's world of post-Cartesian dualism, the mind has no connection to the body, its values worth nothing there, and so it cannot logically concern itself with the body's problems." Fletcher concludes that "whatever the truth of the matter, one thing is certain. Beckett has ranged freely among the writings of the philosophers, where he has found confirmation and justification of the metaphysical obsessions that haunt his work: the gulf set between body and mind, the epistemological incertitude.

His genius has achieved the transmutation of such speculative problems into art." But, according to Coe, one must keep in mind that "Beckett has renounced his claim to erudition. The main theme of his work is impotence, of mind just as much as of body." The problem of analyzing and interpreting Beckett's work, on the other hand, has been met with a somewhat surprising amount of scholarship and erudition. But David Hesla's criticism, in which the novels are considered as the expression of Beckett's personal enigma, is equally effective. Hesla notes that the dilemma which confronts the contemporary writer, according to Beckett, "is constituted . . . by the fact that the writer must take seriously two opposed and apparently irreconcilable claims to his allegiance. On the one hand, he must recognize that the principal fact about modern man's life is that it is a 'mess,' a 'confusion,' a 'chaos.'

On the other hand, the writer, as artist, has an obligation to form. But to admit the 'mess' into art is to jeopardize the very nature of art; for the mess 'appears to be the very opposite of form and therefore destructive of the very thing that art holds itself to be.'" Hesla quotes Beckett as saying: "It only means that there will be a new form; and that this form will be of such a type that it admits the chaos and does not try to say that the chaos is really something else. The form and the chaos remain separate.

The latter is not reduced to the former. That is why the form itself becomes a preoccupation, because it exists as a problem separate from the material it accommodates. To find a form that accommodates the mess, that is the task of the artist now." Hesla notes that with *Watt*, "Beckett [began] a process of removing from his artificial world those tangibles by which the reader usually is able to orient himself in time and space, and those causal relationships amongst the incidents of the plot by which the reader is able to discern the conditions of necessity and probability which—be they never so strained or extraordinary—determine in part the structural coherence and the 'meaning' of the story.

In *Watt* he has found the form which permits 'the mess' to enter art without destroying it. He has developed a literary method—the negative way—which is capable of accommodating chaos without reducing it to form. Furthermore, in developing this method he has developed an instrument of greater precision for the explication of a world-view which was only roughly sketched out in *Murphy*. Beckett's work after *Watt* has, in a certain sense, consisted largely in refining and adapting both the manner and the matter of his new art."

Most critics agree that it was the 1954 English-language publication of *Waiting for Godot* that established Beckett's prominence in the United States. Many, in fact, still consider this play to be his most important work. H. A. Smith calls it "the most comprehensively and profoundly evocative play of the last thirty years," and William R. Mueller and Josephine Jacobsen write: "*Waiting for Godot,* of all of Beckett's dramatic works, expresses most clearly and explicitly the fundamental tension—to wait or not to wait—which is found to a lesser degree in his other writings.

The human predicament described in Beckett's first [major, staged] play is that of man living on the Saturday after the Friday of the crucifixion, and not really knowing if all hope is dead or if the next day will bring the new life which has been promised." Allsop found the play's message less ambiguous.

He writes: " *Godot* is a hymn to extol the moment when the mind swings off its hinges. . . . Beckett is unconcerned with writing requiems for humanity, for he sees life as polluted and pointless: he merely scrawls its obituary, without bitterness or compassion because he cannot really believe it is worth the words he is wasting." Gassner also found the play to be a straightforward pronouncement, but he did not accept it as a prediction of certain doom. "To all this tohu and bohu about the profundity and difficulty of the play," he wrote, "my reply is simply that there is nothing painfully or exhilaratingly ambiguous about *Waiting for Godot* in the first place.

It presents the view that man, the hapless wanderer in the universe, brings his quite wonderful humanity—his human capacity for hope, patience, resilience, and, yes, for love of one's kind, too, as well as his animal nature—to the weird journey of existence. He is lost in the universe and found in his own heart and in the hearts of his fellow men." Bert O. States adds parenthetically: "Convicts and children love it!"

Kenneth Tynan believes that the implications of *Waiting for Godot* are significant not only in themselves, but for all of contemporary theater. He writes: "A special virtue attaches to plays which remind the drama of how much it can do without and still exist. By all known criteria, Beckett's *Waiting for Godot* is a dramatic vacuum. Pity the critic who seeks a chink in its armour, for it is all chink. It has no plot, no climax, no *denouement;* no beginning, no middle, and no end. Unavoidably, it has a situation, and it might be accused of having suspense. . . . *Waiting for Godot* frankly jettisons everything by which we recognise theatre.

It arrives at the custom-house, as it were, with no luggage, no passport, and nothing to declare; yet it gets through, as might a pilgrim from Mars. It does this, I believe, by appealing to a definition of drama much more fundamental than any in the books. A play, it asserts and proves, is basically a means of spending two hours in the dark without being bored. . . . It forced me to re-examine the rules which have hitherto governed the drama; and, having done so, to pronounce them not elastic enough."

Some critics found 1957's *Endgame* to be an even more powerful expression of Beckett's negativism. Gassner wrote: "Nothing happens in *Endgame* and that nothing is what matters. The author's feeling about nothing also matters, not because it is true or right but because it is a strongly formed attitude, a felt and expressed viewpoint. . . . The yardsticks of dialectical materialism and moralism are equally out in appraising the play. Dialectical materialism could only say that *Endgame* is decadent. Moralism and theology would say that the play is sinful, since nothing damns the soul so much as despair of salvation. Neither yardstick could tell us that this hauntingly powerful work of the imagination is art."

Although critics discuss his plays more frequently than his novels, Beckett himself was said to have considered his novels to be his major works. Alec Reid notes: "For Beckett each novel is a journey into the unknown, into an area of utter lawlessness." And a *Times Literary Supplement* reviewer, in his discussion of *Imagination Dead Imagine,* summarizes Beckett's work thus: "[This novel] certainly describes two people in an imaginary situation and it is equally certainly a work of large implications and a desolate, cruel beauty. It might not seem so, however, if it had not been apparent for some time that Mr. Beckett's prose narratives compose a single, long saga of exclusion and heroic relinquishment as well as of the desperate, perhaps unavailing, pursuit of finality." A. I. Leventhal writes: "When Beckett changes to writing his novels in French he leaves behind him much of the humour, grim as it was, in his previous work. He has less interest in making his characters indulge in games to pass the time as in *Waiting for Godot*. They are now concentrating on their *penible* task of dying."

Frank Kermode offers this analysis of the novels: "In Beckett's plays the theatrical demand for communicable rhythms and relatively crude satisfactions has had a beneficent effect. But in the novels he yields progressively to the magnetic pull of the primitive, to the desire to achieve, by various forms of decadence and deformation, some Work that eludes the intellect, avoids the spread nets of habitual meaning. Beckett is often allegorical, but he is allegorical in fitful patches, providing illusive toeholds to any reader scrambling for sense."

Bersani hasn't discovered the toeholds (and laughs behind his hand at those who have), nor does he think he will, if, as he says, he continues to take Beckett "seriously." Bersani writes: "The most interesting fact about Samuel Beckett's novels is that they are, at their best, almost completely unreadable." Bersani, citing Beckett's expressed desire to fail (to be an artist, for Beckett, is to fail), finds his "extreme attempt to render literature autonomous" to be not only "an ironic reminder of the ultimate dependence of literature on life," but also a generally suspicious undertaking.

"The attempt to eliminate 'occasion' from art," he writes, "is in itself an occasion, and insofar as this attempt is a process of what [Ruby] Cohn has called progressive 'retrenchment,' the process rather than the achievement becomes the subject of Beckett's work."

The fact that most of Beckett's important work was originally written in French is far more than coincidentally significant to his stylistic achievement. Coe explains: "Beckett, in the final analysis, is trying to say what cannot be said; he must be constantly on his guard, therefore, never to yield to the temptation of saying what the words would make him say. Only when language is, as it were, defeated, bound hand and foot; only when it is so rigorously disciplined that each word describes exactly and quasiscientifically the precise concept to which it is related and no other, only then, by the progressive elimination of that which precisely is, is there a remote chance for the human mind to divine the ultimate reality which is not.

And this relentless, almost masochistic discipline, which reaches its culmination in *Comment c'est,* Beckett achieves by writing in a language which is not his own—in French." John Barth explains, however, that Beckett's denuded French is yet only another step in his creative process and must not be construed as a total achievement. Barth writes: "Beckett has become virtually mute, musewise, having progressed from marvelously constructed English sentences through terser and terser French ones to the unsyntactical, unpunctuated prose of *Comment c'est* and 'ultimately' to wordless mimes.

One might extrapolate a theoretical course for Beckett: language, after all, consists of silence as well as sound, and the mime is still communication, . . . but by the language of action. But the language of action consists of rest as well as movement, and so in the context of Beckett's progress immobile, silent figures still aren't altogether ultimate. . . . For Beckett [in the 1960s, toward the end of his writing career], to cease to create altogether would be fairly meaningful: his crowning work, his 'last word.' What a convenient corner to paint yourself into!"

In 1967 the Firehouse Theatre of Minneapolis, directed by Marlow Hotchkiss, performed *Act without Words I* and *Act without Words II* simultaneously. Also in 1967, Jack Emery composed and performed an hour-long, one-man programme consisting of "a selection of the desperate reveries and furious tirades of half a dozen of Samuel Beckett's dying heroes," including Malone, Hamm, and the Unnamable. A *Punch* reviewer writes: "Many of the passages are fatiguing to follow in the original novels but so conversational are the rhythms of Beckett's language and so eloquently does Mr. Emery speak them (except when he essays a scream) that the effect in a dark, hushed theatre of this grim gallows humour is electrifying. There is more to life than talking of waiting for death, but Beckett has phrases—'Vent the pent!'—that resound in the mind with the urgency of great poetry." Emery's programme, which premiered at Arts Theatre, London, was also produced in Glasgow, Edinburgh, and Exeter. Two years later, in 1969, Beckett won the Nobel Prize in Literature.

Although unpublished for sixty years, Beckett's first novel, *Dream of Fair to Middling Women,* finally made it into print in the United States in 1993. The author composed the book as a young man of twenty-six during a summer spent in Paris. The protagonist of *Dream* is the adventurous Belacqua, and the story centers on his varied experiences in Dublin and Paris.

Beckett's style here, according to Colm Toibin in the *London Review of Books,* "is a rambling stream of consciousness, full of asides and associations, with a tone of half-seriousness and oblique mockery. . . . The writing is self-conscious: it reads as though the writer wrote it merely to read it himself." Beckett himself described *Dream* as "the chest into which I threw my wild thoughts." And, as J. D. O'Hara comments in the *New York Times Book Review,* "he reused them, often word for word." In the end, George Craig asserts in the *Times Literary Supplement,* "this is Beckett's earliest venture, and it shows. . . . But . . . something important is going on: the search for [his] voice."

Similarly, Beckett's first play, *Eleutheria* (the title means "freedom" in Greek), collected dust in the author's trunk for nearly fifty years before being published in 1995. The dark, three-act comic piece concerns a privacy-obsessed writer who tries in vain to escape from his family and friends, spending most of the play fighting off their efforts to mend what's left of his life. *Eleutheria* was written just prior to *Waiting for Godot,* but it demanded rather complex staging (seventeen characters and two sets, both which are shown simultaneously in the first two acts before one disappears into the orchestra pit in the final act) and so was not produced in the 1950s when *Godot* burst onto the contemporary theatrical scene.

"No one . . . disputes that Beckett did not want *Eleutheria* published," explains Jonathan Kalb in an article for the *Village Voice.* Its publication in 1995 prompted considerable controversy among members of the literary establishment, with opponents appalled at the thought of the author's final request for its suppression—from his deathbed, no less—being ignored. Kalb notes that the play is neither "a hidden masterpiece" nor "a catastrophe," but rather "a fascinating, rare instance of Beckettian excess. . . . At times windy, redundant, even confusing, it will certainly take its proper place as a minor, formative work that is bouyed by eloquent and hilarious passages and the tantalizing seeds of great themes, devices, and characters to come." As Mel Gussow puts it in the *New York Times Book Review,* "*Waiting for Godot* is revolutionary; *Eleutheria* is evolutionary."

Few critics have discussed Beckett's ideas (or the man himself) apart from their manifestation in his work. And Beckett would doubtless have it so. As Robert Wernick writes, "so striking is the personality that emerges from [his] gloomy plays and so striking [was] the occasionally glimpsed, gaunt pterodactylous face of the real-life Samuel Beckett that many people assume[d] the two [were] identical.

A whole folklore of anecdote has grown up around Beckett, in which he appears as a fanatic solitary, brooding eternally . . . on the black mystery of the human race. . . . It is true that he . . . built a wall around his country house, but he denie[d] that he built it, as people contend, to shut out the view. It is true he avoid[ed] all the trappings of the celebrity life, [gave] no interviews, attend[ed] no cultural congresses. But then, why should he [have]?" Alec Reid met Beckett in New York during the making of *Film* and described him as "a close-knit person, all of a piece." Reid says that Beckett "believe[d] that physical movement conveys at least as much as the words. . . . Once the initial reserve . . . evaporated Beckett reveal[ed] a genius for companionship, a remarkable ability to make those around him feel the better for his presence."

Ecole Normale Superieure, Paris, France, lecturer in English, 1928-30; Trinity College, University of Dublin, Dublin, Ireland, lecturer in French, 1930-32 (resigned because "he could not bear the absurdity of teaching to others what he did not know himself"). During the early 1930s he, among others, helped James Joyce, who was then nearly blind, by taking dictation and by copying out parts of *Finnegans Wake.* (Beckett never served as secretary to Joyce as many believe.

A. J. Leventhal, writing for Beckett, stated that "there was never any question of a formal position. . . . It's very hard to kill this story.") From 1932 to 1936 Beckett traveled extensively in England and Europe, residing briefly in London and in several European cities. He settled permanently in Paris in 1937. From about 1940 to 1943, Beckett was involved with the French resistance movement and had to hide from the Germans. He spent these years working as a farmhand near Roussillon, an isolated region in southeast France. From the early 1940s on, Beckett devoted most of his time to writing.

Chapter 2

Acoustic Art in Samuel Beckett's Embers

The Beckett who began to write radio plays in the mid-fifties was no stranger to the medium: in Roussillon, where he lived in hiding from 1942-45, the radio transmitter was *the* crucial information conduit for Resistance groups, and the BBC, which was to commission *All That Fall* (1956) and *Embers* (1959), its main source.

Half a century later, as the *Columbia Encyclopedia* reminds us, radio is still primarily information medium, a conductor of *messages*, whether news flashes, announcements of events, weather reports, and today the ubiquitous "sigalerts" that advise the driver about freeway conditions and traffic accidents even as they are taking place.

All the more reason, then, for the radio artist—and Beckett is surely one of the finest —to turn this information function, this relaying of messages from A to B, inside out. "Communication," writes Michel Serres, "is only possible between two persons used to the same forms, trained to code and decode a meaning by using the same key." But communication is never without disruption: "in spoken languages: stammerings, mispronunciations, regional accents, dysphonias, and cacophonies . . . . In the technical means of communication: background noise, jamming, static, cut-offs, heteresis, various interruptions. If static is accidental, background noise is *essential* to communication".

"To communicate orally" is thus "to lose meaning in noise." Only at the level of mathematical abstraction, when form (e.g., the symbol *x* or the addition sign +) is distinguished from its empirical realizations, is dialogue entirely "successful."

But "to exclude the empirical is to exclude differentiation, the plurality of others that mask the same", and it is those "others"—the interference and noise that everywhere blocks the straightforward A > B model of transmission— that really matter in the communication paradigms that we actually use. "The transmission of communication," writes Serres, "is chronic transformation. . . . the empirical is strictly essential and accidental *noise*".

The notion of "noise" as "the empirical portion of the message" is by no means confined to radio, but we see it heightened in this medium where everything depends upon sound, primarily the sound of the human voice as communicator. Martin Esslin, who worked closely with Beckett on his BBC productions and has written extensively on the radio plays, argues that "radio is an intensely visual medium. . . . Information that reaches [the listener] through other senses is instantly converted into visual terms. And aural experiences, which include the immense richness of language as well as musical and natural sound, are the most effective means of triggering visual images."

This may be true of the more mimetic variants of radio drama—Beckett's first radio play *All That Fall* is a case in point— but what happens when, as Klaus Schoening points out in a discussion of the new acoustic art, words are combined with "nontextual language, nonverbal articulations, quotation, original sound [i.e.,ambient sound], environmental noises, acoustic objects trouvé, musical tones, [and] electronic technology"? What do we visualize then?

Beckett's radio experiments did not, of course, go as far as, say, John Cage's *Roaratorio* (one of Schoening's key exhibits) in undermining the conventional linguistic base, but he was surely aware that if the transmission of information is one pole of the radio experience, soundscape is the other. Indeed, as Don Druker puts it in a discussion of radio, "it is necessary to consider *sound itself* as the raw material for analysis." One must, for that matter, listen to radio more intensively than one does in the theater, where there is always something to *look at* as well.

On the other hand, radio text also differs appreciably from the print media. When reading, one has the luxury of stopping to reconsider this or that point on a previous page, or one skims a given passage and moves ahead. Radio is much more coercively temporal; the sounds succeed each other, and the listener is challenged to take them in, one by one, and construct their relationships. Even when, as is usually the case, the radio piece is heard on tape or compact disc, so that one is free to fast forward and reverse, the listener remains deprived of the visual stimulus taken for granted by the theater goer or television viewer.

Even more important: because radio is essentially an information medium with what appears to be a linear structure, the listener feels compelled to pay close attention with the expectation of "finding out" something. But what does Beckett's radio audience find out? Here the theme of disembodiment put forward in my second epigraph becomes important.

If radio (or the phonograph) has the capacity to bring *voice* into someone else's public or private space, the disembodiment of that voice, Beckett was quite aware, is a signifier of *absence,* of not being there, indeed of "death." Then, too, voice alone— or at least voice between puberty and extreme old age or serious illness— cannot define its owner's stage of life or status as can the visual image of a human body.

As a dramatic medium, radio is at its best when it takes this indeterminacy and absence into account. After *All That Fall,* whose characters are still represented as "real" people in a "real" Irish country setting, Beckett's radio art becomes more abstract and mediumistic, engaging in a dialectic of disclosure and obstacle, information and noise, in which the soundscape — which includes silence— provides conflicting, and hence tantalizing, testimony.

In what follows I want to consider how this dialectic works in what I take to be, in Hugh Kenner's words, "the most original use to which Beckett has put radio, and one is tempted to say as original and moving a use of any to which radio has been put." The play is *Embers*, written for the BBC and first broadcast on 24 June 1959.

"NO SOUND"

Beckett commentators generally speak of *Embers* as a "skullscape" or "soulscape." "The universe which the radio audience is confronted with," declared Clas Zilliacus in the first extended discussion of the piece, "is a totally subjective one: it is one man's world. The interplay between Henry and other characters takes place in Henry's mind" (CL 82). The same point is made by Martin Esslin:

The background—a background of sound, the sea, Henry's boots on the shingle—is still real, but the voices are all internal: Henry's internal monologue as he tries unsuccessfully to conjure up his dead father's presence, and later the voices of his wife and daughter and her instructors, which materialize in his memory.

And in a survey of Beckett's radio and television plays for the recent *Cambridge Companion to Beckett*, Jonathan Kalb remarks that "*Embers* has no surface narrative other than that of a haunted man talking about talking to himself, telling stories that he never finishes, and sometimes experiencing (along with us) the ghostly people and things in his story." Kalb gives the following precis:

Henry, who may or may not be walking by the sea with his daughter Addie nearby, addresses his dead father, who may or may not have committed suicide in the sea. The father fails to respond . . . and Henry tells a story about a man named Bolton (perhaps a father-surrogate) who has called for his doctor Holloway one winter night, for obscure reasons that may have to do with wanting to die. Henry then speaks to a woman, also apparently dead, named Ada, his former companion and mother of Addie, who speaks sympathetically but distractedly back to him.

For most of the remainder of the action Ada and Henry reminisce about old times, some of which are dramatized as auditory flashbacks involving other characters. Henry complains several times of not being able to rid himself of the sound of the sea, and Ada suggests that he consult Holloway about both that and his incessant talking to himself. When Ada no longer answers him, Henry tries unsuccessfully to command the sound effects again, returns briefly to the Bolton story and then ends by seeming to make a note in his diary: 'Nothing all day nothing."

This account of *Embers* as memory play taking place inside Henry's mind is accurate enough in its broad outlines, but it seems to ignore the use of radio as medium, even though Beckett himself, in a much cited statement about his first radio play *All That Fall*, insisted that the distinction between media had to be honored:

> *All That Fall* is a specifically radio play, or rather radio text, for voices, not bodies. I have already refused to have it "staged" and I cannot think of it in such terms. A perfectly straight reading before an audience seems to me just barely legitimate, though even on this score I have my doubts. But I am absolutely opposed to any form of adaptation with a view to its conversion into "theatre." It is no more theatre than *End-Game* is radio and to "act" it is to kill it. Even the reduced visual dimension it will receive from the simplest and most static of readings . . . will be destructive of whatever quality it may have and which depends on the whole thing's *coming out of the dark*.

"To 'act' it is to kill it": "radio text," Beckett here reminds us, is par excellence an art that depends on sound alone and hence cannot be converted to the stage. Furthermore, the sound in question is not just that of the human voice but includes a complex network of nonverbal elements, musical or otherwise. It makes little sense, then, to complain, as does John Pilling, that Beckett should have included the voice of Henry's father, along with Ada's and Addie's voices, in the play:

> The puzzling thing is that Henry's control over voices does not extend to the most crucial figure of all, his father. . . . The failure to incorporate into the physical existence of the play its most important figure is not so much a failure of

conception—though it might have served to link Henry's life to his story of Bolton— as of tact. There seems to be no good reason for the omission.

But there is a very good reason for the omission, which is that, unlike the theater, radio makes it possible to represent characters by means of metonymic sound images: The ghost of Henry's father is indeed "heard" throughout the play: not only when his son acts the role of medium, imitating such parental exhortations as "Are you coming for a dip?", but also in the recurrent "Please! PLEASE!" that Bolton addresses to Holloway, and, most important, in the voice of the sea itself. Indeed, Henry's is not quite an interior monologue like Malone's or the Unnamable's, for it moves easily in and out of the narrator's specific consciousness and depends heavily on the elaborate patterning of phrasal, verbal, and phonemic repetition.

Henry's first halting words in *Embers* are "On," "Stop," and "Down," each one spoken twice, the second time more emphatically, as the exclamation points indicate. The predominant vowel sound is a long open "o" competing with the sound of the sea: [*Sea, still faint, audible throughout what follows whenever pause indicated.]*" The "o" sound now modulates into the longer unit "Who is beside me now?" and after the response "[*Pause.*]

An old man, blind and foolish. [*Pause.*] My father, back from the dead, to be with me. [*Pause.*] As if he hadn't died. [*Pause*]," we hear the words, "No, he doesn't answer me." "No," which will soon become one of the key words in the Bolton narrative ("no, hangings," "no light," "no, standing," "no sound," and then the variant "not a sound," (which will be Henry's final words in the play), is, of course a reversal of the opening "On."

From "On to "No": this is the trajectory of Henry's speech, his Omega (note that both "Bolton" and "Holloway" contain long "o"s as well) in conflict with the Alpha of his wife's name "Ada," and the diminutive of Ada in the child's name "Addie." The narrator Henry, for that matter, whose family name we never know, is so to speak caught phonemically between

Alpha and Omega. When one hears Ada speak lines like "Laugh, Henry do that for me" (E 97), the /e/ and /I/ phonemes stand out as distinct from the other names.

But it is not quite accurate to say, as Pilling does, that Henry has "control" over the voices in the play. For the dominant voice is not Henry's but the voice of the sea. It is that voice that punctuates each of Henry's questions about his father—"Can he hear me? Yes, he must hear me. To answer me No, he doesn't answer me [*Pause*] Just be with me"—and that is presented as a character in its own right in the following strange speech:

That sound you hear is the sea. I say that sound you hear is the sea, we are sitting on the strand. I mention it because the sound is so strange, so unlike the sound of the sea, that if you didn't see what it was you wouldn't know what it was.

The "you" here can be taken to be the dead father, with whom Henry is sitting on the strand. But if so, it makes little sense since, as we soon learn, the father lived at the sea's edge all his life and presumably would know how the sea sounds.

Henry's information thus functions ironically, or even metalinguistically: on the one hand, it shows the narrator having a brief moment of power over the father whose death haunts him; on the other, we can read the speech as an aside to the audience, especially in connection with the next sentence: "if you didn't see what it was you wouldn't know what it was"—an absurd statement given that of course the radio audience cannot "see" the "sea" (note the pun); nor can it, as Henry puts it a few lines further, "Listen to the light."

Such self-consciousness about the use of the medium and the constructedness of the narrative is the "noise" Beckett introduces into the channel. We are warned that the sea sound effects are not accurate and exhorted to "listen to the light." The "story" is thus immediately established as unreal in the sense of unverifiable.

If *Embers* were staged or televised, the seashore setting would be so designated, whether more or less abstractly. But when sound is our only guide and the narrator tells us that the sound we hear is "unlike the sound of the sea," we cannot be sure where we are. It follows that we cannot be wholly involved in Henry's private mental drama. The sea, we are told a little bit further along, is the scene of his father's probable suicide, "the evening bathe you took once too often."

But the next sentence tells us that "We never found your body, you know, that held up probate an unconscionable time, they said there was nothing to prove you hadn't run away from us all and alive and well under a false name in the Argentine for example, that grieved mother greatly. [*Pause*]". Indeed, Henry's obsession is not with the sea as such but only with its *sound,* which he cannot escape, even when he tries to "drown it out" by telling himself endless stories. "I often went to Switzerland to get away from the cursed thing," he recalls, "and never stopped all the time I was there." Ada cannot understand why Henry finds the sea's sound so oppressive. "It's only on the surface, you know," she tells Henry, as if this would comfort him.

"Underneath all is as quiet as a grave. Not a sound. All, day, all night, not a sound. [*Pause*]." And when Henry explains that he now walks around with a gramophone so as to drown out the sea, Ada responds common-sensically, "There is no sense in that. [*Pause*]. There is no sense in trying to drown it" (E101).

Again, the ironies here are multiple. The silence of the sea below the surface, "quiet as a grave," cannot comfort Henry who knows that the sea *is* a grave—his father's. And the use of gramophone or voice or rival sounds to "drown it," has no chance against the sea's own drowning power—power brought home to the listener by every sea-sound-filled pause.

Yet, as Henry says, "It's not so bad when you get out on it. (E 101). Again, an ambiguous wish: it might not be so bad to "get out on it" because one would no longer be alive to feel the pain it evokes.

No sooner have the acoustics of water been established than Beckett introduces its opposite, fire, and the outdoors gives way to the indoors, as Henry tells the story—a story "never finished.

I never finished anything, everything always went on for

ever"— of "an old fellow called Bolton." It begins as follows: Bolton [*Pause. Louder*] Bolton! [*Pause.*] There before the fire. [*Pause.*] Before the fire with all the shutters . . . no, hangings, hangings, all the hangings drawn and the light, no light, only the light of the fire, sitting there in the . . . no, standing, standing, there on the hearth-rug in the dark before the fire in his old red dressing-gown and no sound in the house of any kind, only the sound of the fire. [*Pause.*]

Standing there in his old red dressing-gown might go on fire any minute like when he was a child, no, that was his pyjamas, standing there waiting in the dark, no light, only the light of the fire, and no sound of any kind, only the fire, an old man in great trouble. [*Pause.*] (E 95, ellipses are Beckett's)

The dominant feature here is the degree of verbal and phrasal repetition: the word "fire" appears eight times in combination with "light" and "sound," "only" and "no," as in "no light, only the light of the fire," "no sound of any kind, only the fire," and punctuated by the use of "no" as correction: "all the shutters . . . no, hangings," "sitting there in the . . . no, standing." "waiting in the dark, no light." And "pause" also acts as a kind of "correction," for each pause is filled with the sea voice so that "no sound and not a sound" are not accurate descriptors.

Beckett's dense network of repetition places a curious burden on the sparsely used visual images in the passage. So abstract is the vocabulary, that when we are suddenly introduced to the figure "on the hearth-rug in the dark before the fire in his old red dressing-gown," we hang on to the bright colour image as a kind of signpost in the midst of shadow. Red is also the colour of the fire, and then the embers, and phonemically both "red" and "embers" chime with the "Henry," who is not overtly present at the scene in question.

But the power of visualization, activated momentarily in Henry's monologue, is repeatedly countered by rhythm, in this case the broken phrasal rhythm of "white world, great trouble, not a sound, only the embers, sound of dying, dying glow, Holloway, Bolton, Bolton, Holloway, old men, great trouble, white world, not a sound" (E 95). The sound structure here, as in many of Beckett's later works, is phrasal and linear, with two primary stresses per line:

whíte wórld
greát troúble
nót a soúnd
ónly the émbers
soúnd of dying
dying glów

followed by the chiastic line, "Hóllowaỳ, Bólton | | Bólton, Hóllowaỳ," and then the same refrain with the lines in slightly different order:

óld mén
great troúble
whíte wórld
nót a soúnd

The effect of this elaborately stylized schema is again to occlude the information channel with noise. The message from sender to receiver, which radio, practically speaking, is designed to foreground, becomes progressively less well understood.

For what is the Bolton story about and how does it relate to the death by suicide of Henry's father? John Pilling has complained that *Embers* "has a structural slackness deriving from the two main topics [the father-son plot and the Bolton-Holloway plot] failing to blend" (PIL 98); Bolton, Pilling posits, is "simply an image in the imagination" (PIL100), a reading that accords with Zilliacus's supposition that Bolton is somehow Henry's alter ego or Donald Wicher's that he is "the fictive projection of the self."

But such thematic readings slight the piece's use of sound and silence, speech and pause. Just as outside, there is no way of "drowning" the sound of the sea, inside, the only sound is the sound of the fire and then its embers. However often Henry tells himself that there is "not a sound," whether on the shingle along the beach or in Bolton's sitting-room, in both cases, sound is steady and unstoppable.

The only way of interrupting the continuity of water and fire sounds, it seems, is to introduce another sound, one that is finite (and hence controllable) rather than continuous. Thus Henry summons "Hooves!" in the opening sequence and although the hooves *"die rapidly away,"* he longs for a regular metrical rhythm, a beat that could "mark time. . . . a ten-ton mammoth back from the dead, shoe it with steel and have it tramp the world down! Listen to it!" (E 93). The parallel in the Bolton story is the drip:

Holloway, Bolton, Bolton, Holloway, old men, great trouble, white world, not a sound, [*Pause.*] Listen to it! [*Pause.*] Close your eyes and listen to it, what would you think it was? [*Pause. Vehement.*] A drip! A drip! [*Sound of drip, rapidly amplified, suddenly cut off.*] Again! [*Drip again. Amplifications begins.*] No! [*Drip cut off. Pause.*] Father! [*Pause. Agitated.*] Stories, stories, years and years of stories . . . . (E 95).

Again we have the exhortation "Listen to it!" and the auditory image of a sound that, unlike the sound of the ocean, which is present here again in the repeated pauses, can be identified, timed for frequency, and stopped. It is when the drip is finally "cut off" that Henry, supposedly telling a story unconnected to his family drama, cries out "Father!" So much for the unrelatedness of the two narratives.

Indeed, the verbal, imagistic, and acoustic symbiosis of the two "plots" is worked out with musical precision: they cross in the central sequence of the play which is Henry's dialogue with Ada, and, by extension, with Addie. Jonathan Kalb, in the comment cited above, says Henry and Ada "reminisce about old times," but this hardly gives the reader a sense of the hopelessness and futility that characterizes their exchanges or the epiphany toward which their desultory conversation moves.

Ada's vocal entrance follows the snatch of dialogue with Addie, whose presence, as Henry recalls it, evidently interfered with his need need to "talk," to tell himself stories. Walking in the fields holding his child's hand in what sounds like a parodic version of such Wordsworth poems as "We are Seven," Henry says, "Run along now, Addie, and look at the lambs." But when she says "No papa," he turns "*Violent*": "Go on with you when you're told and look at the lambs!" which triggers

Addie's *"loud wail"* (E 96). Addie's world, a pastoral world of fields, lambs, and the child Jesus, is one the sea-dweller Henry cannot abide. And it is in this context that Ada is remembered:

Ada, too, conversation with her, that was something, that's what hell will be like, small chat to the babbling of Lethe about the good old days when we wished we were dead. [*Pause.*] Price of margarine fifty years ago. [*Pause*] And now. [*Pause. With solemn indignation.*] Price of blueband now! [*Pause.*] Father! [*Pause]*

Another water sound— the "small chat to the babbling of Lethe"—that despite its promise to help the narrator forget, cannot counter the ongoing sound of the sea. Ada and Addie live in the mundane, everyday world where the price of margarine or blueband is the topic of discussion—a world that was, for a short time, Henry's own, as his rhyme "Daddy! Addie" (E 100) suggests. All the odder, then, that when Ada makes her entrance, there is, for once, no sound. and further "[*No sound as she sits.*]" For the radio listener she is simply there; she may indeed have been there all along.

The Henry-Ada sequence is not simply flashback, for there are many time periods covered: their first love making in the "hole" "Where we did it at last for the first time" (E 101), a moment long ago (is that the same moment?) when, as Ada recalls, "It was rough, the spray came flying over us. [Pause.] Strange it should have been rough then [*Pause.*] And calm now" (E 98), Henry and Ada's parental dealings with their young daughter who takes music and riding lessons, a somewhat older Ada given to nagging— "Did you put on your jaegers, Henry?"(E 97); "Don't wet your good boots" (E 99)—and then to warning Henry that "You will be quite alone with your voice, there will be no other voice in the world but yours" (E 102).

And finally what is evidently the present moment in which Henry tells Ada, "I was trying to be with my father," and she says sardonically, "No difficulty about that." To which Henry responds, "I mean I was trying to get him to be with me. [*Pause.*] You seem a little cruder than usual today, Ada" (E102).

But so fluid are the shifts from one time frame to another that there is no use in trying to establish a meaningful temporal sequence. When Henry says, in what seems to be the present, "let us get up and go," Ada responds, "Go? Where? And Addie? She would be very distressed if she came and found you had gone without her" (E 98).

But when, a few minutes later, Henry asks Ada "What age is [Addie] now?" it is Ada who demurs, "I have lost count of time" (E 101). When Henry counters, "Twelve? Thirteen? [*Pause.*] Fourteen?", the audience is even more confused, for Henry and Ada seem to be talking of a time in the distant past. Moreover, the one specific time signal given throws us off even further:

ADA: [*Twenty years earlier, imploring.*] Don't! Don't!
HENRY: [*Ditto. urgent.*] Darling!
ADA: [*Ditto, more feebly.*] Don't!
HENRY: [*Ditto, exultantly.*] Darling! (E 100)

If this prototypical "young love" scene took place twenty years before the present of the play, how could Addie now be twelve or thirteen? Beckett everywhere underscores the foolishness of such questions. And the radio medium makes it possible to shift ground at a moment's notice and to collapse time. Past and present are often indistiguishable, even as sound distinctions are rigidly maintained: sea-sound versus "hooves" in the first sequence, "drip" in the second, and finally the dashing together of stones in the third. When Ada insists that "there's nothing wrong with it [the sound of the sea], it's a lovely peaceful gentle soothing sound," Henry goes wild:

Thuds, I want thuds! Like this! [*He fumbles in the shingle, catches up two big stones and starts dashing them together.*] Stone! [*Clash.*] Stone! [*Clash. 'Stone!' and clash amplified, cut off. Pause He throws one stone away. Sound of its fall.*] That's life [*He throws the other stone away. Sound of its fall.*] Not this. . . [*Pause*] . . . sucking!" (E 100, ellipses Beckett's).

The sound of stone falling *stops*, whereas the sea's "sucking" continues. "Sucking," with its harsh spirant and voiceless stop, now extracts Ada's monologue which is, from the point of view of plot, the key to the play, providing, as it does, the crucial information Henry has sought all along. The climactic scene in question begins with Henry's challenge: "I can't remember if he [Father] met you," and Ada's immediate reply, "You know he met me" (E 102). Henry demurs: "No, Ada, I don't know, I'm sorry. I have forgotten almost everything connected with you." Now comes the following dialogue:

ADA: You weren't there. Just your mother and sister. I had called to fetch you, as arranged. We were to go bathing together. [*Pause.*]

HENRY: [*Irritably.*] Drive on, drive on! Why do people always stop in the middle of what they are saying?

ADA: None of them knew where you were. Your bed had not been slept in. They were all shouting at one another. Your sister said she would throw herself off the cliff. Your father got up and went out, slamming the door. I left soon afterwards and passed him on the road. He did not see me. He was sitting on a rock looking out to sea. I never forgot his posture. And yet it was a common one. You used to have it sometimes. Perhaps just the stillness, as if he had been turned to stone. I could never make it out.

HENRY: Keep on! keep on! [*Imploringly.*] Keep it going, Ada, every syllable is a second gained. (E 102)

Ada cannot remember anything else but she insists that "there are attitudes remain in one's mind for reasons that are clear" (E 103) and that she cannot forget "the great stillness of the whole body, as if all the breath had left it" (E 103). It remains for Henry to finish Ada's story for her: she sees, or so Henry imagines it, the old man sitting on the rock but keeps on toward the tram stop, gets on the next tram into town but feels "uneasy," and gets off again. She retraces her steps: "Very unhappy and uneasy, hangs round a bit, not a soul about, cold wind coming in off sea, goes back down path and takes tram home" (E103).

The critics have made very little of this whole sequence. "When Ada leaves Henry's mind," writes Cohn, "he tries to weave a story about her encounter with his father, but Ada 'takes tram home,' and Henry drops her" (RCJP 84). But then why is this the only moment in the play when Henry urges Ada to "drive on!," "keep on!"? That "Every syllable is a second gained"?

Note that for the first time it is revealed that Ada was the last person to have seen Henry's father alive. It is she who witnessed the scene at Henry's house when "they were all shouting at one another. Your sister said she would throw herself off the cliff." She who knows that Henry's "bed had not been slept in." And it is after the scene she witnesses— "your father got up and went out, slamming the door"— that she sees his figure "turned to stone" on the rock overlooking the sea." There is something so wrong with this picture that, having boarded her tram home, she gets off again and returns to the scene of the crime. But now there is "not a soul about."

This is the "message" Ada relays to Henry but what does it mean? Evidently father and son had had a quarrel— "Your bed had not been slept in"—evidently something terrible has happened, but what? What would make the sister threaten to throw herself off a cliff? Why is everyone shouting? Why does the father go out, slamming the door? What drives him to drown himself? Why is the body, in a detail perfectly suited to radio, "never found"? Henry evidently knows some or all of these things, which is why he cannot drown out the voice of the sea. When Ada retells her tale, a tale she herself doesn't understand, his sense of guilt reaches fever pitch. If Ada could only remember more! "Every syllable is a second gained."

The Bolton story, far from being unrelated, provides the clue. Bolton has summoned Dr. Holloway, an old family friend, to help him in some desperate venture. Holloway finally offers to give his old friend a shot, but Bolton wants something else that Holloway won't give him: "We've had this before, Bolton, don't ask me to go through it again". Does Bolton want Holloway to perform euthanasia?

Or perhaps, given Ada's reference to Henry's sister's threat, an abortion? Or some other act of mercy? There is no way of knowing what Bolton's "Please! PLEASE!" refers to except that it is evidently something Holloway might dispense from his little black bag. The turning point, in any case, comes after the third "Please, Holloway!": Candle shaking and guttering all over the place, lower now, old arm tired, takes it in the other hand and holds it high again, that's it, that was always it, night, and the embers cold, and the glim shaking in your old fist, saying, "Please! Please! [*Pause.*] Begging. [*Pause.*] Of the poor. [*Pause.*] Ada! [Pause.] Father! [Pause.] Christ! [*Pause!.*]

"*Your* old fist": with the sudden and startling shift from third to second person, the text suddenly opens up. For who is Bolton but the father now immediately invoked in the sequence "Ada!," "Father!," "Christ!," each appelation punctuated by a pause bearing the sound of the sea? Far from being a projection of Henry's imagination, or Henry's alter ego, Bolton stands in for the father who, having failed in his unspecified and final plea to Holloway ("Please! PLEASE!"), takes his own life. And it is Henry who, for reasons never made wholly clear, cannot stop feeling he is to blame. No removal to Switzerland, no memories of "normal" family life, no retelling of Ada's uncomprehending story of what happened the fatal day of his father's death, no invocation of horses hooves' marking time, of water dripping, of stones struck together with a loud grinding sound, can drown out the sea's endless sounding.

What is perhaps the key word linking the two narratives in *Embers* is the word "washout," which appears in Henry's opening monologue. He has just gone over the Bolton-Holloway story for the first time and has recounted Holloway's refusal to do what Bolton wants: "ghastly scene, wishes to God he hadn't come, no good, fire out, bitter cold, great trouble, white world, not a sound, no good. [*Pause.*]" At this point, "No good" is repeated, now referring back to Henry himself:

No good. [*Pause.*] Can't do it. [*Pause.*] Listen to it! [*Pause*]. Father! [*Pause.*] You wouldn't know me now, you'd be sorry you ever had me, but you were that already a washout that's the last I heard from you, a washout. [*Pause. Imitating father's voice.*]

'Are you coming for a dip?' 'No.' 'Come on, come on.' 'No.' Glare, stump to door, turn, glare. 'A washout that's all you are, a washout!' [*Violent slam of door. Pause.*] Again! [*Slam. Pause.*] Slam life shut like that! [Pause.] Washout. [*Pause.*] Wish to Christ she had.

The terrible irony here is that if Henry is figuratively a "washout," his father is literally one. But "washout" also refers to Henry's own death wish, his wish never to have been born coupled with his wish that he himself had never become Addie's father: "horrid little creature, wish to God we'd never had her". An important intertext here is Beckett's late prose composition *Company*, specifically the following childhood memory:

You stand at the tip of the high board. High above the sea. In it your father's upturned face. Upturned to you. You look down to the loved trusted face. He calls you to jump. He calls, be a brave boy. The red round face. The thick moustahce. The greying hair. The swell sways it under and sways it up again. The far call again. Be a brave boy. Many eyes upon you. From the water and from the bathing place.

The reference here, as James Knowlson notes in his biography, is to the "famous deep 'Gentlemen Only' Forty-Foot" into which Bill Beckett, a superb swimmer, enjoyed diving from the high rocks at Sandycove when his son Sam was small (JKDF 32). In *Beckett Writing Beckett*, H. Porter Abbott rightly points out that the scene in question is of "an action that does not take place—no jump occurs":

Nor, and this is equally important, is it the record of a refusal to jump (nothing in the scene indicates such a construction either). It is the not-taking-place of a following a father's command. It is the not-taking-on of an identity ("*Be* a brave boy"). It is the nonoccurence of a baptism of total immersion with a father before the witness of many ("Many eyes upon you").

For Abbott, it is thus an example of Beckett's characteristic "Unwriting [of] The Father" (BWB 11), his intentional "sealing" of central autobiographical moments—his own Wordsworthian "spots of time"—"from meaningful, sequential narrative connection with any of the other spots in *Company* (BWB 17).

Abbott convincingly separates Beckett's "autography" from full-fledged autobiography on the one hand, fiction on the other. *Company*, one might add, works more like a lyric poem than any kind of narrative, and the diving incident cited above is best understood in relation to another scene just a few pages earlier in the text, in which the author's father sets off on a mountain hike so as to avoid "the pains and general unpleasantness of [his wife's] labour and delivery," the delivery being Beckett's own. The father's urge is to get away: "Hence the sandwiches which he relished at noon looking out to sea from the lee of a great rock on the first summit scaled" (C 13). The father who absents himself for the moment of his son's birth is not unlike the father of *Embers*, whose posture on a similar rock above the sea provides the death motif. And the son who cannot respond properly to the loved father's request to "Be a brave boy," and to "jump," is forever a "washout."

Knowlson records how devastated the twenty-seven-year old Beckett was when his father died in 1933. It happened during the worst period of Beckett's life—the inability to leave home or to find a viable form of writing, the heavy drinking, the terrible fights with his mother. But his father, who made few demands on his son, was "a great source of strength to him" (JKDF 164). As Beckett wrote his friend Tom MacGreevy:

> Lovely walk this morning with Father, who grows old with a very graceful philosophy. Comparing bees and butterflies to elephants and parrots and speaking of indentures with the Leveller! Barging through hedges and over the walls with the help of my shoulder, blaspheming and stopping to rest under colour of admiring the view. I'll never have anyone like him. (cited in JKDF 165).

It was just a few months later that Bill Beckett collapsed with a heart attack: within a week he was dead. "I can't write about him," Beckett wrote MacGreevy, "I can only walk the fields and climb the ditches after him" (JKDF 166), and more than fifty years later, he told his biographer: "After my father's death I had trouble psychologically. The bad years were between when I had to crawl home in 1932 and after my father's death in 1933. I'll tell you how it was. I was walking down Dawson Street. And I felt I couldn't go on. It was a strange experience I can't really describe. I found I couldn't go on moving" (JKDF 167).

The acute sense of guilt that produced this paralysis is not surprising when we consider that, at the time of his death, Beckett *père* could not know that his son would ever emerge from the bad phase he was in, a phase that gave his mother so much pain. And it is the son's guilt about this situation which is the subject of *Embers*. The sea-sound is forever linked to the dying embers, white world, and "no sound" that greets Bolton's "Please! PLEASE!" Beckett has written a searing play about what Dante called the "great refusal."

INFORMATION, PLEASE

The question remains: what did Beckett gain by presenting this autobiographical drama of filial guilt as a *radio* play? If, as we have seen, *Embers* is closely allied to such of Beckett's later fictions as *Company*, which shares many of its actual images and incidents (and a similar case could be made for *Krapp's Last Tape* and *The Unnamable*, both of them written just a few years before *Embers*), why was Beckett so adamant in refusing to let his plays "for voices, not bodies," be staged or so much as read in front of a live audience? Why his insistence that "to 'act' it is to kill it"?

The answer cannot be that radio gave Beckett the best possible vehicle for "skullscape" or "soulscape," for certainly *Company* and *Krapp's Last Tape* are soulscapes too. Nor is it enough to say, as Beckett does of his radio plays, that the "whole thing *com[es] out of the dark.*" Rather, I would like to suggest that the "radio-activity" of *Embers*, as of *Words and Music*, *Cascando*, and *Rough for Radio I* and *II* which followed in its wake, is that its sounding of disembodied voices makes it the perfect vehicle for the dance of death that is its subject. The dialectic of sea-sound / no sound, within which the sound of hooves, of a water drip, of stones grinding against one another cannot "drown" the continuity of the sea without and the fire within, is the vocal equivalent of a world in which all the characters—Ada, Addie, Henry's father, Bolton, Holloway, and Henry himself—are revenants, ghostly presences. When Ada tells Henry he "ought to see Holloway," she adds, "he's alive still, isn't he?"

But alive at which of the many discrepant times presented in this play? The Holloway we meet in Henry's monologue is an old man who says to the equally old Bolton, "for the love of God, Bolton, do you want to finish me?" (E 104). As for Henry himself, his living testimony exists, as it were, *in absentia:* his self, as Charles Grivel puts it in the passage that gives me my epigraph, lives *without him.*

At the same time— and this is the paradox—*Embers* is an exciting whodunnit. Inevitably, the audience tries to construct the plot, doled out in dribs and drabs of information. Why is Henry so obsessed with his father? How did the father feel about Ada? What, if any, role did she play in his death? What does Bolton want from Holloway and why won't Holloway give it to him? And so on. Normally and conventionally, radio is the purveyor of messages: who killed whom and why? when and where did it happen? what are the latest police findings? What does the coroner's report say? But in *Embers,* there are no findings, no announcement, no "late bulletin." Indeed, it is these features of radio discourse that Beckett parodies: the radio audience's demand for fact is consistently undercut by verbal and phrasal repetition, by unanchored visual image (e.g., red dressinggown, blue eye), and by rhetorical and sonic excess.

So stylized is the play's language, with its invocation of seemingly unrelated sounds and sights, that we all but miss the moment when disclosure actually occurs, when the noise dies down for an instant, allowing a bit of the "message" to come through. That moment occurs when Ada recounts her visit to the house where "None of them knew where you were. Your bed had not been slept in." Her speech is significantly framed by Henry's "Drive on, drive on! Why do people always stop in the middle of what they are saying?" and "Keep on, keep on! [*Imploringly.*]. When Ada stops, unable to remember anything else, Henry has to finish the story for her, a story that imperceptibly and inevitably modulates back into the Bolton narrative. And the narrator repeats the words, "Not a word, just the look, the old blue eye".

But if there is "Not a word, just a look," the radio narrative is over. "Every syllable" is indeed "a second gained," for if there is really no sound, the listener must assume that the receiver isn't working, that there is either failure in the particular channel of transmission or a mechanical failure that has somehow turned off the set. On radio, in other words, the only way to simulate silence is via sound. And it is this characteristic of the medium Beckett must have had in mind when he refused to allow his radio plays to be *visualized* in any form.

In a recent internet debate of the John Cage Discussion Group, participants were discussing how to perform Cage's famous "silent" piece of 1952 called *4′ 33*". The title refers to the four minutes and thirty-three second length of the performance, designed for any instrument or combination of instruments, which are, in fact, not played during the "silent" performance. Daniel Farris suggests:

When one records silence, one must make a number of decisions. As when recording sound, one must decide whether or not to mic it up close or at a distance. The purpose of close mic placement is to reduce the amount of intrusion caused by nearby instruments and ambient sound and not necessarily to capture the most accurate representation of the performance. The purpose of distance mic placement is to capture the complete sonic environment both completely and accurately. Both techniques are useful and the decision about which to use is a subjective but important one. . . . Given the average Western audience's predisposition toward movement and respiration (and occasionally more at a hot gig), if an audience were present, one would need to actually deploy microphones and roll tape. We could call this 'the live version.'

Here Farris reminds us that silence is never in fact, silent: to record it for radio or audiotape therefore presents special problems. On stage or in film, "silence" is represented by having some sort of visual movement (as in Beckett's own *Film*) during which nothing is "said." But on radio, there is no such option and so "silence" must be sounded as it is in *Embers*.

The final sentence in the play, "Not a sound," thus denies its own assertion in ways that underscore the piece's overarching sense of emptiness.

For Henry can't even have the silence he longs for and anticipates; there will always be another "syllable," but not the one he is looking for. Radio would seem to be a unique medium to achieve this particular pathos.

Chapter 3

Special about Samuel Beckett

Literature which celebrates his seventy-fifth birthday, where a hitherto unpublished text of a somewhat unusual nature may be found. It consists of two paragraphs and is untitled except for a symbol identical to the number "8" above the first paragraph and the symbol for infinity above the second. The first symbol is identified in the editor's note (but not by Beckett) as signifying an "indefinite number," a usage unknown to my colleagues in mathematics.

Moreover the title "Crisscross to Infinity" which heads the text is not Beckett's. Since the text describes a sandy figure-eight path up and down what is presumably a hill in the first section, and a similarly-shaped path winding back and forth across barren bedrock in the second, the symbols might well both represent infinity. What is clear is that each of the two sections is structured so as to suggest infinite repetition of the text itself, both as individual units and in relation to each other. It is a text which will be of special interest to those concerned with physical movement and structure in Beckett's work.

The somewhat odd location of this text toward the very end of the issue may be the result of an intentional juxtaposition with the "Notes and Discussion" section which immediately follows.

Intentional or not, the confrontation is a happy one, for Joseph Hassett's brief note on the central concept of "strange loops" in *Gödel, Escher, Bach* by Douglas Hofstadter, seems to offer a direct commentary on Beckett's new text as well. The bulk of the issue is, of course, devoted to scholarly essays, and begins with Enoch Braters analysis of the problematics of narrative perspective in *Watt*. Brater suggests that a careful reading of the novel reveals the impossibility of identifying a single narrator for all four parts, thus denying the general assumption (repeated, for example, by John Fletcher later in this same issue) that "Sam" is the narrator of the whole.

The essay is unfortunately marred by numerous typographical errors. Readers should be warned that few of the quotations are given with complete accuracy, and on occasion render a sense directly opposite to that of the original text. The complex discussion of the chronological sequence of the four sections of *Watt* is marred by similarly confusing typos, the order 1-2-3-4 being given twice, for example, when 1-2-4-3 was intended.

Since *College Literature* is meant as an aid to classroom teaching in American universities, its pages are unlikely to offer much new to the specialist. Michael Mundhenk's attempt to justify an interest in Beckett from a Marxist perspective seems aimed primarily at unenlightened Marxists. I assume his references to Marxist critics are more accurate than his assertation that Murphy died by asphyxiation. J. D. O'Hara's lively and informal style comes as a welcome relief in the following essay, on Beckett and Schopenhauer. I found the first half in particular an excellent overview.

Philosophically-inclined readers should note that Joseph Browne's detailed and useful bibliographical essay in the same issue includes two articles which had already dealt in a major way with Schopenhauer and Beckett, neither of which is mentioned by O'Hara. John Fletcher's survey of Beckett's literary development, based solely on the prose works, provides the best general essay for potential classroom use. Fletcher divides Beckett's work into three periods, revealing a progression away from an interest in the world, toward an increasing absorption with language itself, a view which would be readily agreed to by many Beckett scholars. (The stages themselves are uncannily reminiscent of the three sections of Canetti's *Auto-da-Fe*, a novel which has been tellingly compared with *Murphy* by Marilyn Lovett.) Although *Company* clearly departs from Fletcher's schema, he nevertheless rounds off his discussion nicely by pointing to it as a return to the beginnings, prompted perhaps by the appearance of the Bair biography. *All That Fall,* a text which Fletcher would have found a thorny problem had he included dramatic works in his discussion, is briefly treated by Gregory A. Schirmer in the remaining essay of the issue. Criticism seldom surprises.

There are not that many ways in which the things that Beckett's critics are 'trying in vain to say' may be 'tried in vain to be said'. In this respect it is refreshing to read the special Beckett issue of the *Irish University Review,* an aptly subtitled 'Journal of Irish Studies' which considers Beckett from a specifically Irish perspective, and as part of a tangibly Irish cultural tradition, rather than as an immaculately conceived representative of 'all humanity'.

Arguably, the 'Humpty-Dumpty' approach is best. The critic needs to sit on the wall, or fence, separating the national and the immaculate, in order to savour both. For example, *Krapp's Last Tape* may well be celebrated as a piece of pure, technological, Post-Modernity, or as a quintessential revelation of Beckett's obscure ethical symbolism, without reference to Ireland or anything Irish. But as Christopher Murray points out, in his survey of 'Beckett Productions in Ireland', the play may also be defined as so much Irish.

Taunted by the actor Cyril Cusack's complaint that *Krapp* was a 'piece of Irish Protestant sentimentality', Beckett apparently retorted: 'That's what it's intended to be'. Over and over again, references such as this redirect one 'Back to Beckett's Ireland', rather than simply 'Back to Beckett'. At best, the briefer contributions make the most of a few more of the Beckettian pebbles that punctilious criticism cannot leave unturned.

Roger Little's discussion of 'Beckett's Mentor, Rudmose-Brown', comes up with Beckett's confirmation that Rudmose-Brown 'had no part in the Dante revelation'; David Berman's meditations upon 'Beckett and Berkeley' ponder upon Beckett's assertion that he 'was not influenced by Luce's work on Berkeley'; while Derek Mahon's lucid musings upon the more general qualities of Beckett's poetry sporadically focus upon such minutia as Beckett's claim that he 'never thought' of the ambiguities which Lawrence Harvey imputes to 'Saint-Lô'.

T. P. Dolan's patient analysis of Beckett's departures from 'standard colloquial English' in *All That Fall* establishes Beckett's 'capacity to represent authentic Hiberno-English dialogue', while J. C. C. Mays's study of 'Young Beckett's Irish Roots', considers the extent to which *Murphy* is 'a *roman à clef*, which satirizes and says farewell to the Dublin literary scene'. Tracing the curious dialectic between Beckett's 'dismissal of things Irish', and the omnipresent 'Irishness' arising from 'his detachment from literary forms and language', and from 'the streak of cruelty and violonce that runs through his writing along with the humour and elegance', Mays concludes that Beckett partakes both of what one might think of as the peculiarly Irish, diachronic tradition of 'disinheritance', and of the more recent, synchronic tradition of Modernism, which Beckett shares with an international brigade of 'experimental' writers.

Approaching the paradoxes of 'Beckett's case' from the perspective of R. D. Laing's *The Divided Self*, Patrick Wakeling argues that both Beckett's travels and literary travails spring from his 'schzoid make-up'.

According to Wakeling, Beckett's destruction of his correspondence from Joyce and other mentors after his mother's death signals his escape from 'inauthentic' social transactions, and marks the 'illusion of independence' precipitating his mature work; while the disturbing experiments of this work persistently testify to Beckett's 'divided self'. With this pattern in mind, Wakeling concludes that the 'particularity' of Beckett's 'schzoid' vision precludes the claim that his works speak for humanity, or 'those whose minds are less divided than his own'.

Arguably, though, it is precisely the bewildering osmosis of the private and the public which makes Beckett's writing so compelling. It hooks us with its general archetypes, and then lures us upon the wild-goose chase of attempting to share what Estragon might define as Beckeft's 'private nightmares'.

Seamus Deane's essay on 'Joyce and Beckett' dismisses the concept of 'schizophrenic writing' in order to emphasize the regionality of Beckett's work, insofar as 'Ireland, with its dead language, its deadening politics, its illiberal legislation is the historical correlative of the personal state of nirvana-nullity for which Beckett's people crave'.

From this premise, Deane goes on to compare and contrast Joyce and Beckett, both in terms of what they have in common—'exile, experimentation, heroic dedication and Dublin', and in terms of such familiar dichotomies as their respective preoccupation with 'incorporation' and 'impotence'. Rejecting this attempt to place Beckett's work within a national social and literary context, Ben Barnes' account of 'Aspects of Directing Beckett insists upon the ways in which Beckett's plays demand 'de-personalization' (and one might add, 'de-nationalization'), 'in the service of the accentuated image'.

Without ever explicitly saying as much, Christopher Murray's provocative account of 'Beckett Productions in Ireland' consistently exemplifies this process of 'de-personalization' in a number of striking anecdotes and allusions, such as his reference to A. J. Leventhal's criticism of the "Dubalin" intonation in a 1955 production of *Godot*, on the grounds that 'the author had in mind a universal rather than a regional vision of mankind'.

Still more evocative, perhaps, is Murray's quotation from a letter of 28 January 1958, in which Beckett sternly defined his ideal of a 'straight reading' of *All That Fall* in terms which prophetically anticipate the impersonal utterances in *Play*, observing: 'The ideal for me would be a stage in darkness with a spot picking out the faces as required'.

Murray also alludes to Beckett's aforementioned confirmation that *Krapp* epitomizes 'Irish Protestant sentimentality', and for good measure, adds Cyril Cusack's claim that *Happy Days* was, by Beckett's own admission, 'influenced' by his wife, Maureen Cusack's request that he 'write a happy play' after *Krapp*. Further discussion of *Happy Days* leads Murray to quote the *Cork Examiner's* admiration for 'the slightly mad resignation' of Winnie, and this in turn overlaps with the emphasis that writers Aidan Higgins and John Banville similarly place upon the evanescent optimism within Beckett's work. According to Higgins, Beckett's sense of negation is neutralized by his compulsion for contradiction: 'one doesn't know that [his work] means anything, but he is able to put it in such a way that it is not possible to say that it means nothing either'.

In Banville's terms, 'He knows, with Kafka, that so long as we can say, here is the worst, then the worst has not arrived'. While Banville almost certainly inflates Beckett's and Kafka's confidence in what 'we can say', Higgins also surely errs when he suggests that Beckett's characters 'do not complain', as they linger, 'alive after a fashion, even if buried up to their necks'. For Higgins, Beckett's characters are first and foremost survivors; a 'miracle' that 'they must talk about'. Arguably, the reverse obtains. Involuntary survivors, denied the 'miracle' of death, and, as Higgins remarks, 'preserved in their memories', Beckett's characters talk, not to celebrate survival, but to keep life and memory at bay.

Winnie must talk to evade introspection. In this respect, happiness will only be hers when, like the newly dead 'Mouth' in *Not I,* she is buried from toe to top, rather than merely up to the neck. 'Mouth' experiences the reverse of Winnie's trajectory. Rather than sinking into silence, 'Mouth' rises from the grave, reluctantly suffers mental resurrection, and survives again, to complain, again and again.

Like Micheál Ó hAonghusa, a theatre historian, who, as Murray remarks, makes 'no attempt to appropriate Beckett as an Irish writer, one might well define Beckett's ghostly plays as the product of the first dramatist of the space-age', or as plays 'set on the edge of nowhere', where 'society does not exist and man is in a void'. Ultimately, though, this judgement oversimplifies Beckett's achievement. The sense of existing 'nowhere' or anywhere, somewhat like Jarry's *Ubu,* certainly gives Beckett's work its compelling, archetypal mystery.

But at the same time, a certain muted Irishness, and still more muted autobiographical overtones, also give Beckett's work that poignant 'Beckettian' flavour for which space-age fictions offer little substitute. The Beckett issue of the *Irish University Review* offers the perfect catalyst for further meditation upon Beckett's national, international and extra-national qualities.

Beckett regulars will wonder why thirty years after *Godot,* a Nobel prize, and a very fortunate set of critical introductions to his work there is any need for more Beckett criticism at an introductory level. In the case of the new *Samuel Beckett Reader* edited by Beckett's publisher, John Calder, the answer is clear. Since the appearance of Calder's popular and useful 1967 reader, Beckett has produced works in new forms with difficulties for the general public as great or greater than those of the earlier works. The selections and introductions in the new *Reader* successfully relate the recent works to the earlier ones and provide justification and understanding of Beckett's whole corpus by comparisons to music, painting, and Romantic literature.

The reason for Professor Bert O. States's *The Shape of Paradox* is less evident. The book is another theological and philosophical "essay" on *Waiting for Godot.* In each of six brief chapters States develops a single thesis and illustrates it with a primary example from the text. His hundred pages are notably overstuffed with references to the intellectual furniture of Western civilisation. His index looks like a precocious but predictable graduate school reading list—Kirkegaard, Auerbach, Kermode, Levi-Strauss, Barthes, Augustine, Robbe-Grillet, Schopenhauer, Lukács, Jon Kott, Bert States, etc. But behind this veil of authority and profundity, the perfectly obvious is constantly charging. This book is a classic example of the currently rampant method of scholarly presentation which set up an artificial context of heavy-duty intellectual references to camouflage the banality of the authors observations. Most of States's many references to world-renowned authors serve only ostensibly to place Beckett in a wider intellectual framework.

The comparison in most cases is not really to Beckett's work but to States's argument. By adducing these analogous passages from other critics on other authors, States strives to give the impression that the quality of his thought is on a par with the distinguished thinkers he quotes. Unfortunately, it is not. States devotes his first two chapters, entitled "The Language of Myth" and "Generic Time and Place," to establishing that the spareness of the language of *Godot* and the lack of unique references to time, place, and specific personal milieu for the characters give *Godot* a universal or "mythical" dimension.

Because they are not limited by specific associations, the characters and situations readily take on extended associations. *Mons laborat!* But the creature astir here is not entirely harmless. States fails to see the difference between Beckett's statement that *Waiting for Godot* is a play which "strives at all costs to avoid definftion" and his own irresponsible invitation to "liberty of inference or free association." He finds *Godot* "so docile, so amenable to adjustment: it will surround what food it is given, like an amoeba." In a flurry of metaphor, he compares the play to a Rorschach blot inviting a freedom of reader response which he calls a critical "Rapture of the Deep."

Scuba divers know the deceptions and fatal dangers of that kind of rapture in reality. States should heed the Implications of his own metaphor. In Chapter Three, "The God in the Plot," States advances the proposition that Pozzo is to be compared to Godot and both seen as representations of the Divine. Professor States's appreciation of his audience's ability to apprehend what Beckett has made clear in the text of his play must be minimal indeed if he believes that he has to instruct them on this point.

Pozzo's lines; "...Poz.:o! Made in God's image.... Who is Godot? ...You took me for Godot." are clear enough without States's overblown deductions. States's argument in Chapter Four, "The Fool of Time," is for once not so blatantly self-evident from the text itself. Because Pozzo begins in good fortune in Act I, exhibits pride, and ends in a state of suffering and misfortune in Act II; States argues that he is the archetype of the tragic hero. According to States, Pozzo's hubris consists of delivering the speech on night in which he reduces time to the mechanical setting of the sun.

This establishes Pozzo's sin and punishment as "actual sin" committed in time and finding retribution in time. It is a personally earned destiny in contrast to the original sin of having been born which places Estragon and Vladimir in an "Imposed Situation"—the subject and title of Chapter Five. The larger argument of the book as developed in the last two chapters contends that the subplot of Pozzo and Lucky presents in a linear, temporal development a more personally specific kind of tragic destiny within the universal human predicament represented by the main plot of Vladimir and Estragon.

Together the two contrasting fates complement each other and offer a complete version of human destiny. The relationship of the subplot to the main plot gives "Godot" the "shape" referred to in States's title. He represents this structure by a diagram showing the "comic" action of Vladimir and Estragon as straight lines: one slanting upward in Act I and another slanting downward in Act II.

The "tragic" action of Pozzo and Lucky is represented in each act by a circle tangent to those lines. That (STOP THE PRESSES!) is the structure of the play: the "comic" action of Didi and Gogo impinged upon briefly once in each act by tangential contact with the "tragic" action of Pozzo and Lucky. It is the shape of a "paradox" because, as with the two crucified thieves, salvation and damnation are meted out unaccountably by the same Divinity.

For some, grace is given; for others, it is denied. Tragic roles and comic roles are assigned arbitrarily. States's argument that the Pozzo-Lucky sub-plot is a kind of "tragic relief" within a comic plot is moderately instructive. There can be no doubt that the passage of time brings suffering to Pozzo and Lucky in a way that it does not to Vladimir and Estragon.

The contrast in their fates is worth considering in this light. Pozzo says pointedly in Act I in a line which Beckett makes much of in his own direction of *Godot*, "For surely I shall suffer." But States's insistence that the fates of the characters have different origins is based upon a fundamental misreading. In the central speech of the play, Pozzo says that his blindness and Lucky's dumbness came upon them "one day"—the day of their birth and of their death. States acknowledges the passage as the "crucial hinge" of the play but misreads it as Pozzo's inability to remember correctly and to distinguish past, present, and future.

The point, of course, of the collapse of all time into a single day and finally a single instant is not that Pozzo cannot distinguish the moments of his existence. He does have that problem, but that is not essential. The essential fact is that the condition which brings about his suffering is constant and ever present. Time is not, after all, a whirligig which brings in its revenges for the misdeeds of the past. The afflictions of Pozzo and Lucky are not brought about by their own actions in time, as States asserts.

Nor is the change in their condition merely the random result of the slow diminution of capacity with time. The fate of Pozzo and Lucky may be manifested more obviously overtime, but it is no more a consequence of actions in time than the fate of Vladimir and Estragon. Physical affliction, like unfulfilled wafting, is the consequence of an absolute universal condition present from the moment of birth until death. Time is only the undifferentiated medium in which destinies are enacted. "Have you not done tormenting me with your accursed time," Pozzo shouts, "When! ... One day, is that not enough for you..." By stressing "*one* day" Pozzo is emphasising the fact that the condition of time is *universal* rather than the fact that the date is unknown and therefore immaterial.

A single causality reduces birth and death to one moment. And that moment is the same for all humanity—as Beckett indicates with one of his characteristic grammatical progressions: "... one day he went dumb, one day I went blind, one day *we*'ll go deaf [Pozzo and Lucky], one day we were born, one day we [everyone] shall die.... They give birth astride of a grave..." (Emphasis added). Even for those coming to Beckett and *Godot* for the first time, States's book will be of little use. It belabors what any intelligent reader would perceive on his own, misleadingly invites uncritical response, and misinterprets the "birth astride a grave" passage which presents the central philosophy and one of the central images of the play. In contrast to States's book, John Calder's *A Samuel Beckett Reader* provides a useful and needed introduction. His selections are mostly the same as in his earlier reader but with the addition of works published after its appearance.

The novels and short fiction are far more liberally represented than the plays—more for reasons of copyright than anything else one suspects. There are lengthy excerpts from all the major novels and also from the less well-known works like *More Pricks Than Kicks, Mercier and Camier,* and *First Love.* Although the collection contains less drama than fiction, the longer excerpts from the pre-1975 plays *Godot, Endgame,* and *Happy Days* are augmented by the Introduction containing short passages of the plays since 1975 to give an adequate overview of Beckett the dramatist.

And the complete text of *Come and Go* compensates in part for the absence of fuller examples of the minimalist mime and monologues of the recent plays. Calder's choice of selections illustrates Beckett's types of writing and main themes—including his humour, feeling for animals, treatment of love, and Gothic fascination with ghosts—so characteristically that the question of editorial bias never arises.

The selections are presented according to an intelligent and informed chronology of composition rather than by date of publication so that readers can really see the position of individual works in the pattern of Beckett's development. The section on Beckett's poetry—unquestionably the most underestimated of his writings—will be of special interest to those who know him only as a novelist and playwright.

Even from the few examples here, readers can get a sense that although he is not a prolific poet, Beckett is nevertheless a poet of the first quality. In his introductory material Calder is as concerned as Professor States with establishing an intellectual and cultural context—not, however, as a means of giving importance to his own perceptions, but as a means of providing a framework in which Beckett's works can be recognized and appreciated more readily. Many of Calder's points are broad, personal generalisations open to challenge, but they effectively illuminate the works. His comparison of Beckett's later plays and short prose to music goes beyond the by now familiar observation that the cadence, timing, and minute details of pattern require attention like that given to chamber music—an analogy which Beckett himself has used often.

More importantly, Calder's comparison of Beckett to Schubert and Beethoven offers a corrective for the audience which finds in Beckett an unacceptably pessimistic world view and situations too stark and somber to look at. In response to those like critic John Simon who recently challenged Beckett's supporters to look him in the eye and say they enjoy performances of the newest plays, Calder writes: "Beckett is often criticised for the blackness of his vision, and the question is asked why he feels it so necessary to write to depress us. The same question is not asked of Beethoven's *For the Faraway Beloved* or of Schubert's *Winterise,* two song cycles of overpowering sadness and perfect beauty, which audiences flock to hear sung by their most famous contemporary interpreters. If there is a huge sadness in Beckett's work, it is akin to the great Romantic music of the past in its evocation of beauty, in the way phrases haunt the mind, and in all the other qualities that he introduces, including humour, flashes of joy, moments of contemplative peace.

"The point, though broad, is valid. Not only are the principles of construction in Beckett's work like those of music, but Beckett should be accorded the same right to portray the sadness of life in an aesthetically effective mode as his acknowledged influences, Beethoven and Schubert. The comparison with Beethoven is developed at greater length. Calder sees in both artists a pattern of three periods of development. Like Beethoven, Beckett began with an early period of "nonemotional" extension of the current artistic possibilities.

As a young man he was "a mannerist delighting in an eccentric use of language, portraying the world he observed but did not feel very much a part of, exploring the comic possibilities of human relationships and especially of love."

To this period belong *Murphy, More Pricks than Kicks* and everything else he wrote before the war and *Waiting for Godot*. And, like Beethoven, in a second period Beckett exhibits in his works a "new dynamic where emotion constantly breaks out of the framework of form, thereby increasing the possibilities of style and content. "This is the period of *Godot, Endgame,* the Trilogy, *How It Is, Krapp, Happy Days,* and *Play.*

It is marked by great purity of style which allows Beckett to depict a world "recognizably the real world, but stylized to catch those moments in life that are most important or most revealing." Finally, Beckett has a late period in which, like Beethoven, he "turns away from the world into himself—to find "an introspective peace" in which he could escape his own suffering and "make a statement about the human condition."

"Extreme brevity and concentration, and a perceptible change in tone and atmosphere" distinguish the works of this period. They include among others the plays since 1975: *Footfalls, Ohio Impromptu, Rockaby,* the television scripts: *Ghost Trio, But the Clouds,* and the new, short poetic prose works: *Imagination Dead Imagine, Ill Seen Ill Said,* and *Company*. Much of Calder's introduction seeks to situate Beckett within the tradition of European Romanticism—a source of interest in Beckett's own reading which has directly influenced his writing from the beginning to the present.

His first poetry, *Echo's Bones,* for example, begins with an image he has pointed out as drawn from Goethe's *Der Gaier* (*The Eagle*). And the rehearsal notebook for *That Time* acknowledges the influence of Hölderlins's *Hyperion Fragment*. The entire text of *Nacht und Traüme* is the poem of the minor German romantic poet Matthäus von Collin set to music by Schubert. Calder finds Beckett's characters notfar removed from Goethe's Werther and Wilhelm Meister— "creations who lived to suffer and to learn through suffering." For him, Beckett is a late romantic who depicts with Goethe the need for love, the warmth of human friendship, the regret for lost opportunity, and the evocation of sadness for its own sake." Ultimately, Calder sees Beckett as a great "neo-mannerist" who by distortion, caricature, and ambiguity reflects and presages the great social and political ills and uncertainties of his time. While ever insisting on purely historical or political readings, Calder sees and constantly calls attention to Beckett's awareness of the apocalyptic moment.

Beckett thus becomes for him the special, outstanding spokesman for humanity confronted with unprecedented horror and the imminence of its own demise. Beckett's importance, Calder points out, does not come from fictionalized documentary of war, concentration camps, or nuclear bombs. It comes from his haunting depiction of humanity faced with the great suffering of twentieth-century holocaust in a final moment of consciousness between the beginning of the individual or collective end and the extinction of sensibility.

Other traditions as a context for Beckett's work might have occurred to other readers and might have served as well; Beckett's background and interests in music, visual arts, and literature is vast. But Calder's choice of European Romanticism is at least as close to the direct concerns of Beckett himself as other contexts one might have chosen. And the time is also right for a look at Beckett from this perspective.

In the years since *Waiting for Godot*, Beckett has assumed a role much like that of Joyce in the second quarter of this century. No longer the exclusive property of an elite avant garde, he has become the established master, a major influence on other authors. He is an accepted and popular figure. Two different runs of evenings of new one-act plays have sold out in New York's theater district. And the theater in which they played has been named The Samuel Beckett Theater.

He is the subject of set exams in Britain and busloads of students are brought to special matinees of *Godot* to prepare for them. But attraction does not not confer understanding, and Beckett's ever larger and wilder audience is often confused by what it has so eagerly chosen to see or read. In his innovation Beckett is still beyond his time. What Richard Ellmann said of Joyce is true of Beckett, we are still learning to be his contemporaries. By locating Beckett's emotional equivalents in music, painting, and German Romanticism,

Calder's introduction is a helpful step for both the new readers and theatre-goers first engaged in the struggle to be Beckett's contemporaries—to accept his work for what it is—and also for those who have been at that task for some time.

At first glance, this special issue of *Revue d'Esthétique*, entirely devoted to Beckett and coming out in April 1986—right on time for the author's eightieth birthday—might remind us of the *Cahier de l'Herne* n. 31, directed by T. Bishop and R. Federman and published in 1976 just after Beckett had turned seventy: both volumes have more or less the same format, the same aspect of a dossier complete with new excerpts from Beckett's unpublished works, critical essays or articles, interviews or conversations, personal letters, reminiscences or testimonials, nice and appropriate illustrations, bibliographical and chronological data.

Yet, past these apparent similarities in their general outlook and make-up they remain, to a large extent, quite different from each other in their respective choices of/ and approaches to Beckett's works. In other words, *déjà vu* perhaps, but *déjà lu* certainly not. To begin with, the number of texts in *L'Herne* dealing with Beckett's novels or other forms of narratives was almost the double of those concerning his plays; whereas nearly all entries in *Revue d'Esthétique* have to do either with his theater and other forms of audio-visual works or with the theatricality of his fiction and, especially, with non-dramatic pieces such as *Le Dépeuplaur* and *Compagnie* that have already been the object of various stage adaptations.

Furthermore, most studies in *L'Herne* that dealt with Beckett's plays tended, through a mainly thematic approach, towards philosophical interpretations. Indeed, only two texts under the heading "Au travail avec Beckett"—one by A. Schneider, the other an interview of R. Blin by T. Bishop—were directly concerned with such a practical problem as the actual staging of Beckett's plays. Well, if this issue of *Revue d'Esthétique* may still be seen as a kind of offshoot of the *Cahier de l'Herne*, it can only be with regard to that specific approach, for it could bear as a general subtitle what was just a particular, and rather undernourished, caption in the latter: "At work with Beckett." At the very start of his "Présentation," P. Chabert wants to make things perfectly clear: "Ce numéro *Samuel Beckett* est consacré au travail, à la pratique non au commentaire. /.../ On n'y parlera donc ni d'absurde, ni de transcendance, ni d'être là, etc. /.../ Le propos est plus simple, plus direct, plus près de la vie /.../: Beckett au travail, aux prises avec l'oeuvre, l'oeuvre à accomplir—avec ses différents collaborateurs, décorateurs, musiciens, cameramen, acteurs, metteurs en scène."

And, in accordance with his purpose, he did indeed call upon the participation of such collaborators as mentioned above: out of sixty-four contributors, at least thirty belong—like himself, of course— to *le monde du spectacle*. But although the others are more readily identified as critics and, generally, members of the academic community (or in some cases like S. E. Gontarski *et al*, with a foot in both worlds), they too favour and exemplify here the same practical approach to Beckett's works. Now, it is true that there are a few exceptions that seem to contradict Chabert's categorical assertion whereby no philosophical interpretations and, particularly, no mention of *absurde, transcendance,* or *être-là* are to be found in this volume: after all, T. Todorov in "L'espoir chez Beckett" (where he contrasts the infamous cylinder in *Le Dépeupleur* with Plato's famous cave) does speak of a "monde désespéré et absurde" (p. 29), of "l'illusion de l'absurde", and à propos of *Compagnie* of a world that "cesse d'être absurde." (p.35); for his part, M. Esslin, in "une poésie d'images mouvantes, "speaks of Beckett's "exploration de l'Etre" (p.391), of "problème de l'Etre", of "expérience existentielle", and even brings in Schopenhauer.

However, the stress in these two particular essays is still much less on Beckett's philosophical ideas per se than on the way he expresses them through what Chabert calls his "travail de composition et d'écriture." (p. 14) Actually, in the long list of contributors there is only one lonely philosopher identified as such—Gilles Deleuze whose short entry on *Film* (pp. 381-382) is curtly, and somewhat unfairly, summarized thus: "According to Gilles Deleuze, *Film* derives from Berkeley and his principle 'esse est percipi'." (p. 471) which, to me, makes his contribution sound a lot like a fine example of *l'art d'enfoncer une porte ouverte...* At any rate, this new Beckett dossier is divided into six main parts. Following a short but vibrant testimonial from H. Pinter, P. Chabert's detailed and forceful "Présentation," and a brief survey of Beckett's literary evolution and artistic innovations by E. Fournier (who is also credited for translating into French most of the texts originally written in English), Part I is entitled "Roman, Théâtre/ Théâtre, Récit."

It comprises nine entries, all but two of which (Todorov's essay and E. Klausner's interview of L. Janvier and A. Vaquin—Janvier about their translation of *Watt*) are devoted—by D. Anzieu, L. Janvier, A. Ubersfeld, A. Simon, M. Saison, M. N. Delorme and L. Breuer—to the question of interrelationship between Beckett's plays and narratives. Part II— "Dramaturgie"—is headed by D. McMillan's informative and perceptive article on *Eleuthéria* as being Beckett's comical version of the Cartesian *Discours de la Méthode,* that is to say as a *miseen- doute* through *mise-en-oeuvre* of several past or present theatrical traditions and conventions, and, therefore, as a play that clears the way for *Godot* where Beckett will discover his own "méthode de l'art dramatique."

Then comes one of the most valuable documents in this *dossier*: a series of long and so far unpublished excerpts from *Eleuthéria* itself, whole scenes from Acts I, II and III, plus Beckett's "note sur la disposition de la scène et l'action marginale." The next entry is a substantial essay by E. Jacquart on the genesis of *Fin de Partie,* on the changes from the first typescript to the last version that show how Beckett is always at work trying to find, paradoxically, a "forme-Dieu caché de l'oeuvre—qui accommode l'informe."

Finally-after A. Didier-Weill's mercifully short note on time, death and waiting, in *Godot*—S. E. Gontarski demonstrates once again, through a close examination of the successive versions of *Pas* (and not of *Comédie,* as stated in the "résumès"), Beckett's creative process as a "combat contre l'explicite" and the search for a "schema formel."

With thirty-seven entries altogether, Parts III, "Représentations," IV, "Musiques," V, "Samuel Beckett, metteur en scène," VI, "L'image (T.V., film)," constitute the major corpus of this volume, but since I could not possibly review them in detail I shall only indicate here that—to the editor's content and, I assume, the reader's—they *all* tackle essentially the problems, always practical and often technical, of directing, staging, adapting and acting, whether the contributors are primarily theater/television professionals or academics/critics.1 Although the entries that follow M. Esslin's essay are listed in the "Sommaire" (p. 5) as components of Part VI, they really belong to a separate filled with compilations of updated bio-bibliographical facts and a whole series of diverse chronologies all specifically relating to the staging of Beckett's dramatic or non-dramatic works throughout the U. S. A. and Europe (France, England, Italy, Spain, West Germany), thus providing very useful informations to Beckett scholars in need of quick and reliable references.

Reflecting, in various degrees, the four main orientations in Beckett most recent criticism which E. Jacquart sums up in an introduction to his bibliography—"Le travail théâtral et audiovisuel," "La problématique de la traduction de soi," "L'étude des manuscrits," "Les 'dramaticules' récents,"—this special issue of *Revue d'Esthétique* adds a new dimension to the area of Beckett studies or, at least, extends it significantly. Also, and notwithstanding a few mixups here and there (like for instance, besides the ones I already mentioned, a certain discrepancy between the order of the "résumés" and "l'ordre du sommaire" with which they are supposed to agree), this impressive and elegant volume has been, in general, quite carefully edited, so that my only—but serious— reservation is more of a material nature, for it concerns its extremely poor binding quality.

After opening flat and leafing through my own copy just a couple of times, most of its pages came off loose at the seam, which makes its use, as a research tool, very *impractical* indeed. *Dommage!*

The characters tell stories "to reveal deep and difficult

thoughts and feelings while at the same time concealing them as fiction or at least distancing them as narration." For the great talkers of Beckett and Pinter, "telling becomes a form of doing," and "storytelling... is itself the action." Frequently the characters tell their stories to escape from the pain of their existence; "evasion itself is often the main action." Morrison canters play by play through the canons of Beckett and Pinter.

She is a good practical critic, sensitive to the delicate psychological nuances of her two playwrights. The analysis of *Krapp* and his tapes and of Winnie and her memories is impressive. She is just as persuasive discussing the complex monologues of Pinter's *Landscape* and *Old Times*. Indeed *Canters and Chronicles* always has interesting things to say about Beckett and Pinter.

Morrison writes with clarity and relish about even the most obscure, miniature plays of the two authors. Her yoking of Beckett and Pinter also yields at least one interesting side-effect, for a disturbed sense of human sexuality seems to be at the centre of most of the works she discusses. Still, I must confess that though I began *Canters and Chronicles* with the belief that narrative is very important in the plays of Beckett and Pinter, I was rather less convinced when I had finished the book.

The fact is that Morrison simply does not "refer only to actual narrations ... delivered during the course of the play by one of the characters." Her interpretations regularly veer away from her avowed topic in the direction of more general criticism. "There are frequent references, especially in Beckett's later plays, to a face," but so what? While it is no doubt "useful to note two important related elements" in *No Man's Land*—the suggestion of homosexuality, the hostility toward women—such elements have precious little to do with Morrison's consideration of narrative.

Similarly her account of *A Slight Ache* focuses on the "anxiety of death" in the play rather than on Edward's "attempt to retell his life story." Too often she seems merely to be offering generalized literary analysis. It's as if her intended subject, storytelling, doesn't give her enough to hang her critical hat on. Furthermore, the argument suffers from a disconcerting looseness in its definition of narrative. No matter how accurate are the Biblical and literary allusions Morrison identifies in *Waiting for Godot* and *Happy Days,* it is farfetched to describe these allusions as versions of narrative. She also discusses Pinter's long set-piece speeches as narratives whether or not they contain a story.

An argument about storytelling that can accommodate Ban's instructions to Gus in *The Dumb Waiter* or Mick's aggressive ideas of Interior decorating in *The Caretaker* seems to me fatally blurred. Mick does indeed dazzle "Davies with language," but it isn't always the language of narrative. Even when Morrison is genuinely focusing on her narrative target, she keeps reaching the same conclusion over and over. E.g., "personal anecdotes" in the later Beckett "both reveal and conceal, shielding the character while at the same time showing where he is most vulnerable."

A Piece of Monologue, written as a prose piece rather than a play, raises interesting questions about a writer in whose work the distinctions between monologue and fiction tend to capsize (and so do most of Beckett's fictions from *Molloy* onwards). These are questions that Morrison never begins to address.

The scant single paragraph of conclusion at the end of the book is all too symptomatic. The practical criticism is very good; the theoretical underpinnings are negligible. There is much to be said in praise of a book that offers many instructive insights into the difficult plays of Beckett and Pinter. Any serious student of the two playwrights will profit from Morrison's interpretations. Still, in a comment on Pinter's *Silence,* she does inadvertently write her own epigraph: "plenty of stuff to occupy the analytic mind, but none of it quite coheres." their way into libraries and archives.

The manuscripts that are here carefully examined, dated, put into chronological sequence and analysed include: *Fin de Partie, Krapp's Last Tape, Happy Days, Play, Film, Eh Joe, Ghost Trio, "...but the clouds...", Not I, That Time, Footfalls, A Piece of Monologue, Rockaby, Ohio Impromptu, Quadra I + II* and

Catastrophe. In addition Gontarski gives a detailed account of a hitherto unpublished sketch for a story or play *Kilcool* that contains some of the germs of *Not I*; and prints, as facsimiles of the manuscripts of two unfinished mime-plays, *Mime du Reveur A* (which anticipates elements of *Endgame*) and *J. Mime*, (written for Jack McGowran and pointing towards *Quadrat I & II*). Gontarski has performed an admirable piece of textual scholarship.

He has dated the different drafts, typescripts as well as holographs, and established their chronology so that the history, the development of these texts can be reliably—and illuminatingly—reconstructed. What emerges from this tracing of the genesis of some of the finest works of the literature of our time is, precisely, what Gontarski calls Beckett's "intent of undoing"—undoing, that is, the elements in his work which are grounded in, and reflect his own personal life-experience or other elements derived from "reality"—people Beckett encountered or places he knows.

It is thus, undoubted, fascinating to realise that, for example, the world "after the flood" that we encounter in *Endgame* directly springs from Beckett's experience in 1945 as an ambulance driver in the St. Lo military hospital, surrounded as it was by ruins, desolation and churned up earth; again and again Gontarski shows how Beckett after having started from such "realistic," even "descriptive" beginnings, gradually but systematically erases the traces of descriptive or personal detail in order to arrive at, in the end, distillations of reality, structures, which, having been purged of much that is purely individual and accidental, can become genuine images of the "condition humaine."

These refined and distilled images still contain concrete detail—the objects Winnie cherishes in *Happy Days*, the social set-up that still shines through the fragmented scraps of recollection in *Play*, the memories the listener rehearses in *That Time*, but having been dislocated into mere broken fragments of narrative, they become themselves generalised metaphors of the objects and incidents that—absurdly—constitute our existence. Another aspect of Beckett's method of composition which Gontarski's research highlights is the extent to which, increasingly throughout his career, Beckett has become preoccupied with structuring his material according to rigorously formal, even mathematical, principles of permutation and variation.

While much of Beckett's earlier work notably the "trilogy," could be seen as a stream of consciousness, a torrential inner monologue, which, carefully shaped as it was, nevertheless suggested the chaotic outpourings of an inner voice, his writing has become increasingly rigorously structured and geometrical, culminating in highly formalised structures like *Lessness* and *Quadrat I & II.* All these insights are masterfully presented and documented in Gontarski's book.

Yet the very success, the very illumination his work provides, seems to me to raise some highly interesting and intriguing theoretical questions: how does this type of research, this type of insight into the genesis of individual works of art, into an authors general development as a craftsman, square with the contemporary tendency to discount the importance of the author as creator of a text, to proclaim the autonomy of the text as a "given," existing in its own right, and, once available as a written artifact, referential neither to its creator nor to any reality outside itself?

If the text exists in its own right, as an artifact to be judged solely as what it is, not how it became what it is, if, indeed, it is argued that, after all, we do not know the genesis of the texts of Sophocles or Euripides, or, less convincingly, Shakespeare, and therefore should be able to read these without reference to the biography or working methods of their authors, then knowledge of how a text grew out of first drafts, revisions and corrections should be irrelevant, or even positively misleading; after all: the reader who reads the completed text, the playgoer who confronts it, does not have the privilege, or, indeed, the time, to take the subtleties of the composition of that text into consideration while experiencing the impact of the finished product.

And, indeed, it might be argued, Beckett's persistent

refusal to discuss his own intentions, or to comment on the meaning of his text, on the grounds that the text as it stands must say all it says, otherwise it would be a deficient text, being in need of supplementary elucidation. ("if I knew who Godot was, I should have had to put into the play") seems to point towards the post-structuralist view.

Indeed, if he has gone to such lengths to erase the process of the genesis of the germ of his texts as well as the actual method of their composition, is it fair to reveal it all to the gaze of the curious? This, it seems to me, crystallizes in an extremely clear, manner, some of the dialectics of the present theoretical debate. Both standpoints, I feel, have something to be said for them nor do they necessarily seem mutually exclusive.

The dogmatic assertion that a text should be judged independently of its author or of its historical referentiality is, on closer inspection, overstated and *eo ipso* less than wholly realistic. Even Barthes and Derrida have their names on the title-pages of their writings, and these writings themselves are peppered with references to authors like Racine, Balzac, Freud, Nietzsche, Rousseau, Artaud and innumerable others. And even texts of whose authors we know little or nothing have, and need to be perceived as having, historical referentiality. We should not possess the texts of the *Iliad*, the Greek tragedians, the medieval mystery plays, without historical—and hence referential—research which has established these texts themselves.

We should not be able to read, say, the Greek classics, without a knowledge of the meaning of the words they used—knowledge that has been gained by historical and archaeological research. We should not have the texts of Shakespeare (which are now proclaimed not to need any referentiality to any real world) if their "biography" and printing history, their sources and historical, social and cultural context had not been established by scholars just as meticulous as Gontarski, if less fortunate than he who had access to Beckett's early drafts as well as to their author himself.

Nevertheless the champions of the autonomy of the text,

as text now existing in its present form, have a very strong case, particularly if, as Gontarski so convincingly shows, the author has gone to immense lengths to erase the traces of its genesis. It is irrelevant to the meaning and impact of a piece of writing whether the author laboured over it for years or threw it onto the page in an instant, "never blotting a line."

And this is especially true of texts like Beckett's who deliberately opens up his work to a multitude of widely diverging interpretations, precisely in order to force the reader or spectator to experience the uncertainty and ambivalence of the images. Beckett himself has built the need for deconstruction into his own texts: let each individual reader or spectator make of them what he wants! let the ultimate "meaning" of them be found in the tensions and gaps between the possible contradictory interpretations to which they open themselves up! What then do we gain by knowing how they originated? Might it not be a positive loss if our knowledge of their genesis narrowed the range of possible interpretations? This, I feel, is undoubtedly so.

And yet the need to inquire, the "obligation to express" the findings of research into these texts, remains, simply as an aspect of the irresistible urge to find out, to increase our knowledge, to yield to the basic human instinct which is the source of civilisation itself: simple curiosity. The contradiction is there. Yet, it seems to me, it resolves itself if we manage to look at the two opposing viewpoints as no more than two totally different fields of inquiry.

The one is *criticism*—the activity to respond to a work of art and the endeavour to express this response and make it the basis of new thought, new vision, new insight. The other is *history* or the *psychology* of the creative process, or a multitude of other fascinating and rewarding scholarly pursuits. While a detailed knowledge of how Michelangelo acquired his paints, what he paid for them and by what technique he applied them to the ceiling of the Sistine Chapel has no relevance whatever to our response to the images we see there, that information is valuable in itself and well worth unearthing.

Equally, there will be some value in knowing what kind of person Michelangelo was and how he lived. We would be less than human of we did not want to satisfy our curiosity about those matters. Yet it is essential that we should be aware of the fact that the two different spheres—the contemplation of the work of art as it is, on the one hand, and the research into its genesis on the other—should not be confounded or merged.

For it is here that the "biographical" or "intentional" fallacy of literary criticism tends to originate. Let us beware of the temptation to use biographical knowledge as a substitute for the genuine impact of the work of art upon us. I dread the moment— almost inevitable now that Gontarski has revealed the origins of the play—when the set of a performance of *Endgame* will include a photographic representation of St. Lo after the Normandy landings, (and we have, alas, already had the subway station afterworld War III which is almost as bad) just as I have suffered more than once from the tree in *Waiting for Godot* looking like a painting of the crucifixion.

There is another danger that lurks in the exploration of the process of creation of a poet like Beckett: namely that the *ex post factum* reconstruction of how it was done should be mistaken for a prescription for "how to do it." Ever since the schools of rhetoric of antiquity there has always been a perilous implication in literary criticism to turn an inquiry into the structure and creation process of works of art into a prescriptive methodology for *producing* new works of art. Much dead and mechanical art has been engendered by the consequences of this fallacy which is at the basis of all "academicism" and, even worse, much harm has been done by the imposition of rules of "how to do it" which, throughout the centuries, have restricted and stifled genuinely original creativity.

If Samuel Beckett creates his works in a particular way and if we can follow his creative process, that is fascinating knowledge which opens up exhilarating insights into his psychology and the psychology of the creative process itself.

But that does not mean that any other artist does, or

should, follow similar ways of creativity. It is one of the merits of Gontarski's outstandingly researched and brilliantly argued book that, beyond its engrossing detective work, it opens up and helps to clarify these general aspects of the theoretical debate. The exhibition which it accompanied was one of the highlights of an important international conference "Translating Beckett / Beckett Translating" held at the University of Texas in 1984.

Over 430 items were on display, many of them unique, including the original manuscripts of most of Beckett's major novels and plays, together with several rare illustrated editions seldom seem by the public. Although most Beckett scholars are well aware of the rich holdings in Austin, it was breathtaking to see firsthand the range and depth of material exhibited. The catalogue is a record of the exhibition; it was not intended as a definitive bibliography, nor even as a full listing of the complete holdings of Beckett's works in the HRC—there would not have been enough display cases for everything they have. Nevertheless, no important manuscript or first edition in the HRC collection was missing from the show.

In selecting and describing the holdings, Carlton Lake chose to "let the books and manuscripts tell their own story, only sketching in background, where it seemed useful, in order to help them do so." The result is an unusually coherent bibliographical overview of the development and progression of Beckett's work through 1983. Lake's seemingly modest role is in fact a difficult and crucial one—to summarize and interweave the often complex lives of the texts and the author. Lake's touch is light, and with exception of one or two unnecessary swipes at the national character of the French, he manages to entertain and enlighten the reader without undue over-simplification.

Read carefully, the catalogue offers a wealth of detail which often corrects or enlarges upon our knowledge of the history of the texts. The descriptions are particularly good at identifying and specifying the relationship of variants, "false starts," and other varieties of pre-publication excerpts to later complete printings of individual works, as well as at identifying the contents and various stages of manuscript drafts.

Linda Eichhorn seems to have been instrumental in this latter task, "a considerable achievement," as Lake points out, "blended of persistence and percipience, which has helped to remove several hand-me-down misconceptions." Those using Richard Admussen's admirable *The Samuel Beckett Manuscripts: A Study,* will want to double check the additions and revisions provided in the Austin catalogue. Lake and his assistants, Eichhorn and Sally Leach, were not restricted to the evidence of books and manuscripts. They also had at their disposal a wealth of personal correspondence to, from, and about Beckett, from which Lake has chosen to quote quite liberally.

This material is often particularly revealing. Although it is clear that Lake did not wish to weigh the catalogue down with footnotes and citations, it would have been extremely helpful if some concise system of indicating when such material is being quoted for the first time had been employed. Other minor cavils with regard to documentation may be raised as well. The information provided for each entry is not always consistent.

The colour of bindings is sometimes indicated and sometimes omitted; the presence or lack of a dust-jacket is not always indicated. Inevitably, a few dates and statements regarding priority of printings are inaccurate. The text provisionally titled "The Way", listed as unpublished, had appeared in *College Literature* over a year before the catalogue came out.

The reproductions of sample manuscript and typescript pages are clearly not intended for scholarly use, reduced as they often are to a point just below that at which they might have been deciphered. Although the numerous illustrations are a welcome visual record of the exhibition, their function is limited for the most part to the iconic. Such objections are minor when placed beside the considerable achievement of *No Symbols Where None Intended*. That the quality of its layout, typography and paper offers such pleasure is an added bonus.

It is clearly the most important bibliographical tool to appear since Admussen's study of the manuscripts, and as such will prove an indispensable aid to any Beckett scholar.

Modern Dramatists series, intended for "people interested in modern theater who prefer concise, intelligent studies of drama and dramatists, without jargon and an excess of footnotes." What looms large in many volumes of this type—a biography of a writer and the socio-theatrical context of his plays—attracts little attention here, the essentials of Beckett's life and work are condensed within a few opening pages, and parts of the chapter on *Waiting For Godot* situate Beckett's achievement in the context of the Parisian avant-garde of the fifties.

The rest of the book is devoted to the elucidation of Beckett's plays. Factographical details are restricted to a minimum, and here Mr. Lyons refers the reader to the bulk of Beckett criticism, from which he himself has drawn extensively. The length of the bibliography will certainly not frighten a novice in the field, although the inclusion of a bibliographical study and a book-length monograph of Beckett's late work (e.g. Knowlson's and Pilling's *Frescoes of the Skull*) would have been useful. Lyons's aim is to "concentrate upon the text of each of Beckett's major plays as it operates in performance". Meant to be general, this study highlights only certain narrowly-restricted problems.

The mode of discourse is subordinated to the main task: to set for the reader a perspective which will help him understand Beckett as a playwright, not as a thinker. Therefore only the most vital aspects for the argument are illuminated, while the argument itself focuses on form, technique, poetics, and evolution. Lyons situates Beckett's drama within the tradition of the history of poetics (rather than the history of ideas), using examples from ancient drama, Shakespeare, Racine, Ibsen, Strindberg, Chekhov and modern dramatists, to illustrate his argument.

He conceives of Beckett's work in terms of evolution, as it develops in the process of "refining and distilling," or in the "simplification and intensification" of theatrical images.

The conviction that this evolution reflects Beckett's understanding of the physical resources of the theatre and the assumption of the organic integrity of Beckett's plays form the foundation of Lyons's reasoning, The author seems to be telling us that if we want to understand Beckett's theater, we should analyse the implied poetics of his works, and especially the way their internal structure contributes to generating a network of meanings.

He is interested in the subtle and complex interaction of a variety of potentially significant elements in the plays as they are to be perceived and explained by a hypothetical viewer. This is, we might infer, the ultimate source of involvement of the audience, quite the opposite of the *Mitspiel* strategies based on direct participation of the audience in the evolving action. Narrow as his perspective is, it is used in his argument with regard to three universal categories (Lyons call them "theatrical images") of time, space (scene) and character, which also appear as subtitles in each chapter.

In order to show us the principles according to which works operate, Lyons frequently embarks on what might be called a description of a space for interpretation. This space is indicated by a series of indeterminancies established by the text and affecting the spectator's imagination in such a way as to provoke "a particular kind of speculation."

To show a repository of such possibilities, Lyons patiently enumerates the possibilities certain issues evoke (e.g., the five possibilities of explaining the rapport between Hamm's story and the situation on stage or the seven levels of Hamm's possible characterizations) and collects a variety of suggestions which particular passages bring forth. But he concludes with a statement that "actions and words hold a range of possible significance, but any significance remains potential," and since "the text itself provides no final clarification [...] any fixed resolution violates the play".

Thus the author says of *Waiting For Godot*: "The value of the image derives from its use by Vladimir and Estragon as an hypothesis on which they base their behaviour. Beckett establishes a critical absence, n:)t on the stage physically but within the cognitive processes of the two principal characters'. And of *Endgame*: "...the play is the theatrical embodiment of the uncertainty and equivocation implicit in the concept of selfhood and the relationship of the self to the presence of another." Although such remarks maybe considered "thematic," (one might argue that they refer us to specific problems of a particular branch of psychology), they are general enough that they do not seem to reduce the appeal of the play or to unduly narrow the range of experience of the spectator.

In fact, Lyons explicitly identifies the principal subject of Beckett's fiction and drama as: "the consciousness of an aging person grappling with his clouded perception of the space he inhabits, attempting to reconcile images of the past that revolve in his imagination, questioning his own identity and the authenticity of his own existence".

This definition does need qualification— for it does not apply to most works written between *Whoroscope* and *Endgame*—but it confirms our impression that Lyons tends to look at Beckett from the point of view of the later works. "The limits of consciousness form the boundaries of Beckett's sense of reality". This remark too is more readily applicable to the late works with their tendency towards "the absence of an image of character' than to plays like *Waiting for Godot* and *Endgame* where characters act on stage as distinct persons. Lyons acknowledges this and in the course of his book describes the changing poetical mechanisms employed to subvert naturalistic convention (or realistic, as Lyons prefers to call it).

In the earlier plays this convention is broken by repetition, a poetic device used extensively by Beckett, thanks to which the immediate event is deprived of its insignificance by the denial of its uniqueness. Lyons distinguishes here between enacting and performing; the Beckettian characters, instead of enacting a story, are engaged in performing a repetition. They rely on repetition in that it promises to uphold their sense of identity. In *Krapp's Last Tape*, a "physical or scenic division between character and memory" takes the form of confrontation of the person on stage and the disembodied text. With *Words and Music* and *Cascando* this pattern changes when "individual consciousness becomes the arena for action." The essential structure of Beckett's late drama is binary. The text (or rather, verbal structure, for it may also be memory or recollected images) is set against the character (their relation being equivocal), who "revolves it in consciousness."

The text becomes dominant, and indeed may even fully eclipse the character, as in *Not I.* The categories of time, space (scene) and character not only serve Lyons's discussion of the polymorphous structure of Beckett's plays, but also provide co-ordinates in the authors attempt to find a formula for continuity and integrity in Beckett's entire dramatic *oeuvre*, and, at the same time, to show a possible source of the uniqueness of his later works.

Seen within these coordinates, the Beckettian evolution is the process of acquiring freedom from "a specific (scenic) location" and shifting to "non-space or functional space". In the end, a major change ensues: "the character becomes scenic, a location to house the repetition and place of narration.". How can a character become a location to house the repetition and place of narration? some common readers may ask. Those hoping for a general introduction to and a "concrete reading" of Beckett's work (i.e. the establishment of what recent theory calls all-fixed transcendental signification) may find these somewhat more abstract explanations as to how the system operates (not what the text says, but how it works) too dry and speculative.

After all, they have the right to be moved by the poetry of what the text says rather than by how it is believed to move them. Professor Lyons may reply that he has been interested in nothing more—and nothing less—than how it *is* in Beckett's theater. We may feel that the solutions to specific problems invite, and indeed demand, more discussion, although certain issues may seem clouded only because the limited size and the specific character of the book does not allow for more extensive clarification.

But in this concise study the author has succeeded in

showing us once more the value of the custodian of method over the purveyor of doctrine. Lyons has placed Beckett's oeuvre in a perspective that does not deny us the chance of explaining the entirely new notion of theatricality proposed by Beckett in his late drama.

By rights, we should welcome this book, given all factors that promise both competence and accessibility. Written by a university professor but clearly not someone dedicated to the impassionate dissecting of texts, it is the fruit of personal involvement and research supported by the experience of teaching and staging Beckett's works. Written by a Shakespeare scholar at a time when an extensive monograph on Shakespeare's lasting inspiration for Beckett has yet to be undertaken, it focuses on the self-reflective nature of Beckett's "theaters" (his plays for the stage and the media), something vitally important to Beckett criticism as it enters it fifth decade.

Both in his studies of Shakespeare and of Beckett, Sidney Homan advocates the metadramatic approach. It is tantamount, as he claims, to focusing on "theater's own workings," with emphasis on what he labels the aesthetics of metadramatic metaphor, something born out in the immediate theatrical experience.

The author thus describes the scope of his inquiry: "...the imagery I will be looking at most closely is that based on anything within the gamut of our theatrical experience: the playwright, his craft, the physical theater, the theater itself as a metaphor, actors, the concept of dialogue, metaphor or simile, the audience, and most important, the energies generated among that trinity of playwright, actor, and audience in sustaining a meaningful illusion on stage". As to the "meaningful illusion on stage," Mr. Homan makes a well-founded observation in his last book on Shakespeare, noting that in Beckett's work the "artificial world challenges and external reality that the playwright discredits in a way that Shakespeare never does nor could do. [...] The interplay within the dualistic notion of the world as a stage and the stage as a world that informs Shakespeare was simply not there, since Beckett's 'macrocosm' is not the public world, or the nature that Shakespeare would have mirrored, but our own idiosyncratic internal world.

The study postulated by Homan should be useful in every respect, for it is precisely the complex, paradoxical nature of Beckett's "artificiality" on stage that has given to his texts the "power to claw," and that lies perhaps at the very core of Beckett's originality. I am not convinced, however, that his book, in the shape in which it has been presented here, has succeeded in achieving what seems to be its goals: to give a cohesive interpretation of Beckett's dramatic work in "a more practical performance criticism," or "to put down in logical order the components [...] of Beckett's aesthetics".

It is not surprising that this all-inclusive approach is a "loose" system, "drawing on metaphors generated by a variety of elements in the theater. However, we are surprised that in confronting this rich variety, the author is so unceremonial in his use of principal terms. One looks in vain for definitions, even approximate ones, and for the delineation of related terms, which at times not only overlap but are interchangeable. Impromptu characterizations are affixed with offhand qualifiers and used in ad hoc oppositions. Homan's ever-present rhetorical device is to place two of more terms next to each other without specifying the nature of the semantic relation between them.

The most widely used—in fact abused—distinction is that of thematics and aesthetics. As early as the preface we are given a taste of this art of substitution. The closest Sidney Homan comes to defining the two is when he speaks of the lack of separation between "what is said (thematics) and how it is being said (aesthetics)" (p.1 9).

One wonders what distinguishes it from the traditional distinction between content and form. A little further on we hear about separating "form from content, or metadramatics from thematics" and the familiar quotation from Beckett's essay on Joyce appears. Later on, aesthetics is juxtaposed with thematics, thematics, "or content," with "metadramatics," content with form, then form with substance, and content with style. Both principal terms appear as convenient modifiers:

attributive, as in a statement on the art of radio: "in this medium, when one does not speak, one goes from thematic loneliness to aesthetic nonexistence"; or adverbial, as in a statement about *All That Fall*: "Aesthetically, the play is not about falling, but rising, about the yeastlike optimism of a birthday".

On occasion, the two terms are given a companion, as when Mr. Homan enumerates three levels of tension in *All That Fall*: "the prosaic one of whether Mrs. Rooney will see her husband; the thematic one of whether Mr. Rooney murdered the child; and the third and greater mystery, one of form rather than substance". So there may be mystery of form, rather than substance in Beckett's works, but as far as obscurity goes, "If there is obscurity in Beckett, it is thematic, I think, not aesthetic".

If one agrees with Mr. Homan that his method is "loose," one is inclined to doubt that his interpretation is "light". Even if it is indeed a reading of Beckett's plays "on the very terms by which they operate," we can hardly grasp it as such. To paraphrase Homan's own words, his book seems to be "a tremendous outpouring of formed and half-formed statements," and this quality makes reading the 250-page volume an arduous endeavor. Often, in this state of weightlessness, we have the feeling that we have approached an understanding of the authors intention, yet we regret the lack of a more solid frame of reference.

If there is anything valuable, beyond piecemeal observations, it can be perceived only with much effort or by chance. Does the "inner" discourse then, despite the book's style, reveal "the very terms by which Beckett's works operate"? The common conclusion of Homan's interpretive strands is a vague statement about energies generated among that trinity of author, actor, and audience in sustaining a meaningful illusion on stage. "Given this theater turning to itself, it is inevitable that the three ingredients for any production—artist, actor, and audience—should be prominent in Beckett's works", says Homan; "given" and "should be" are the key words here. The commentary (often showing a lack of sensitivity to Beckett's irony) usually leads to stretched points and forced analogies, invited by the ubiquitous presumption of the union of "the trinity." Here is one example taken from the chapter on *Krapp's Last Tape*: "As he interacts with one certain and affirmative element of his life, the interaction is aesthetically affirmative even if the event itself, an abandonment of love, a separation, is thematically negative.

The medium of the theater here relies not on the story itself but on the audience's interaction—Krapp's and ours—with that story. The play is about the union of audience (Krapp, us) and actor (Krapp, Krapp on tape, the tape recorder that bears his voice), and about a thematic union as well, of man and woman, of a man in the present with a man in his past, of the cerebral or imaginative with the physical and time-leaden. [...]

By definition the theater demands union, of actors and audience; a play can exist only if it is heard and seen". Why is the interaction aesthetically affirmative and thematically negative? Why is the play about the union of man and woman, present and past, rather than about the abyss, the unredeemable gap between them? Are "cerebral" and "imaginative" in opposition to each other, or merely in "apposition," in this sentence? And what is "the story itself"? The recorded text, the text spoken by Krapp on stage, or the "plot" of the play? Certain conclusions seem to be at odds with interpretative common sense, dictated by experience in reading Beckett's texts.

Why should we link sexual creativity to artistic creativity if on numerous occasions Beckett has made a clear distinction between them? The only reason to do so would be the critic's search for something to fit into his own scheme. If theatre—by definition—demands union, everything can be put under the comforting sign of the trinity, every disparate aspect can be domesticated. Much of what is said in Homan's book is not susceptible to proof.

One of his interpretive "threads" deals with sexuality. The elucidation of Mrs. Rooney's remark about the rim of Mr. Tyler's wheel—the outside of the vagina that Tyler is too old to penetrate" (p. 118)—may be overstated, although as someone whose native tongue is not English, I yield to Mr. Homan's feeling for word play.

However, I would not subscribe to the view that in *Embers*, "the music master's method of instruction [...] hints at crude sexual intercourse", or that the character evoked in the Bvoice of *That Time* is masturbating" trying like the man in *Eh Joe* to come sexually, but unable to do so, the spent penis displaced by the hollow tree". Can it be proven that in *Eh Joe* 'the actor is masturbating off-camera since only his face is shown"?

Regretfully, this passage is rather vague: "More than one actor and spectator has suggested that Joe is masturbating." At any rate, the statement, "Like the semen, the story comes within Joe only to make its way out" seems to be in keeping with this sexual misreading of Beckett. While such readings cannot be definitively refuted, there is no evidence for many of Homan's observations, and some are clearly mistaken. We cannot prove that the ball in *All That Fall* is not Krapp's black ball, yet I insist that there is no mention of colour in the radio play. We cannot prove that "Eff" in *Embers* does not stand for "fuck," nor that Minnie might not be Winnie's daughter, but there is undoubtedly no mention of an emmet in *Endgame*.

While we have no proof that Bianca is not a whore, not that it was not the case that "Krapp's book *Effi* has failed, with only a few copies sold," I insist that neither the sentence: "The engraver in *Endgame* sees nothing in his art, and Beckett has argued that the playwright's impossible task is to write about nothing—as if it were something", nor the footnote referring to the *Three Dialogues*.... is accurate. It is striking that in this book of "performance criticism," the author prefers lengthy discussion on subjects clearly belonging to what he labels thematics, to an analysis of stage implications in the dramatic works.

For example, in his commentary on *A Piece of Monologue*, he analyses only the spoken text, not dwelling on its relation to stage action. References to Beckett's own productions are rare, and Mr. Homan seldom takes into account solutions by Beckett's most outstanding "theatricians," but revels instead details of his own involvement "with two professional theater companies: Bacchus Productions and Hippodrome Theater". "Staging *Waiting for Godot* for the prisoners of Florida State Penitentiaries," he confesses, "was an exhilarating experience, clearly at one with the simple fact that men waiting were watching a play about men waiting. It led to my putting Shakespeare aside for a spell and, over the next six years, throwing myself into Beckett..." [*Shakespeare's Theater...* p. 13].

If not for publications on Rick Cluchey and the San Quentin Drama Workshop, the remarks about prison performances would be strikingly original—some twenty years ago. I do not intend to discredit the value of playing Beckett to prisoners or workers (because I also believe that "Beckett is not for a coterie," p. 124), but the subtitle *Interpretations for Performance* promises more than the book delivers.

Notably, actors who turn to this book for ideas will discover that the author, while commenting on particular plays, drastically narrows the range of stage interpretation. Mr. Homan writes with directness and verve, which makes this book attractive to students. Yet, as a *vade mecum,* it provides too little systematic information, and presumes close familiarity with Beckett's work; indeed, references to minute details sometimes fall like passwords, clear only to the initiated.

The book undoubtedly has value as a testimonial of a long involvement with Beckett's works, but considered as a book of memories it has far too many footnotes. These, in turn, should be more scrupulous and accurate. I may not be doing full justice to Mr. Homan, for his study is not lacking in interesting perceptions and useful observations. If I emphasize its shortcomings, it is because the faults are more conspicuous than the merits.

The remarkable experience which we surmise to be at the foundation of this project has born too little fruit. *Abysmal Games in the Novels of Samuel Beckett* is a study in clarity and crispness. It is also an important addition to Beckett criticism. The intention of the work is stated on the first page: "This essay, in two parts, analyzes how Beckett's novels undermine textual linearity, on the one hand, and the myths of self-transparency, on the other, by turning words into toys, writing into abysmal play."

Using play in several senses—as the narrative play of displacement and fragmentation that characterizes Beckett's fiction, that "steeping in and out of levels of discourse," as Moorjani describes it; as psychoanalytic play, Freud's fort/da game wherein the child substitutes the toy for the absent mother, displacing and returning it as he works through his own frustration at abandonment by the parent; and as play techniques described by Melanie Klein—Moorjani analyzes Beckett's fiction, particularly *Murphy*, *Watt*, and the trilogy.

Given such broad categories as narratology and psychoanalytic theory, it is to Moorjani's credit that the book, a concise 151 pages including a 14-page bibliography, while amply referring to current writing in both areas, and supplying excellent notes suggesting subsequent and more detailed forays into areas of interest, stays with Beckett, using the theories to illuminate the texts, and not, as in some studies, allowing the fiction to become lost in the welter of theoretical apparatus.

What emerges are clear, structured discussions of the major novels and, in the case of *Molloy*, one of the best psychoanalytic readings available. "Infinite reduplication" is what Moorjani calls Beckett's preferred abysmal game, and in the section on narrative repetition, she offers examples of the unending forms such play takes, likening Beckett's narrative fragmentations of his novels to Piranesi's *Carceri* where labyrinthian constructions reduplicate and imprison without seeming end.

Watt is described as a series of games, each a replication of the initial one Watt enjoys as he waits in the kitchen of Mr. Knott's house on the eve of his entry there. The play with colour, a "come and go" game, becomes the model for repeated encounters: Watt fading before the eyes of Hackett, as he fades before the eyes of Sam and of the station master in part 4. Each of these games leads not to unity or meaning but to further displacement, an unending series, mirror within mirror, box within box, or what Moorjani calls a *mise en abyme,* which breaks a syntagmatic chain by means of a paradigmatic series of events, sights, mental forays. Knott's house becomes a narratological "dizzying mirror house and resonance chamber."

The best discussion in this first section—as it is in the second part on thematic reduplication—is on *Molloy*. In both sections Moorjani offers helpful avenues into the text by applying her theory of abysmal play. Building from the discussion of *Watt* as a series of variations on a primal game, she reads *Molloy* as a narrative of the unconscious and the conscious, Molloy and Moran, fragments of one being, "simultaneous versions of the same story on different levels, "Molloy alive in the mind of Moran, the unconscious preceding the conscious in the text, but within the mind of Moran in the psychic framework of the novel. She also sees what she calls the preamble, the A and C section of the opening, as the third part of the work, the attempted meeting of the two.

Thus Beckett, she argues, again fractures the linearity of his story by this narrative displacement as he fractures the self of the character into two: Molloy identified with mother, the unconscious seeking fusion once more with the primary parent, Moran allied to the father, the law, yet finding himself moving toward his unconscious desires as he moves toward Molloy. Moorjani continues the psychoanalytic reading of the novel in the second section of her bock, and if there is a fault in her study, it is the separation of the two parts which would read better if connected rather than as discrete chapters causing the reader to move back and forth to gain a complete analysis of any novel under discussion. It is in the second part, on theme, where Moorjani provides a detailed systematic reading of the elements in *Molloy*, "psychoanalytic topology," in relation to the game theory of Freud and Klein and Oedipal parallels.

Describing how the child may receive conflicting messages, identifying with the father "be like him," warned against taking his place with the mother, "don't be like him,"

Moorjani sketches the movement in the novel as a series of conflicting comings and goings of the male-oriented conscious level personified by Moran who identifies with the law—with religion, with order, with rules—yet at the same time desires to undermine his role and the laws he ascribes to, imputing to his son his desire to disobey, to kill the father, to run away.

The inner story of the unconscious personality, the Molloy section, is described as a commensurate battle of the self and identification with the mother, the primary scene of which is played out in the protracted section in Lousse's garden. Here Moorjani's reading is wonderful, carefully putting the pieces of the fractured encounter together: the killing of the dog named Teddy, Greek for God, the replacement of him by Molloy, the double messages "stay/don't stay" all part of the oedipal myth, the son's desire for and repulsion toward the mother.

Moorjani concludes that while the oedipal myth is at work in the structuring and thematic unity of this part of the text, Molloy is actually an antioedipus, unable to solve the riddle of the Sphinx, receding from upright position to crawl, from Mothers room back to the ditch "the dead yet unborn." In her reading, Molloy's and Moran's meetings with spectre figures in both parts of the novel mirror the same psychic come and go of the fort/da game, the pull of don't/do with commensurate desire to kill and embrace. Thus the images and orders of Youdi and Gaber can be read as the functioning of the law, ordering, contradicting, rescinding, expelling and returning the figures to their starting places.

While Moorjani does not push her reading too far, she does make a strong case for the imagery that sustains the oedipal duplication in the work: the sixteen sucking stones (suck an image related to the mother-oriented Molloy) paralleled by the sixteen theological principles of Moran (law the province of the patriarchal father-connected Moran). She also compares the paradisiacal refuge of Lousse with the patriarchal garden and home of Moran. In both the fictive selves first seek refuge and then retreat. While *Molloy* is clearly the centre of this book, the work also has illuminating things to say about other Beckett novels, particularly about the chess game in *Murphy*, described in detail by Moorjani as yet another variation on a game of mirrors, a fort/da game with Murphy seeking a recognition of self that is impossible for him to achieve.

She also beautifully describes the ending of that novel, Mr. Kelly flying his kite as a fort/da game. Another interesting point that she unfortunately does not pursue except in passing refers to *Watt*. Twice she comments on the novel being a compilation of Watt's Augustinian, Sam's Cartesian, Hackett's empirical, and Arsene's pre-Socratic logic—an archeology of western thought. This idea is worth developing in connection to the theme of game, particularly Beckett's favourite game of devaluing philosophical theories.

In the concluding section of the study, Moorjani illustrates her theory of abysmal game once more by applying the term to the more recent fiction *Company* and *Mal vu mal dit*. This section of the work is less successful than the preceding discussions because of its brevity. More space would have given the author sufficient room for expanding what she does have to say about the two works. Overall, *Abysmal Games* is a fine work, an important addition to Beckett criticism, offering a model of how allied theoretical investigations can provide ready tools for the analysis of fiction.

Beckett's works clearly lend themselves to this type of investigation. After reading Moorjani's book, one has new ideas about the possibilities for further investigation, but does not have the feeling, so often experienced after reading a theoretical approach, that the theory has left the fiction buried below. Throughout this study, Beckett's works remain paramount—a credit to Moorjani's sensitive reading.

Chapter 4

Beckett and the Temptation of Solipsism

Of all philosophical positions and forms of speculation known to mankind, solipsism is perhaps the most extreme and paradoxical. The remarkable thing about affirming the existence of the *solus ipse* as the only known and testable instance and source of existence for the universe is that this affirmation seems to be reached as an extreme logical conclusion of both idealism and empiricism, two otherwise irreconcilable doctrines of thought.

There are few, if any, consistent doctrinaire solipsists in the Western tradition (while they literally abound in Eastern philosophical systems). The best known instances of solipsistic talk (not always accepted as such) are given by George Berkeley and, closer to our days, by Husserl and Wittgenstein. While Beckett is certainly not indebted to the last two (at least not in this respect), he owes much both to some logical persuasions, and to Berkeley.

Berkeley, in his turn, owed a lot to Locke's description of ideas and even to Hume's relational concept of matter. Unlike Locke, however, the Bishop of Cloyne flatly denied the existence of a material substance. "All I can do," he wrote, "is to frame ideas in my own mind. I may indeed conceive in my own thoughts the idea of a tree, or a house, or a mountain, but that is all. And this is far from proving that I can conceive them existing out of the minds of all spirits."1 Few thinkers, writers and ordinary men resonate with the idea of solipsism to the point of, say, enjoying its inner attraction/repulsion, consistency/inconsistency. Among them Samuel Johnson, in a letter to Berkeley, confessed: "The reading of your books has almost convinced me that matter as it has been commonly defined for an unknown Quiddity is but a mere non-entity. That it is a strong presumption against the existence of it, that there never could be conceived any manner of connection between it and our ideas.

That the *esse* of things is only their *percipi...*" The laconic dictum, '*esse est aut percipi aut percipere*,' which summarises the impossible central solipsistic position, without properly enlisting adherents in the Western hemisphere, nevertheless haunted several powerful and critical minds, among whom Fichte, Wittgenstein, and Husserl, let alone Husserl's, progeny: Sartre and Merleau-Ponty. None of these philosophers succumbed to the temptation of absolute, mad, yet contrary-to-fact consistency, more than for a fleeting moment. Solipsism as qualifier is, in philosophical parlance, an insult, and even the suspicion of flirting with it stigmatises one with ignominious guilt.3 As a consequence, a philosopher contaminated by it, however slightly, will retreat into philosophically more sound positions by trying to deploy his own kind of realism, phenomenological (cum corpore, cum conscientia),transcendental, communicational, empirical, dialectic, scholastic, etc.

Not so with Beckett who, fortunately, not being a philosopher, can therefore experiment with the dangerous central dictum of solipsism at will. But if philosophical solipsism is no more than a provisional, ephemeral, almost fictional stage in the development of an argument, it appears in Beckett's work as one of the leitmotifs that lend his artistic construct the indelible emblem of an impossible wager. A singular rhetoric will betray this obsession, a rhetoric of the first person singular (sometimes plural), —soliloquy. *Film*—a metaphysical visual joke about perceiving and being perceived, and therefore, being thrust into being without one's consent—operates no longer upon the Cartesian split of mind and body, but on the more sophisticated one between the Transcendental Ego and the constituted self.

The aporia in Film consists actually in the unbearability of "being perceived" (percipi)— presumably by oneself, but the perfect neutrality and admissibility of "percipere," e.g., the room as perceived by O, is normally perceived, described as bearable. It is the perceivedness of O by E which is agonizingly painful, this very form of inspectio sui à la Geulincx. The split in film might also be expressed as one between the for—and the in—itself, in Sartrean terminology; then it will be the fear of reification leading to the pathological flight of the subject in front of the camera. The camera is objectifying, casting, constituting Buster Keaton in being—an image. It makes visible, it sustains in being, it "creates"; but that may be a secondary, "evil" creation, and the character has our sympathy in trying to escape the camera. It is an evil voyeur engaged in an eternal pursuit of its "object," by violently "bracketting" that object's individuality, subjectivity, inner privacy, soul.

Philosophically, Beckett's descendance stems from Descartes, although there are quite a few important allusions to Greek and medieval philosophy scattered in his work; but as far as the subjectivistic close-in is concerned, one cannot go further in time than Sr. du Perro, who appears as master-model already in the early poem, *Whoroscope*. The Cartesian track has been explored exhaustively, in all its implications, especially in Morot- Sir's "Beckett and the Cartesian emblems,"4 My contention is that from *Murphy* on—and Murphy is acknowledged as both a prototype for future incarnations and as a Cartesian hybrid (not to say Centaur, or chimera),—the Cartesian ontology is refracted through Occasionalism, mainly that of Geulincx, according to whom the "Cogito" is an assertion of powerlessness associated with an incessant and painful introspection; the ego, unlike the Cartesian subject of "cogitationes," is at best an occasion for, and not an underlying substructure of, thinking.

Geulincx spills out treasuries of rationcination only to prove in the end the spirit's impotency of probing into the abyss of matter and of itself. Occasionalism, while acutely aware of the Cartesian problematic, is also convinced of its insolubility and has indefatigably, obsessively insisted, for years, as in a hopeless waiting (Simone Weil), on incomprehensibility and its correlate, the miracles, in the universe. Beckett's moods, even in Murphy, but certainly more so in *Watt*, sound infinitely more akin to the agnosticism and pessimism of a Geulincx than to Descartes's apodictic certainties, purely Cartesian. But even Murphy, once his conarium (pineal gland) is reduced to zero through ascetic practices, allows himself to be "kicked," both in intellectu and in re, and is therefore shaken off his solipsistic posture. Another pillar of Beckett's solipsism seems to arise from his artistic minimalism which directly leads to the last, minimal, and actually non-reducible, residue of all subjectivity: the ego.

At the risk of appearing pedantic and of projecting a favourite grid upon the reading of Beckett, I would advance that he operates in his work one of the most thoroughgoing phenomenological reductions. His aporetic, the systematic deconstruction of language and of meaning, but especially that of reference, is akin to the tedious and sometimes outright inexplicable steps of the Husserlian époché, as well as to a ladder of successive purifications in any genuine mystical system, e.g., that of Advaita Vedanta. This is not to say, however, that Beckett is intent upon reductions or purifications in a teleological way, with a purpose of gaining anything—certainty, salvation, heaven or hell. Phenomenological reduction comes spontaneously to the artist in quest of essences, of simplicity and, in turn, it yields pure formal translucency. By uncluttering the natural landscape, the artist arrives at bare figures and scarce colors; successive eliminations, far from hurting the mysterious meanings, let them shine through. Sometimes the illumination is produced by baring the descriptions, speeches and stories of all their elemental components and leaving intact their genitor: the "I" that speaks.

That way, the Universe will appear as vanishing or be kept in being by a mouth, traversed by a verb or two, which even then seems to transcend its power of generation. Credibility in the evanescent structures of the universe borrows its evocative strength from the ego that gives it intention and intentionality, direction and vectoriality. Outside the "I" that we can vaguely guess behind, the enfeebled syntactic and semantic game little prods us to pay attention: an I, seldom a we. Sometimes only fleeting images which, we know for sure, are shreds of memories, imaginative rags; yet somebody's. Moreover, this asymptotic pole of the artistically suspended universe tends constantly to negate itself: isn't that the only way to silence the whole, the "blooming, buzzing confusion," to annihilate at last Being. Solipsism might be stirred up by the existential anguish which Heidegger expressed in quite classical fashion: "Anxiety individualizes Dasein and thus discloses it as *solus ipse*.

But this existential 'solipsism' is so far from the displacement of putting an isolated subject-thing into the innocuous emptiness of wordless occurring, that in an extreme case what it does is precisely to bring Dasein face to face with its world as world, and thus bring it face to face with itself as Being-in-the-world." One step beyond that, however, the attempt to supersede anguish brings about the nihilation of the ego itself. This is, it seems to me, the deeper sense of Beckett's mysterious play with the: "not-I"—a repeated negative—which exorcises anguish, as in the mouth of Mouth, in *Not I*, where the "battle of the soliloquy" was won, according to Beckett's own expression in *Mercier et Camier*. The same juggling with "I/not-I" pointing both to the ultimate instance in constitution of the universe of discourse and to its cancellation, is to be found in the *Unnamable*, where a constant irony about, and rejection of, the I are exhibited: "Where now? Who now? When now? Unquestioning. I, say I. Unbelieving. Question, hypotheses, call them that.

Keep going, going on, call that going, call that on." And a little further: "I did nothing. I seem to speak, it is not I, about me, it is not about me."6 "Ah yes, all lies, God and man, nature and the light of day, the heart's outpourings and the means of understanding, all invented, basely, by me alone, with the help of no one, since there is no one, to put off the hour when I must speak of me. There will be no more about them." To transcend the state of solipsism, the *solus ipse* must be killed or just bracketted. In *Company* the situation obviously obtains: a super-instance—the Voice—addresses the character in the dark, describing his spatiotemporal coordinates. But the whole is an act of the imagination. Quick, hushed silence is required in the mysteriousness of the process. One could say that the Voice is the Transcendental Ego, absolutely impersonal, addressing a third, an alter Ego.

The emergence of any third appears as highly improbable—in any event, exceedingly difficult. There are two: the Voice and the one, whose reference frame is spelled out by the Voice and whose mind is passive to the point of not even reaching to the Voice. The voice recites the litany of the little boy, and of his mother, hand-in-hand in the Irish—presumably—landscape. The voice speaks of the blue of the sky, and of the day when the other saw the day, and of the father's regrets about it, themes familiar from *Texts for Nothing, Fizzles*, and other opuscules. But in *Company*, a subtle advance takes place, which, one could say, is the investigation of the need not to be the only one left in the world inventing the voice and the hearer and himself. "Deviser of the voice and of its hearer and of himself. Deviser of himself for company. Leave it at that. He speaks of himself as of another. He says speaking of himself, He speaks of himself as of another. Himself he devises too for company.

Leave it at that. Confusion too is company up to a point." *Company* offers in a nutshell the most extreme, and extremely advanced, modern literary shape of solipsism together with Beckett's central "*trouvaille*," a philosophical one, if anything, about the necessity, the duty even, to live with and within the "mess" (*le gâchis*). The piece is about loneliness (and sole-ness too), a loneliness engendering another loneliness, in order to dispell loneliness, an Ego generating an After Ego and another, and so on up to the genesis of the "blooming buzzing confusion" of the world as the end of any alterity. The vast parable of solitude grows into hyperbole when the comic overtones start taking over. What could possibly "enhance company"? Within this feverish activity, led by the author since centuries, is that of "The conjuring of something out of nothing," a voice, even one's own, perceived as not one's own, a different voice received as mysteriously different, imagination, confabulation, even prayer-with a slight shade of self-mockery: the black (of darkness) apt at keeping company, some shades at least, some postures more capable than others.

But which ones? Some locomotion modalities, although they too might remain unidentified, apparently because they might foster some possibilities of meeting. Whom? A dead rat, for example. Fine example of company: long ago a dead rat! In the impossibilities to fight loneliness coupled with the need for company, Beckett touches on his usual aporia at a most delicate point of the phenomenological balance. The "I" that speaks is obviously alone; at the same time, in the mode of its constituting the world in imagination, it must seek the company of others, of an other at least. The first such to be taken seriously is the body: in its "spectral bone-whiteness," it is the first real companion to the "I." The others, as we have seen, are possibly aural phenomena, not far from the hallucinatory, the voices any poet hears, emanating from behind one's own, or from within, but nonetheless pure, disembodied. Finally, there are the even less real, sometimes mock companions, like the vanishing woman in *Company* (which, by the way, seems to carry the mood obverse to that of the woman in *Premier Amour*), the sea, or the tide, the dead rat, etc. This concrete literary experience in solipsism is floating amidst a sea of pessimistic if not outright nihilistic moral connotations.

Obviously, meditating on the evils of mankind, one may emerge as a solipsist—a pathway current in Oriental metaphysics. The idea that every other is a projection of self transcends, however, the implicit moral meditation and takes one abruptly into a hard-to-accept ontological statement. But Beckett had anticipated this aporetic demonstration through symbols much earlier, in the poem "Echo's Bones," in *Murphy*, and *Watt*. Only a reader capable of accepting this progression or regression of thought from search of soleness to its less-than-conditional final assertion can take an opus like *Company* at all seriously. Yet *Company*, along with the stress on the counterfactual of absolute solitude, paradoxically populates the world of the writer and the reader with innumerable phantoms, all results of the fantasmagoric capacity of the I to proliferate and create more similes to one's own self. Modern solipsism, in shifting emphasis from everyday experience and the man in the street to an "author in search of characters" or of subject-matter, proves undeniably subtler, more elusive but also more "realistic," if this word be permitted now, than the classical one.

It is a solipsism of language and meanings, not one of being and knowledge. But why speak of solipsism? Isn't loneliness sufficient as a critical category? The Paradox of solipsism exhibits almost literally the same shape as that of Beckett's ultimate and most profoundly stated aporia: impossible, therefore, unavoidable. I can't, I shall. It is impossible to think of myself as the sole source of being, yet this is inescapably true for the poetic universe, the only one delivered by the writer, anyway; and it is rigorously correct, both experientially and logically. Thus the absurd lies at the core of Beckett's dramaticules, not as sheer non sequiturs, nonsense and flat denials of meaning, but as the logical paradox which moves the writing hand out of its inertia. What logic and reflection affirm, ordinary experience is sure to deny, if we accept Locke's rambling thought that "the mind, in all its thoughts and reasonings, hath no other immediate object than its own ideas, which alone it can contemplate," we must also admit as evident "that our knowledge is only conversant about them."

It appears thus that the possibility of a would-be pragmatic solipsism is at the very roots of modern philosophy, and not at all a post-modern contraption. It is true, however, that the wager of transmogrification of an abstract epistemological argument into the stuff of prose, drama and poetry was won by Beckett, our contemporary, with far-reaching consequences for the notion of art itself. I mean solely that Beckett stands at the frontier between the minimalist experiment and its self-cancellation altogether. Thus, the crave is for a real close-in, and then again for an expansion to the size of the universe as if the skull, once folded in upon itself in deep reverie or reflection, could then, at will, produce or reproduce the whole universe. A passage from *The End* mimics that: "The sea, the sky, the mountains, and the islands closed-in and crushed me in a mighty systole, then scattered to the uttermost confines of space."

So the roots of Beckett's solipsism are in classical British philosophy, although not exclusively there. Here is also his skepticism equal in power and stringency to that of a Nagarjuna or Sextus Empericus. Beckett's pessimism is of Buddhic intensity, whether acquired indirectly through Schopenhauer,16 or independently. Beckett's version of cosmic pessimism is couple with an abhorrence of Self and the sheer mystical bent to destroy Self whenever feasible. The solipsist character par excellence, Murphy, who is also the prototype for all future "egological" characters in Beckett's prose, sleeps well, the first in along time, when he succeeds in conferring upon the self he hates, the aspect even to Ticklepenny's expert eyes, of real alienation.

Another concomitant or perhaps mandatory correlate of solipsism is Beckett's minimalism, which I would characterise as the conscious progression, in his art, towards, experiencing the minimal structures still able to account for an aesthetic effect. In this perspective, the *solus ipse* (in the act of writing) emerges as a minimal, vestigial structure, a bedrock source of difference, and the last irreducible residue (of subjectivity) out of which the universe— dilated or contracted at will — can be engendered. Similarities between Beckett's progressive simplification of the world and the phenomenological reduction have been pointed out by Hesla, and others; it is a procedure he shares with many of the artists in the abstract expressionist tradition.

Yet none of these artists has eliminated the outer world or deconstructed so systematically every objective meaning. "Beckett climbs one more rung in the ascetic ladder" as Jean-Louis Mayoux aptly remarked. The parallel with Husserl, requirement for his époché is striking indeed. Each time

Beckett stages pure voices, void discourses, rather than polyphonic narratives and descriptive paragraphs, it seems bel et bien that it is the Transcendental Ego who speaks, who constitutes himself a body, (mostly a mutilated one), then some kind of persona whom he immediately addresses in the second person, then—why not?—a whole bunch of Alter Egos— the Murphys, the Molloys, the Malones, the Watts, and Worms, and Mahoods, and Macmanns, a whole intersubjective community of monads as Husserl would call it.

All this, however, only to retreat once more into the inaccessible Jar of the Unnamable, or a primordial Womb, Skull, or Tent; yet no sooner is the word "monad" uttered—whether Leibnizian, without window, or phenomenological, somewhat more open to communication, than we are relapsing into the world of absolute closedness, self-containment and self-sufficiency of solipsism.

Beckett's world is a rather unique combination of static and dynamic in the metaphor of the skull, a "hollow sphere hermetically closed to the world without," and the "inside of my distant skull where once I wandered, now I am fixed, lost for tininess or straining against the walls," as the Unnamable would have it. The padded self, like the hollow sphere or the empty chambers, the huts, the caves and the cabins, or, more archetypally, the caskets, are all privileged places that release the imagination and hence the creative power to produce or to annihilate the world. This is the case in *Endgame*. In *Watt*, the Kafkian incident of the piano-tuners, the Galls—father and son—as related by Watt, takes on the value of a symbol for a solipsistic and apriori constitution of meaning. After the younger piano-tuner declares the piano doomed, and they both depart, the narrator starts wondering why the incident did not die in Watt's mind but "continued to unfold, in Watt's head, from beginning to end, over and over again, till it developed a purely plastic content, and gradually lost in the nice processes of its light, its sound, its impacts and its rhythm, all meaning, even the most literal."

Whatever had happened that day, "the scene in the music-room, with the two Galls, ceased very soon to signify for Watt a piano tuned, an obscure family and professional relation, an exchange of judgments more or less intelligible, and so on, if indeed it had ever signified such things, and became a mere example of light commenting bodies and stillness motion, and silence sound, and comment comment." The passage suggests the filmic constitution of a perceptual noema where some allowance is still made for comment on comment" but what a definitely artistic, uninvolved point-of-view, that of the mind that entertains perceptions and "percepi," the type of mind that in *Film* constituted the whole chase of the "I" in rapid, and less rapid, motion. This "fragility of outer meanings" discovered by Watt passes further into no meanings whatsoever, into the very annulment of the pursuit for meaning.

The incident of the Galls which was converted into images "rather belonging to some story heard long before, an instant in the life of another, ill told, ill heard, and more than half forgoften" plays in the narrative the miraculous role of abolishing, for Watt, all possibility of the pre-existence of any "outer meanings" altogether, even of objective correlates of meanings, simultaneously with the occurrence of events, or the encountering of objects. Watt is a drama of "Surds," of utter incommensurability: of Watt to his task; of Knott to his image; of language to feeling; of emotion to reality.

No wonder it ends up, for Watt at least, in the paraphrastic distortion of his language, a total glossolalic effect. It is true that in the end, all the incredible inversions in Watt's speech are straightened out, deciphered, made sense of. But what of Mr. Knott, the master and endgoal of Watt's pilgrimage? Was he discovered? Seen? Understood? Did he succeed in taking away Watt's doubts, down-to-earth habits, empirical convictions, changing him in any way? Well, in this universe of total 'surds,' "Mr. Knott needing nothing, if not, one, not to need, and two, a witness to his not needing, of himself knew nothing, And so, he needed to be witnessed. Not that he might know, no, but that he might not cease...." Actually, to make things more comical, Mr. Knott needs to be witnessed permanently, that is why he is careful to keep two valets, one on the going, one on the coming, lest he be faced with extinction by not being watched. This is the supreme irony directed by Beckett against the very Berkeleyan emblem of solipsism, as there are other ironic treatments of the Leibnizian monadology.

The wager of solipsism which, at times, looks sterner and more earnest than, say, Tertullian's paradoxes, Kierkegaard's fear and trembling, or Pascal's emotional wager of faith, takes on definitely the hue of a literary jocular device, being saved thereby from physical impossibility and ridicule. Telling as these stratagems and devices are in Beckett's art, it would be preposterous to try to inflate his flickering meditations to the size of a philosophical self-conscious thesis, or to dissolve his work into a mosaic of metaphors each of them signifying a philosophical dilemma, an argument, or a counter-argument. Solipsism is not really thematized by Beckett, but only lightly touched upon, toyed with, and, in the end, deconstructed as surely as any other, formal or informal, intellectual proposition that occurs to him; the term "solipsistic" itself appears in the texts qualified in ironic or even oxymoronic ways: "seedy" (Murphy), "peripatetic" (Belacqua), "in love" (*First Love*), etc.

But even as it becomes more qualified, it is negated as such, i.e., text as the willy-nilly accompaniment of the drive to think (along with the impossibility to think) over one's lived experience, as the trace (grammé-Derrida) and/or an allusion to it, never as the thing-itself, humour pulverizing everything, even the hardest of philosophical dilemma, into a shining cloud of stardust. It wasn't perhaps until the 1981 Beckett symposium at Ohio State University, and particularly during the panel on "Beckett's Recent Dramatic Writings," that we in the West were made dramatically aware of the fact that Beckett is alive and well in Poland.

For it was during that session, held in the Drake Union theater where *Ohio Impromptu* enjoyed its world première, that Antoni Libera, fresh off the plane after an eleventh-hour decision, in Poland, to grant him permission to come to Ohio, addressed an audience of several hundred. Libera, who of the ever-increasing number of Beckettians in Poland is certainly the most active representative (as Beckett's chief translator, director of plays, essayist, and editor of special journals), told his audience in no uncertain terms—at least I hope they were, as I was called on at the last minute to act as Libera's translator as he proceeded to read his paper—that Beckett's presence is continuing to make itself significantly felt in Poland, despite the relative isolation of his country from the rest of the Western world.

Under normal conditions, when a contributor is asked to appraise a number of publications for *JOBS*, a meta-critical stance is best. However, given the inaccessibility factor that I am sure applies to most readers of this journal when it comes to Polish publications on Beckett, I have chosen to minimize my own critical afterthoughts, and instead to summarize what I believe are the most salient features to be found in these publications. I hope, of course, that my summaries in themselves will provide Beckett scholars with potential leads for further reflection and investigation.

If nothing else, however, I trust that what follows will help bring to light the scope of Beckettian activities in Poland—a fertile field that has been too long neglected by the majority of Beckett scholars. Mindful of the fact that the Federman-Fletcher Bibliography of 1970 lists only one Polish critic, Jan Kott, I will present each of the more current items in its chronological order. This special monograph issue was composed in anticipation of Beckett's seventieth birthday, as a continuation of the universal homage accorded to Beckett in *Beckett at Sixty*, and in an effort to make Beckett better known in Poland, particularly in terms of his enormous impact on certain key avant-garde currents in contemporary prose writing. Thus, roughly half of the section is devoted to the presentation of previously untranslated prose texts from the Beckett opus.

Other translations include essays by Martin Esslin, Jérôme Lindon, Harold Pinter, Madeleine Renaud, and Alan Schneider. There are, in addition, five original essays and a chronology of Beckett's life and works to 1973. As with each of the items reviewed here, I will focus primarily on the original essays. The logical place to begin, it would seem, is with the concluding essay by A. Libera, "Beckett in Poland". Essentially a plea for a more responsible and consistent practice of translating Beckett into Polish, Libera's purview acknowledges the debt owed to the founding editor of *Dialog*, Adam Tarn, as having done the most, to date, to make Beckett's dramatic works accessible in Poland, as for example in the first issue (1956), which presented translated portions of *Waiting for Godot*.

Thereafter, *Dialog* continues to publish a steady stream of Beckett's plays, as well as translations of reviews of Beckett's works, and, occasionally, pertinent bibliographical information. Equally important in its pioneering efforts is the journal *Twórczoœæ*, which from 1957 on focuses on Beckett's prose works, and provides reviews of non-Polish essays and monograph studies on Beckett, especially from France and the U.S.

But the bottom line of Libera's concluding piece remains a rather urgent criticism of the patterns established by the collective and uninformed attempts to provide "instantaneous" translations of Beckett's works (most notably his theatre); heedless of the problems of form and artfulness in the original language in which Beckett writes his works, such practices too often result in heterogeneous "galimatias," doing grave injustice to the exceptionally homogeneous character of Beckett's language (refrains, key words, similarities of structure, etc.).

Another brief article in this volume is a condensed version of an essay by Alojzy Pallasz ("Motywy okupacyjne u Becketta" ["Motifs of the Occupation in Beckett], *Przegl¹d Humanistyczny*, no. 3,1972), whose title here is "Three cents' worth concerning *Watt*", immediately following Pallasz's translation of the "garden surrounded by a high barbed wire fence" passage in *Watt*. Pallasz offers the readers of this volume a biographical sketch of Beckett during the period in which he was composing this novel (with references to M. Esslin and L. Janvier), and casts Watt as an innocent victim and Christ-like martyr. He concludes, in this spirit, with a reference to

First Love as also reflecting the hellish atmosphere of the early 1940s, a period during which Absolute Evil reigned.

Elsewhere in this volume, Pallasz discusses a fragment of the first manuscript version of *Godot*, where Estragon's name appears as Lévy, and on pp. 233-34 he offers a few observations on "Beckett and Chess," as exemplified in *Murphy* and *Endgame*, with references and comparisons to Borges, Zweig, and Bergman. Clearly the most original and ambitious of the original contributions in this volume, however, is Libera's essay on the structure of *Ping* ("Jak Zbudowane jest 'Dzyń' Becketta?"). Written in 1973, and including a new translation, by Libera alone, of the French *Bing*, Libera's essay tackles the Berkeleyan-Kantian-Heisenbergian riddle of this text (in my opinion, Beckett's most difficult composition), by conducting a minute and painstaking analysis based on a close reading of the nine variant versions.

In his analysis, Libera posits a reconstruction of the "epistemological norms" which are shrouded by the illusory differences (i.e., the variant degrees of whiteness and motionlessness on the one hand, and the unreliable permutations which seek to correlate sensation and perception on the other) that keep the barely perceptive subject and the barely perceptible object in a state of constant tension, one with regard to the other, and that create a metaphoric equivalent of life as a never-ending rite of passage, with occasional "pings" (or "bings" and "hops" in the French version) as the only perceptible signs of progression, bringing the subject to within yet another heartbeat of death and darkness.

Thus, Libera argues (in the first third of his essay), the body of axioms, articulated in the first three phrases, express the Ur theme of the text, constituting a geometric order which (as in the model provided by Spinoza's *Ethics*) is then subject to a series of deductive inferences, seeking to establish their own immanent causality—while at the same time being constantly undermined by the intervention of the uncertainty principle (à la Heisenberg). The second third of the essay examines, in fine detail, the relations between form and substance in "Ping" in terms of its "hardware" and "software," the latter component including three categories (colour; sound; movement), each one of which is programmed (as it were) according to two distinct criteria: inconclusiveness/ conclusiveness.

Thus, the inner articulations, or mechanisms, of *Ping* are so structured and positioned as to constantly challenge—and be challenged by—the globalising efforts of textual finality qua mathematical cohesiveness qua memory bank. ("Ping," or the sound of the loose cog[ito] in the wheel?) In the process of working out *Ping*'s intricate configurations (thematic and declamatory... in the musical sense of the word), Libera draws some interesting conclusions. Among these are: a) the suggested connnections between the seventy semantic units of the text, the opening lines of *The Divine Comedy* where Dante designates the time span of thirty-five years as representing the half-way mark in human life, and *Ulysses*; b) whereas Dante describes the anthropocentric experience of associating with the extraordinary (i.e., the inhuman world of the beyond), Beckett posits the "anti-anthropocentric" experience of extraordinary association, i.e., the inhuman consciousness of an absolute witness... the object of which—"all known"—is the very ground covered by the ten extant versions of the text; c) finally, Libera suggests a philosophically embedded, thematic kinship between *Ping, Ulysses,* and the *Odyssey,* on the one hand, and a similarly related kinship between *Lessness, Finnegans Wake,* and the *Book of the Dead,* on the other hand, with *The Divine Comedy* as the centrally located threshold through which both sets of kinship must pass.

This special programme, dedicated to Beckett on his seventy-fourth birthday, was printed for the opening performances, on 12 April, 1980, of *Krapp's Last Tape, That Time,* and *Not I.* In addition to the complete texts of the translated versions of these three works (with ample photographic documentation), it also includes translations of: essays by James Knowlson, on *Krapp's Last Tape* (from *JOBS,* no. 1, Winter 1976) and on *Not I*; Rick Cluchey's article "My years with Beckett"; Beckett's notes for the staging of *Krapp*; Walter Asmus's rehearsal notes for the German premiere of *That Time* (from *JOBS*, no. 2, Summer 1977, pp. 92-95); excerpts from Deirdre Bair's discussion of *Not I* (from pp. 623-30 of her biography); the J. Knowlson interview with Billie Whitelaw that appeared in *JOBS* (no. 3, Summer 1978); and an original essay by A. Libera, "How I interpret *Not I*" (on the ontological status of Mouth, and the parabolic story it tells, as it searches for the ultimate purge of existence through language).

The second monograph issue from this Warsaw review was compiled in observance of Beckett's seventy-fifth birthday. It too devotes half the space in the special section to translations of Beckett's works. In addition, there are translations of two critical essays, by James Knowlson and Deirdre Bair.

The volume opens with an *état présent*, by A. Libera ("Beckett in the World," pp. 4-130), of Beckett's works published, and plays performed, in Poland, and highlights the significant international milestones in Beckett criticism and scholarship since 1975. In presenting this special issue, Libera states its dual goal as that of broadening an understanding of Beckett's dramatic works in Poland, and of filling the lacunae (and updating) with regard to the 1973 anthology, *Teatr*. Thus, with the publication of this commemorative issue, almost the whole corpus of Beckett's dramatic works is now available in Polish, with the sole exception noted being that of *Words and Music*. (So that if "The Germans ha[d] translated almost everything" by 1977 (the same can now be said of the Poles.)

The second essay is by Marek Kêdzierski, titled "Samuel Beckett over the years"; it reconstructs a bibliobiographical portrait of the artist through his works and critics, and ends with several excerpts from Libera's forthcoming translation of *Company*. Kêdzierski is also the author of an interesting essay, "Descartes, Vico, Beckett," *Przeglad Humanistyczny* No. 5,1979.

Immediately following the thirteen Beckett texts, Libera returns with an essay on "A Piece of Monologue in the light of recent dramatic creations by Beckett" (i.e., *Not I, Footfalls, Ghost Trio, ...but the clouds...*). This original analysis treats the genesis of *Monologue*, from its first conception as a prose text to Beckett's special attention to its staging devices and techniques, as triggered by the 1975 production, by David Warillow, of *The Lost Ones*, by the Mabou Mines. After describing the latter production in detail, Libera traces the evolution of Beckett's staging techniques, which ever since *Eh Joe* have converged to ascribe a new function to the texts, and concomitantly have led to the gradual effacing of the first-person singular from the dramatic dimensions of his characters.

In its place, it is the absent other (the "signified") that assigns a new, ontological status to the staging effects, leading towards what Libera designates as "indirect drama" in which the theatrical signs indicate that what they are signs of (the absent signified) is not directly representable; rather, they can only suggest conjectured forms and mechanisms of the world, as well as of the self, and thus provide poetic insights into the hidden structures of existence.

Libera then examines the architectonics of *A Piece of Monologue*, whose staging itself is a metaphor of the caged form within which the subjective being is confined to its own inner impenetrability, as it contemplates the impenetrable world outside. What connects the two zones of impenetrability is the contrapuntal arrangement of key, spatial delineations (for example, "edge of *frame* [...] out of *frame*"; "*parts* lips [...] *parts* the dark"), enframed within the imagined, introspective landscape, whose boundaries reverberate from one "frame" to another. Within this landscape, Libera calls attention to the "larches," as an autobiographical allusion and symbolic landmark, delineating the point of demarcation between the unadulterated mental perception of youth and the progressive blindness (and foreshadowing of a new, ephemeral and undefinable light) brought about by the debilitating effects of introspection.

What in the final analysis is conjectured into being, in the text of the monologue itself, is an allegorical representation of human existence, whose mechanism is released in the articulation of the opening word of the text: "Birth" (with the ex-plosive b parting the lips, followed by the forward thrust of the tongue, as it expresses sound from the obstructive *rth*, thus instantaneously reproducing the dual phenomenon of conception and childbirth, as word is made flesh at the very instant that it "parts the dark").

What ensues thereafter is an attempt to withdraw (indirectly) into the inner refuge—"the familiar chamber"—of *Film, Eh Joe,* and *Ghost Trio.* The respite, or peace, sought in this inner chamber is at best illusory, for it provides no relief from the unchanging requisite, namely that of creation itself, with no end in view... short of the cemetery, "that place beneath" and beyond the room. This *Piece of Monologue,* then, can only give a premonition of the *monologue of peace,* which, in a world forsaken by God, can't even get off the ground ("he all but said [...]"). (I must add at this point that Libera is in part responsible for this pun, when he refers to the analogous space, or room, in *Ghost Trio*—to which the female voice appeasingly directs our attention: "Look. The familiar chamber"—as an *analogiczny pokój,* for *pokój* means both "room or chamber" and "peace.")

JOBS is highly praised for the scope and quality of its endeavors, especially in the theatrical domain (nos. 1 & 2); summaries of selected essays and book reviews (including the Calder-Israel reactions to Bair's biography) from the first four issues are presented. The Beckett section of the volume concludes with an article on "Staging Beckett in Poland," by Micha Mrozowicki (pp. 248-59). Presented as a survey of the most significant developments, it is chock-full of information. *Literatura,* April 9, 1981, p. 12: A full five-column page dedicated to Beckett's seventy-fifth birthday; includes: a) translations of two "Fizzles' by A. Libera; b) a summary of world-wide Beckett celebrations; c) announces the forthcoming publication of *Company* in *Twórczoœæ* (trans. by A. Libera); d) "Swiat w pulapse Prokrusta" ("The World in Procrustes' Trap"), a pre-publication excerpt from Libera's essay in *Pisma proz*[1], dealing with the two "Fizzles."

Twórczoœæ, no. 4, 1981, pp. 9-17: translation of "Dante and the Lobster," by A. Libera and Ewa Jankowski, also in commemoration of Beckett's seventy-fifth birthday. *Kultura*

(Poland), 7 June 1981: An interview with Libera, by Jadwiga Kurska, entitled *Pociemnialy strop nieba* (The dark cope of sky); this is, in my opinion, as good a summary of what Beckett represents in our Western culture, and as sensitive an insight into his uniqueness, as has seen print anywhere in the world.

This important volume contains translations of numerous prose works written between 1956-76, as well as a long essay by Libera, titled "Beckett's Cosmology". Although the essay is in large part devoted to interpretation and commentary concerning the Beckett works published here, it does much to tie together what might appear as loose ends to the Polish reader who is not current on Beckett's prose; as such, it provides a service that is analogous to that of John Pilling's commentaries in *Frescoes of the Skull*. Composed in 1979, Libera's essay gets its title from Beckett's reference to Milton's cosmology in *From an Abandoned Work* (the opening piece in the volume). Libera begins with an exegesis of "Dante... Bruno. Vico... Joyce," whose chief interest is in the way that it establishes the cornerstones of Beckett's own artistic credo and literary programme. Thus, Libera proposes to guide the reader through the recent prose texts, in view of a reconstruction of Beckett's primary goals as a creative artist-a procedure whose need became manifest with the publication of *Imagination Dead Imagine*.

These goals, as Beckett had outlined in his explanation of Joyce's situation in the evolution of new forms of expression, are: a) to re-instill in man the primacy of his poetic powers, as the only means of providing occasional glimmers of light, and b) to provide the mathematically inspired infrastructure with which to buttress the evocative potentials of language, without which the first goal could not be met; finally, c) with the satisfaction of the first two requisites, to give back to poetic expression its original wholeness. The Beckett opus thus represents a tireless process of language labouring its way, by trial and error, out of the dark labyrinth of unanswerable questions; and in the bulk of his essay, Libera describes and ccomments on this process as it progresses from *More Pricks Than Kicks* to *Fizzles*.

On pp. 110-19, he gives an analysis of the bivalent narrative and multileveled digressions in From an Abandoned Work, and identifies its elements of parable as key metaphors that posit the narrator as a personification of the human race drawing up the balance-sheet of its three-staged evolution in time, in conformity with Vico's anthro-poetical categories, including the tongue-in-cheek Providence which Beckett seized upon in his "Dante... Bruno [...]" essay. This leads to the concluding observation that it's the "tongue in cheek"-ness of a Providential release from the Beckettian pensum that informs Abandoned Work with its ironic, narrative structures (these, to be later radically reduced in "Ping").

The next section (pp. 119-34) explores *Fizzles* no. 1-6. No. 1 is a poetic exploration of a theme in "Dante... Bruno," namely, "The consciousness that there is a great deal of the unborn infant in the lifeless octogenarian." No. 2 exemplifies the narrative hesitancy between spoken and written forms of discourse, and thus highlights narrative uncertainty as to the purported function of discourse itself. Its narrator is a personification of human existence as a hermetic *quality*, taunted by the imagined spectre of elementary will (Horn), which traduces the bivalent relationship of seeing and being.

In anticipation of *Film*, "Horn," by its foreshadowing of the playful manipulations of the Berkeleyian formula, focuses on the theme of "blockage of expression," the latter term referring simultaneously to self-expression and the expression of the self's longing to be identified with a higher order. With reference to no. 3 and no. 4, Beckett's representation of the interdependence between the mortal and the immortal is compared to Schopenhauer's *World as Will and Idea*, Hölderlin's "Rhine," and Simone Weil's *La Pesanteur et la grâce* (1947) and *La Connaissance sumaturelle* (1950).

Well's principle of creation as divine abdication—with humankind bearing the brunt of God's benevolent joke—is seen in no.4 as fusing with Vico's theory of language, to produce the image of immortal being, as conjectured within an inner necessity rather than projected onto the level of the exteriorized sign-as-subjective-disclosure. The world is thus limitless existence, insatiable in its quest for a suitable form at the same time that it is subject to the Procrustean bed of man's own insufficiency. No. 6 is a spontaneous expression of inner resonances, highlighting the theme of unbridgeable, inner separateness between experience and consciousness.

Though its spontaneity is paradoxical, inasmuch as its structure is based on a series of associative links, it is at the same time stressed by the sudden surfacing of a line, in the original foirade no. 5, and just as sudden a disappearance from the English translation, from Canto 7 of the *Infemo: Tristi fummo nell'aere dolce.* Canto 7 also furnished Beckett with the allegorical scenario (the Fifth Circle) for How It Is, a work that represents a solitary, intermediate stage in the evolution of narrative forms, between the *Fizzles* and *Imagination Dead Imagine,* the latter of which opened the way for the full expression of Beckett's earliest formulated goals.

There follows a discussion of *Enough,* which, although written one year after *Imagination* (in the original French versions of both), belongs to the pre-*Imagination* group of texts, as Beckett himself indicated by placing it before *Imagination* in the published collections. Although Libera's positioning of this text differs from Pilling's, for whom the "placing [of] *Enough* in pole position before the other residua" is sign enough of "Its unprecedentedness", the question as to which of these views is more persuasive is, in my opinion, a draw.

On Pilling's side, "it is only in *Enough* that Beckett discovers the prose style that breaks decisively with what has gone before," a prose style characterized by its absence of commas; the Kaminski-Libera translation, on the other hand, presents a challenge to this criterion inasmuch as it reintroduces the commas, following the example of Elmar Tophoven's translation into German,[3] checked and approved by Beckett himself.

Another formal criterion that Pilling notes is "the return to paragraphed prose" as "another index of *Enough*'s individuality," an observation that leads Pilling to conclude that "Enough is in fact somewhat regressive in its reliance on paragraphs" (*Frescoes,* p. 151); and further, to cite Pilling as support of Libera's placing of "Enough," *The Lost Ones* is actually much closer in subject-matter to *Imagination Dead Imagine* than it is to "*Enough*, the work which immediately preceded it". Another, perhaps more interesting, point of comparison between the Pilling and Libera readings of *Enough* is the former's stress on the sexual neutrality of the narrating figure despite the feminine tone and the "accoutrements" which appear in the last line of the text, and the latter's description of *Enough* as the feminine counterpart of *From an Abandoned Work*.

For although Libera acknowledges the importance of narrative androgyny in the original French and English versions, and explains why it is impossible to preserve that neutrality in the Polish translation, for the simple reason that the past tense (in which *Enough* is narrated) of narratives in Polish, an inflected language, inevitably discloses the sex of the narrator, his analysis refers to the narrator in the masculine form (*narrator*, rather than *narratorka*), while he describes the theme of encounter in the story as one which occurs between the narrator as a young female and an old authority figure, the whole story itself being mused over by an old (feminine) narrator left unto her solitary wanderings.

Whatever other ambiguities may lie beneath the narrative surfaces of this text, Libera views it as a condensed Genesis of the relationship of the human species to its maker, from prehistoric eras to the parting of the ways shortly after man's emergence, with "Aquarius hands," from the floods. The "Aquarius hands" (in the fifth paragraph of *Enough*), for their part, emerge as *rêce Wodnika* in the Polish translation; *Wodnik*, or "Water-Bearer,' also designates a water spider, another form of which, in Polish, is *wodnica*; this feminine form is derived from the German *Nixe* (or "nixie"), referring to a female water spirit, or mermaid. The masculine *Wodnik* (filtered through the German) thus preserves at least some of its sexual ambiguity. Ambiguity is perhaps the key issue in this parable.

For man, prematurely forestalled in the process of forming himself when God abandons him, is left pondering the question: "What do I know of man's destiny?" (in the penultimate paragraph of the text). His memory, meanwhile, keeps the time of his pre-abandoned state alive, and it can do so only by driving out of the mind the consciousness that something (or anything) lies in the past, including the written opus itself.

The means for the narrator to achieve this type of oblivion is through his/her narration itself. The paradoxical effect arrived at being that words are made dispensable by the very process of their bringing about a fusion of things as they are with things as they were before the separation; and yet it is through the word, and the word alone, that man can maintain contact with divine being, or, in other words, it is only through the divine word that the past can still be made present. And, as words go, the title word alone—*Enough*—is in itself an ambivalent summa of Beckett's quests in first-person narrative prose.

In the next section, on *Imagination Dead Imagine*, Libera analyzes the depiction of the white rotunda as an allegory of life in the womb, and also of Eden before the expulsion of Adam and Eve (in much the same way, it seems to me, as "*Enough* [which] is pre-eminently a narrative of separation" [*Frescoes*, p. 152] can be seen as representing the same motif, that is to say, life before and after birth). The allegorical dimensions here, however, are only a pretext for challenging the imagination's potential to project metaphorical equivalents of reality by "shaking off the yoke of perception," i.e., by immuring the imagination in the milky whiteness of silence (p. 149). (Note, in passing, Libera's creative translation of "omit" [the second hypothetical imperative of *Imagination*] as "za*milk*nij," or "fall silent.") Finally, *Imagination* is judged to be a paradigm of the Beckett cycle death of imagination-birth of primitive memory-birth of individual existence-death of observer—settling the score with the systems of Bruno and Vico.

The Lost Ones is discussed on pp. 152-63, where Libera explores life in the cylinder from within the two domains of the narrative: informational and factual, on the one hand, interpretative and hypothetical, on the other. An English version of this was presented at the Ohio State Symposium and was published in *Samuel Beckett: Humanistic Perspectives*. With due reference to Dante's *Purgatory*, he describes the cylinder as a highly compressed microcosm of human existence, with the narrative voice representing man's mythical propensity for penetrating the mysteries of his world on the one hand, and the compromises that his analytical abilities are forced to conclude with the unfathomable, on the other.

The frustrations of the lost ones are compounded by the fact that the unfathomable mysteries are themselves excluded from within the confines of the cylinder, as the channel of communication from within to without is obstinately blocked off. This sets the stage for a presentation of the world as being caught up in an incessant dialectic, while man's quests for a way out of the dilemma cut a distinctively regressive path. *The Lost Ones* is thus a poetic variation on Vico's theory, in that what is discovered (Divine Providence, taken here as the will to transform one's mode of existence) in man's never-ending quest is not what was originally sought out.

The section on *Ping* (pp. 163-70), by comparison to Libera's earlier study (in the first volume reviewed here), presents a compact, yet incisive, analysis of this text, whose seventy, semantic units—beginning and ending with "All [...] over"—represent units of time. With *Lessness* (pp. 170-81), Beckett achieves the poetico-ideologico-philosophical summa of his opus (cf. the summa attained in *Enough*), as Libera demonstrates by way of a detailed, formal analysis of the mathematical configurations of the text's internal arrangement (as previously done by J. M. Coetzee and J. E. Dearlove). The text, broken down into six evenly distributed groups of ten sentences each, offers a totalizing image of life, reduced-and exponentially magnified to astronomical potentialities—to a Platonic idea: the world as a shattered pattern, torn apart by the conflicting forces of the need to create and the impossibility of same.

The theme of totalization is seen as an homage to the last Canto of *Paradise*, which, informed with the numerical values of three and ten, posits a three-part synthesis of being: content, attribute (or quality), and sign (or manifestation), and also to Vico's three ages and three institutions.

Libera wraps up his essay with commentary on *Still* (*Fizzle* no. 7)... Still, or 'being there' in three acts: looking, touching, listening. *For to end yet again* (*Fizzle* no. 8) postulates a prophetic vision of the twilight of humanity and eventual replacement by some other form of existence, the latter being open to speculation. And, in the Conclusion (pp. 187-88), Beckett is crowned "cosmologist of transitory climes."

Błoński's eight-part essay, "Samuel Beckett", (pp. 5-51), is an extended version of his Afterword to the anthology *Teatr* and begins this volume. It is a sensitive and intelligent profile of the intellectual and esthetic paradoxes that make up the man and his autonomous creation. Liberally sprinkled with quotations from various works, it discusses the following topics:

- The circularity of Beckett's universe; and the spiral configurations in his works, achieved by the endless variations and resumptions of Beckett's wandering words (with *Molloy* singled out as the masterpiece of Beckett's narrative prose), leading to the inevitability that the patterns charted out by the tenacious processes of Beckett's *inspecto sui,* in the fiction, were to lead to the stage.
- Beckett's stage, though characterized by powerlessness, immobility, and confinement, becomes infused with an increasingly resistant temporality. Time is a palpable substance on the Beckett stage; it sticks to each word and gesture, against which the latter activities (representative of all human activity) rail endlessly by resorting to four essential, and substantially theatrical, processes: rhythmic disruption, annulment, anatomization (or disarticulation), and above all, repetition, albeit anything but mechanical. Beckett's theatre is thus a visualization (or, in the case of the radio plays, an audition) of the reciprocity between the reversibility of events, on the one hand, and the circularity of time,

on the other, a theme that had surely been inspired in the young Beckett's mind by *Ecclesiastes.* Theatrical time, in Beckett, is a static present, leading nowhere, giving rise to nothing save the sole element of surprise possible: that one of the repetitions will be the last.

— The predominant role of corporeality in Beckett's theatre is in large part responsible for his humour, which is compared to that of Shakespeare, Bruegel, and Aristophanes, while his merciless treatment of the erotic impulse smacks of a certain irrepressible puritanism. This creates a paradox, whereby the more "flesh bound" the themes, the more verbose the texts; "in a word, Beckett's metaphysics is always expressed in terms of physical signs", a metaphysics predicated on the inevitability of corporeal loss, and, in the case of the loss of others, on solitude: "Beckett's hell is very anglosaxon, individual, and law-abiding. His victims fall in light of their own will, as they prepare for the self-inflicted punishment to which they have been condemned". An attendant observation by Bloñski is that Beckett's is a truly classless society (the absence of historical consciousness in *Godot* makes the facile identification of Pozzo as symbol of ownership and Lucky as symbol of proletariat invalid), made up of the weak and the strong, the cruel and the submissive; in *Endgame,* on the other hand, evil is revealed in its pure state, inseparably bound with humanity.

— On meaning-lessness in Beckett's literary universe: this is the fundamental condition against which Beckett's characters exercise their will to express, if not to signify, creating an extraordinary pathos, whereby speech is the very sign of existence (no more, no less) all the while it gravitates towards death. Existence is the signified, postulated by the boldfaced lie of literature itself as a signifier of anything at all. The stories it tells are substitutes for meaning, for goals, for order, and are therefore indispensable for the existence of the Beckett man: this is why his existence *is* a dying process.

— The tragic element in Beckett's vision is a purifying motif, as it strips away the moral relativism of historical considerations, and rejoins (in spirit, if not in form) the universality of the tragic in Classical Greece, in that it highlights not so much the tragedy of the paths that lead to death, but rather the ever-shrinking paths themselves. This shrinking process is due to the cunningly calculated refusal, on the part of whatever it is that we are waiting for, to justify itself as the object of the waiting: "To claim that *Godot* is only the sign of the waiting is to wriggle out of the issue. We likewise wait for meat and for the trolley, often to no avail. The significance of the waiting can only come from whomever or whatever it is that we are waiting for. The riddle of *Godot,* however, is familiar to those who have been puzzled by the sacrifice of Abraham, the story of Job, or the parable of the workers in the vineyard. From another angle, and despite the fact that it is not an allegory, *Godot* can be seen as a never-ending Purgatory, a valley of tears; as is true of virtually all of Beckett's theatre, there are no clearly defined symbols here. Instead, we are confronted by an appreciably prevailing metaphysical concern with survival itself—nurtured by the never-ending and admittedly futile quest for dissimilarity, indeed for absolute Otherness—the tools of which are good will and lack of illusions.

— In the face of it all, again, the humour, as a means of periodically distancing us from the pervasive tragedy, a humour which, in itself, does not go unchanged from one version to the other: for example, the English *Godot* is more subtle and spirited than the French. As a rule, Beckett's humour is most effective when, in the circular give and take of the humorous and the tragic, it's the humorous that starts the ball rolling, for it puts us in a more truthful light, and cushions the fall from grace (or what we think was the case) that mankind, in its presumptuous egocentrism, has always complained about.

— Beckett's "fiducial point" is an empty place, after God; the tragic element is provided by man's looking into the emptiness, while the comic element is provided by the emptiness looking back at man. While the tragic element gives rise to the voice of protest, the comic element is the only one of the two that can accommodate man to his lot, on the condition that he give up the notion of his cosmic primacy. The comic is born of the void, and rebounds back to the tragic; the tragic, in turn, addresses its plaint to the void, and rebounds in laughter—each performing its necessary role, in turn, endlessly. This state of affairs is developed to a farcical climax in *Endgame*, an anti-*Godot*, a hell that is life, death, and fate all-in-one.

— Thereafter, beginning with *Happy Days*, Beckett's theatre becomes a subtle panoply of humanity's indefatigable, yet knowing, preoccupations with its own triviality, while it is increasingly submerged in the realization of its unpurgeable suffering on the one hand, holding out, on the other, for the possibility—however minimal—that the word, once it will have absorbed all it can of its own superfluousness, may reveal, in the hollow of its own poetic insignificance, a beauty heretofore unspoken. As Czeslaw Milosz has written,

Civilization is defined by its creations; whosoever wishes to penetrate its essence must take stock of its most honest writer, Samuel Beckett. The greatness of the capitalist West lies in its having produced and claimed as its own a writer such as Beckett—a writer who chose truth with no illusions, [...] a writer who has formulated the mass-scale consciousness of meta-physical Absence. The essay by Kêdzierski, titled "Końcówka" ["Endgame"], opens with critical observations on the prominence of the closed-room motif since *Malone Dies,* and leads into an analysis of *Endgame,* with special focus on Hamm (as Malone-Pozzo-Lucky, rolled-in-one, and strapped into his Cartesian wheelchair), who in his monologue is seen to be echoing metaphysical concerns of Schopenhauer and Calderon, while leaning towards religious significance, as witnessed by distorted allusions to, and citations from the Bible.

In addition, Kêdzierski is setting the record straight, by pointing to key inaccuracies in the J. RogoŸinski translation of *Endgame,* without, however, overstressing his case. Rather, his intention is to trace the "Fundamental sounds" with which Beckett had structured his polyphonic text—"structure" being taken in the way Beckett speaks of the "structural" in "Dante... Bruno. Vico.. Joyce," i.e., a "decoration of arabesques—decoration and more than decoration [... where] form *is* content, content *is* form." Thus, Kêdzierski examines selected passages from the French, and compares them to the English translation, showing how the RogoŸinski translation gives short shrift to the polyphonous, bicameral structures that inform the two versions of the text with their shared resonance.

He also cautions against the "interpretative paranoia" that ensnares those critics of Beckett who, on the one hand, isolate a given work from the surrounding opus, and on the other hand neglect to take account of structural coordinates within the framework of the individual text under consideration, and who, failing thus to recognize the similarity of structural patterns that creates an inner bond from one work to the other, consequently end up viewing Beckett's poetic creations as metonymical, rather than metaphorical.

In the same context, he describes the futility of attempts to follow through with any one thread among the many literary or mythical allusions in *Endgame,* without obviating the interdependency of the two, mutually exclusive, dominant themes at play, namely, *ending* and *playing,* whereby the chaos of forever-unwinding linearity is accommodated by the form of endless circularity. Any critical interpretations of the enclosed space within which this drama occurs must therefore by confined within the network of resonances generated by the arabesque-like reverberations of its "fundamental sounds"—which are themselves reverberations of similarly fundamental sounds in otherly inscribed Beckett texts—whether these be identified as chiefly suggestive of intertextual, biblical, mythological, metaphysical, psychological, or autobiographical motifs. This, Kêdzierski explains, is what Beckett himself had warned, when speaking to the actors of Berlin's Schiller Theatre he equated the "action" of *Endgame* to a game of chess, its execution being determined by its preordained failure.

Dialog, vol. 28, no. 3 (March 1983): table of contents, in English; includes A. Libera's translation of *Ohio Impromptu,* and El¿bieta Jasiñska's translation of S. E. Gontarski's revealing essay, "*Ohio Impromptu*: Play Against Text". Also included is an original play by Feliks Falk, which in the table of contents is listed as *There and Back,* while on page 3 (in the Polish table of contents) its title reads: *Tam i z Powrotem*—which happens to be the title of the Polish translation of *Come and Go.* Finally, the back cover of the issue announces the publication of *Kolysanka* (*Rockaby*) in a forthcoming issue.

Finally, a few words on the translations: needless to say, it would require a great deal of time and space to do justice to the painstaking and masterful feats accomplished by the various translators represented in these publications. The sheer volume and rhythm with which Beckett's Polish translators produce their work is in itself remarkable, and should serve as a reminder that, together with the other languages into which Beckett's works continue to be translated, there is more than ample material for countless studies to be made. The scope of the matter is all the more awesome if one takes into consideration the fact that in Polish alone there are often two or more translations of the same text.

Chapter 5

A Typology of the Posthumous Narrative

For there be divers sorts of death - some wherein the body remaineth; and in some it vanisheth quite away with the spirit.

In one kind of death the spirit also dieth,
and this has been known to do while yet
the body was in vigour for many years.
Sometimes, as is veritably attested,
it dieth with the body, but after a season
is raised up again in that place
where the body did decay.

According to many systems of belief, there is a part of the human being which goes on to lead an independent existence even after physical death has set in. This part, which is usually called the soul, is assumed to be conscious and to bear the characteristic traits of the deceased's personality. Since antiquity, this supposed transformation has been used for narrative purposes.

But even in modern times, when the belief in an afterlife has become less widespread, authors have used it as a convenient fiction for their own ends. However, the ideas of what exactly constitutes death have been somewhat modified over the centuries, as have been those about the soul and the imagined conditions of the afterlife. The smallest common denominator for the declaration of death seems to be the ceasing of the bodily functions, but not necessarily that of consciousness. As a matter of fact, some sort of consciousness

- wherever it is to be located - is a prerequisite for this type of narrative, because otherwise there would be nothing to narrate but what happens to the body after death.

This consciousness, however, may take on many forms, reaching from a seemingly uninterrupted continuation of the earlier form of existence to an (almost) complete break with it. This is partly correlated with the question of how far the dead are aware of the fact that they are dead.

Since the circumstances of the posthumous condition depend largely upon the various kinds of awareness belonging to this condition, the following observations will be structured upon the pattern of the latter. I shall therefore first describe various types of the posthumous experience - ranging from full knowledge and acceptance of death to complete ignorance - and then speculate upon their possible uses. Although I have tried to give historically important examples of the appearance of a particular type, systemisation rather than chronology has been my concern.

"Damned to Fame" is not the first life of Beckett, of course. Notably, there was Deirdre Bair's 1978 biography, which drew on many letters she had discovered from Beckett to his friend Tom MacGreevy. They dispel the notion of Beckett as a philosophical recluse and show him as a man whose troubles shaped his writing. Mr. Knowlson has had full access to the MacGreevy letters, unlike Ms. Bair, and to six notebooks reporting Beckett's mind-altering trip through Germany in 1936-37.

He added dozens of other sources. Beckett died six months after Mr. Knowlson began his work (he retired as a professor of French at the University of Reading in England to take it on). For five months, in brief visits, they discussed his life. Mr. Knowlson's presentation of these materials is academically invaluable. Much more important, he has composed a remarkable portrait of an impressive man. "Damned to Fame" is a magnificent biography.

Beckett's writings hold their audience because they are emotionally intense and disturbing. They are also richly allusive, evocative of literature, art, music, philosophy and psychology. Mr. Knowlson speaks authoritatively about these matters, without ostentation. He gives credit unstintingly; he even mentions me once.

The biography, though sadly shortened from the manuscript, is enlivened by suggestive details. Examples: Beckett's maternal grandmother rebuked a granddaughter who loved chocolates. "You shouldn't love something to eat, my dear. You should only love God." His uncle Gerald Beckett, rather different, called life "a disease of matter." When Beckett's father died, Gerald comforted the widow: "Well, May, he's got it over. What is it all about, in the end, for us all, from the cry go, but get it over?"

Such anecdotes bring alive decades of Beckett's public accomplishments and private doubts, regrets and illness. Mr. Knowlson modestly claims to have found new materials in three areas: "music and art," Beckett's political activities and Beckett's character. Readers will find much more.

Beckett's lifelong absorption in classical music (he was a competent pianist) and his concern for the verbal music of his own writings are matched by his knowledge of art: "He could spend as much as an hour in front of a single painting . . . savoring its forms and its colors, reading it, absorbing its minutest detail." Mr. Knowlson also shows how Beckett's dramatic scenes, figures, gestures and lighting echo these artworks.

The German diaries record Beckett's many meetings with painters, and discussions of paintings. They also convey his distaste for Germany's increasing anti-Semitism and censorship and Hitler's long, shrill speeches.

That topic prepares us for Beckett's activities with a French Resistance group and with the Irish Red Cross in France after World War II. In this grim work he displayed "astonishing powers of concentration, a meticulous attention to detail," Mr. Knowlson says; he could "organize, reduce and sift very diffuse material so as to make it succinct and intelligible." Those qualities recur in his writings. Additionally, "sheer obstinacy . . . was, he commented himself, a constant trait in his character."

That difficult, variable character is Mr. Knowlson's major theme. He describes a model of upper-class Protestant gentility: the 4-year-old praying; the youth playing golf, tennis, rugby and cricket, swimming, boxing, running track and racing motorcycles; and the college student who neither smoked nor drank.

But higher education puts at risk conventional faiths and values: "On the key issue of pain, suffering and death . . . Beckett's religious faith faltered and quickly foundered." A sermon in which a Canon Dobbs said that the only thing he could tell the suffering, dying and bereaved was, "The Crucifixion was only the beginning. You must contribute to the kitty," shook Beckett. So did Dobbs's advice to the unhappy: "When it's morning, wish for evening. When it's evening, wish for morning." Adding Baudelaire, Beckett sharpened that idea in "Endgame": "You cried for night; it falls: now cry in darkness."

Beckett discovered Dante and recent French writers at Trinity College, Dublin. He won an appointment to the Ecole Normale Superieure in Paris, met James Joyce and published a monograph on Proust. His career was under way. But this flawed summary evades the harshness of his writings.

Here Mr. Knowlson is especially valuable, providing persuasive detail. The young Beckett was an arrogant and withdrawn brat: "He confessed later to feelings of superiority and contempt, which led to a depression that came to seem . . . 'morbid.' " Teaching at Trinity, he met his like among colleagues. "Scholarly wit and sarcasm," Mr. Knowlson says, "sounded all too often like exhibitionism, bitchiness and character assassination." As for creativity: "How can one write here," Beckett complained, "when every day vulgarizes one's hostility and turns anger into irritation and petulance?"

Those perceptions, and psychosomatic illnesses, led to painful psychological insight. Beckett abandoned teaching and entered therapy after his father's death in 1933. Mr. Knowlson is eloquent about the effects of that death. The therapy lasted about six months, Beckett told him. (He once told me three.) "In reality his treatment lasted nearly two years," Mr.

Knowlson says. What Beckett would not tell him he had written to MacGreevy. In March 1935, after some 150 sessions, he wrote an amazing letter. With bitterness and detachment he summarized what he now knew about his illness. Mr. Knowlson specifies its causes: "the intensity of his mother's attachment to him and his powerful love-hate bond with her." Later, fleeing his mother and Ireland after a dreadful quarrel, Beckett offered MacGreevy a memorable phrase: "I am what her savage loving has made me."

Accurate analysis is not therapy. The relationship and its effects continued. Even in his last months, Mr. Knowlson says, "Beckett's feelings of love for his mother and remorse at having, as he saw it, let her down so frequently, struck me as still intense, almost volcanic." About his remarkable wife, Suzanne, who died some months earlier than he, he suffered similar guilt and remorse.

But that hard-won knowledge of his psyche had altered him. Mr. Knowlson describes his letter of self-analysis as "the first convincing explanation of how the arrogant, disturbed, narcissistic young man . . . evolved into someone who was noted later for his extraordinary kindness, courtesy, concern, generosity and almost saintly 'good works.' "

Beckett's outer world is not neglected, although space limitations restrict discussion of the trilogy of novels, "almost certainly the most enduring works that Beckett wrote." Mr. Knowlson is insightful about the plays and detailed about their performances. A playwright gives hostages to fortune. We hear of many misfortunes and some near misses, especially with "Godot." Imagine Buster Keaton as Vladimir and Marlon Brando as Estragon.

The inner world persists. Beckett remains painfully aware of his faults, unable to mend them and struggling to compensate for them, as Mr. Knowlson guides us through the powerful writings in which he dramatized the blackness in his psyche.

Beckett becomes his own finest character. Mr. Knowlson is with him to the final curtain, unblinking: "Beckett became frailer and thinner. His hands were now noticeably distorted.

. . . Greeting him with a fond embrace, you noticed how prominent his shoulder blades felt . . . and how thin his wrists and forearms had become." Born on Good Friday, April 13, 1906, he died on Friday, Dec. 22, 1989.

What is the meaning of this complicated life? Mr. Knowlson reports discussing with Beckett his brief autobiographical novel "Company": "We laughed uproariously at the idea of reaching 'truth' in so shifty an area as a human life." Weeks before he died, William Butler Yeats wrote: "When I try to put it all into a phrase I say, 'Man can embody truth but he cannot know it.' I must embody it in the completion of my life." "Damned to Fame" splendidly preserves the truths embodied in Beckett's life.

VARIETIES OF DEATH

The Conscious Dead

The traditional account of what happens after death is that the immaterial soul of the deceased detaches itself from the body and goes on a journey to some other place, often characterised as heaven or hell, where it will then dwell forever. One of the earliest fictional representations of the postmortal life in English appears in a work that is usually seen as a precursor of the novel proper: John Bunyan's *The Pilgrim's Progress* (1678). Here, we find a visionary account of an after-death experience in the form of a journey which starts in familiar surroundings, but moves into less and less familiar territory until it finally reaches - or at least comes into sight of - a goal, which - when reached - will be the place of fulfillment. The main intention is, of course, to exhort the reader to look at his life and to mend his ways.

It is remarkable, however, that the novel proper hardly ever takes the idea of the afterlife in this form seriously, but rather uses it for satirical or polemical purposes, although this does not exclude a didactic element. Such is the case in Henry Fielding's *A Journey from this World to the Next* (1743), where in the first part the anonymous narrator, a newly departed soul, relates his adventures on his voyage to This affords much opportunity for satiric swipes at doctors and tourist-guides in the style of a travelogue, since the soul is still at a transitional stage and has not yet become accustomed to its new state. The judge guarding the gates of paradise is Minos, whose criteria for admittance resemble strongly those precepts for human benevolence advocated by Fielding in his other works. The souls who fail to gain admittance are, as a rule, sent back to earth to try again. The narrator, however, gains admittance.

In the second part the narrator relates interviews with several famous persons that he meets inside paradise, and which throw quite a different light upon their characters. The last part of the work is the story of the life of Anne Boleyn, told by herself, in which she appears "more sinned against than sinning" and is admitted into paradise in compensation for what she has suffered. The whole narrative, then, attempts to be a broad satiric mirror for the various walks of life.

It is in this satiric vein, too, that Hawthorne uses the form in "The Celestial Railroad", in which the protagonist reenacts Christian's journey in the *Pilgrim's Progress*, only this time modern advancements in religion speed the traveller along without any trouble - the only drawback being that he will never reach the Celestial City.

An interesting variation of this type of narrative is represented by David Danziger's *The Devil in Miss Jones*, where a 30 year old catholic virgin called Justine commits suicide, because yet another frustrated boyfriend has left her after six months of a platonic relationship. She wakes to find herself in a sort of clearing house between heaven and hell. Since she has led a life free from sin, she would normally go straight to heaven, but of course her suicide is unforgivable. She is, however, given a week's respite on earth in order to really earn hell. Before she is allowed to return, she is given a thorough training in all the varieties of sex, which she then practices with abandon during her week on earth. When she is finally consigned to hell, her punishment consists in being forever encarcerated with a man whose sexual interest she is unable to arouse. The satirical butt of the novel is obviously the catholic religion and its prohibitive attitude towards sex.

Even more bitingly anti-religious is Stanley Elkin's *The Living End* which could also be called the ultimate posthumous narrative, because it ends with the destruction of creation as we know it. It tells of three men whose deaths are linked through the almost accidental murder of one of them at the hands of the two others and who meet again in hell. They all know that they are dead - but they cannot accept the consequences. The victim, Ellerbee, was the very model of a "good man" who cared more for others than for himself. The greater his surprise, when St. Peter at the pearly gates tells him to go to hell - and hell really is hell in every way. He later meets one of his murderers who died a natural death at the age of almost one hundred. The manifest injustice of this incites Ellerbee to blasphemy which actually gets him God's attention. Asked for an explanation of it all, God tells Ellerbee that the latter did neither honour the Sabbath nor his parents (whom Ellerbee never knew, being an adopted child), that he took God's name in vain, and - worst of all - that he thought, Heaven looked like a theme park.

All ideas of a God who, if not merciful, is at least just, are here put to ridicule. Veneal and cardinal sins alike assure everlasting damnation and punishment. Admission to heaven, on the other hand, depends only on God's whim. At a final great party, God gives a glorified account of his career and then reveals the ultimate motif behind everything he has done: "It was Art! It was always Art. I work by the contrasts and metrics, by beats and the silences. It was all Art. Because it makes a better story is why."

With artistic aplomb, God has chosen the perfect moment for his disclosure, for it marks the beginning of Doomsday and bodily resurrection. But not for long, since a disillusioned God proceeds to annihilate everything, giving as his reason: "Because I never found My audience." This, presumably, is then really the end. These narratives have in common, that their protagonists are searching for a meaning - if not for their lives, then at least for their deaths. This search is presented to the reader either in a didactic vein, as in *The Pilgrim's Progress*, or with satirical intentions, as in the other stories. But even

Bunyan uses the form to show up vices, and there are certainly also didactic elements in the satirical narratives.

The Puzzled Dead

The previous examples showed the dead as being fully aware of their state and behaving in the traditionally expected manner - albeit with certain variations. In the following cases, the dead find it much more difficult to understand and to come to terms with their new state. Generally speaking, "real" death only sets in, when it has been accepted as such, because only then there is a sense of closure and a more or less peaceful state can be reached.

Sometimes the dead do not realise for quite a while what has happened to them. Only after they have been confronted with incontrovertible evidence do they accept the fact of death. Such is the case in Ambrose Bierce's "An Inhabitant of Carcossa". The anonymous first-person narrator finds himself of a sudden in unknown and completely deserted surroundings, somewhat reminiscent of a former cemetery. He remembers having been ill and believes he has somehow recovered his health, but has lost his way. A lynx and a savage cross his path, buth they don't seem to notice him. Finally, he encounters his own tombstone, and when the sun rises and he does not cast a shadow, he realises that the ruins around him belong to the town of Carcosa, in which he formerly lived.

In Mervyn Peake's "Danse Macabre" there is a husband who notices one night that his dinner suit leaves the wardrobe all by itself and has a clandestine meeting in the woods with his wife's evening dress. The next night, husband and wife decide to find out about this and go to bed dressed in their respective clothes. They are lead into the woods, and when the husband returns the next morning, he finds himself and his wife both dead in bed.

The indications that something strange is going on are far more subtle in Muriel Spark's *The Hothouse by the East River*, where the first hint is conveyed by the present tense in which the story is told throughout, thus indicating the timelessness of the events. Another strange feature is Elsa, the main protagonist, whose shadow, as her husband Paul maintains, falls in the wrong direction, i.e. towards the source of light instead of away from it. But the possibility that either or both are insane cannot be ruled out for quite a while, and their friends act strangely too. There are different versions of their common past, which they try to work out. It is finally revealed that they have all been killed by a V2 in London in 1944, but they strenuously try to deny this.

Various features are remarkable in all these stories: the dead person has no direct experience of his or her death, but there are certain things that appear strange - there are starkly improbable events, disorientation, and direct contradictions of physical laws. But only when the evidence becomes incontrovertible is the fact of death acknowledged, and this is then invariably the end. So these narratives tell of a transitory state, which still bears many marks of the previous life, but they keep silent about what happens after.

This transitory state is also the beginning of Alasdair Gray's *Lanark*, in which the eponymous protagonist finds himself unaccountably in a rather drab city. The only thing he remembers is arriving in a train and being given a name and some money. This experience is apparently shared by everyone he meets, as are also certain physical peculiarities, especially an illness called "Dragonhide", which eventually covers the whole body in some hard scaly substance. Lanark escapes through a giant mouth that swallows him entire and wakes up in an underground hospital to find that he has been cured. There he finds out about his past as Duncan Thaw, who killed a girl and then committed suicide. He decides to leave the hospital and becomes involved in a fight between good and evil.

This story is remarkable not only for its detailed working out of the afterlife, which seems to consist mainly of the more unpleasant aspects of the previous existence, but also for apparently giving the protagonist another chance in a new realm: the realisation of death does not entail the end, it is rather a new beginning.

In all these narratives the protagonists at some point

become aware of their state, and are thus able to achieve a certain degree of closure, i.e. they acquiesce in their condition and presumably find some sort of convenient arrangement, but there are also those who fail to find out what has happened and therefore are doomed to wander - often literally - in circles.

The Ignorant Dead

Since only the acknowledgment of death opens the way to escape from eternal repetition, those who cannot make this step - for whatever reasons - are doomed to a hell of their own making.

Flann O'Brien's *The Third Policeman* (1967) comes in the guise of an *apologia pro vita sua*: the first-person narrator gives an account of his life and doings, beginning with the startling revelation that it was him that committed a particular murder. It is less a desire to justify this murder than a wish to explain how it was done that prompts him to his narrative. The reader, however, soon has reason to doubt less the narrator's veracity than his ability to assess the import of what befell him and what he himself is doing, for he neither seems to realise that his mother was a (part-time) prostitute nor that both his parents have died - he rather thinks, they have just gone away. In very much the same vein he devotes his life to the pseudo-philosopher de Selby and strikes up a partnership with the parasitic layabout John Divney with whom he murders old Mathers for his money, only to be killed himself later by a bomb that Divney has planted for him.

His death, however, is solely perceived by the reader, but not by the narrator who continues blithely on his way into an ever stranger world and straight into a police station, where he is arraigned for the murder of Mathers - apparently only because he just happens to be there. Among the strange things that happen to him while he awaits his hanging are a visit to a very odd place called "Eternity" and also several conversations with his own soul, which is called Joe and tells him that they will soon go different ways. (What will happen to itself, it cannot say.) After fleeing from his confinement and confronting a mortally frightened John Divney, who reveals that the narrator has been dead for 16 years, he finds himself back where he was just after the bomb killed him - only this time he enters the police-station together with John Divney.

An important feature of *The Third Policeman* is the anonymity of the narrator: he cannot remember his own name, although he tries out several appellations to see if they fit him. When asked by the police, he says his name is "Nobody", thinking that this is a clever ruse to escape hanging. As a matter of fact, this gets him only deeper into trouble, since the death of "nobody" will be of no import whatever. The nameless narrator has no identity to give up and, consequently, can acquire no new one, as would otherwises be usual after death. Because of this deficiency, he is trapped in an endless repetition of a purposeless existence.

Whereas it is clear in *The Third Policeman* that the narrator is dead, in some stories by Samuel Beckett the reader is left in doubt as to the exact state of the protagonist. However, we do find the apparently eternal repetition of the same, and there is also a circular movement. This is true for How It Is, which has a setting reminiscent of Dante's *Inferno,* and in which the protagonist is apparently damned to wander - or rather crawl - in circles forever, while life's necessaries are providentially provided in a sack containing cans of food and a can-opener. This certainly sounds like eternal damnation. Still, there is a glimpse of hope in the belief of some unreachable beyond.. This is also true for *The Lost Ones,* where the inhabitants of a place that looks very much like hell are not aware of the exact nature of their plight and have a faint hope of escape. This escape might be the acquiescence in their death.

Looking Over the Brink

Some narratives concentrate on the actual moment of death. The dying are usually not conscious of what is happening to them, and, depending on the narrative point of view and the presence or absence of certain signals, the reader may only realise after a while what it is all about. Interestingly, these narratives do not seem to believe in an independent afterlife at all. When bodily death has fully set in, this is the end. A famous instance of the transition from life to death is given in Ambrose Bierce's "An Occurrence at Owl Creek Bridge", where a confederate officer in the American civil war is hanged by the Unionists who have caught him in an act of sabotage.

In his last moments he fantasises a miraculous escape and return home until everything goes black: "Peyton Farquhar was dead; his body, with a broken neck, swung gently from side to side beneath the timbers of the Owl Creek bridge." Here we find a characeristic change of perspective from the inside view of the dying man to the outside view of the narrator. This also occurs in William Golding's *Pincher Martin,* where the eponymous protagonist creates almost a whole new life for himself in the last seconds before drowning.

Another instance where the projected afterlife is a decisive improvement on the preceding one and especially upon the circumstances of death is to be found in D.M. Thomas's *The White Hotel,* where the protagonist, Lisa Erdman, imagines she has been healed of her physical and mental wounds and meets again all those friends she had lost. These examples can be called wish-fulfillment fantasies, created by a wish to evade the inevitable and to replace it with something pleasant and gratifying in order not to have to face the fact of death. Almost the opposite could be said about a number of Samuel Beckett's protagonists who not only do not flinch before death, but seem positively to desire it, although the best they can hope for is annihilation.

Thus, Malone in the novel *Malone Dies* tries three times - unsuccessfully - to tell the story of his life, each time in a different version. At last, there are only incoherent mumblings which indicate the end of his physical existence. What happens after is possibly told in *The Unnamable,* where a ruminating consciousness attempts to come to terms with its state, which is possibly death. It continuously tries on different past identities that it calls "vice-existers", which are connected with different reminiscences, but nothing ever leads to a conclusive answer, so the point of closure is never reached.

In Beckett's story "The End", the first-person narrator

relates the last months of his life, although he does not seem to be aware of his approaching death. There are, however, many indications in the story itself that this is just what is going to happen: there is a pervading feeling of utter disorientation and the complete inability of the narrator to make sense of the occurrences. As a matter of fact, sense is not really what he is after, it is more like a fatalistic acceptance of whatever befalls him. In a final vision, he goes to sea in a boat and drills a whole into its bottom:

[...], I swallowed my calmative. [...] The memory came faint and cold of the story I might have told, a story in the likeness of my life, I mean without the courage to end or the strength to go on.

Characteristically, death is here not a definite event but a continuous process whose beginning and end are hard to specify. The word "calmative" in the quotation above links the story to another one by Beckett which might very well be seen as its continuation. In this story the narrator knows that he has died, but he does not know when this happened, and hardly anything seems to have changed. He wanders about and meets people, but the events are similar to the ones in "The End" in their inconclusiveness. These two stories can thus be seen as mirror-images of each other: both spill over into the realm of the other without there being a strict borderline. This is summed up succinctly in "Texts for Nothing, III", where an anonymous I tries to imagine a body, but this turns out to be impossible: "There is no flesh anywhere, nor any way to die." Death in the old sense seems to have been abolished.

The Undead

The borderline between life and death is also indistinct in the case of the Undead, who continue some sort of physical existence. The ceasing of the bodily functions does not necessarily mean a separation of the body and the mind: there are various cases, in which the two continue together, are in fact inseparable and exhibit certain properties that in other circumstances would be thought to pertain to the living. This seems to violate the criterion of death posited above, and indeed these cases have traditionally been labelled "the Undead", such as vampires and zombies. They can be differentiated from the "proper" dead by the fact that their existence is bound to their body: when the latter has been destroyed (in an appropriate way), they cease to exist. I have here also included ghosts, since, albeit not bound to a body, they intrude into the realm of the living.

Vampires

Vampires suffer the death of their former being, but undergo certain bodily and psychic changes which enable them to lead a different kind of physical and mental existence, one which, however, is dependent upon a continous supply of fresh blood. Their only concern is to maintain their existence, but since their condition is contagious, they potentially eradicate their supply. Before they face extinction through starvation, though, they are usually delivered from their condition through various practices that involve the drastic mutilation of their corpses, as can be seen in Bram Stoker's *Dracula* (1897).

Zombies

Zombies are the bodies of dead persons which are "reanimated" by somebody else, usually a sorcerer, who uses them for his own ends. They are said to possess tremendous bodily powers, but they have no will - and presumably no consciousness - of their own. An exception here is Windle in Terry Pratchett's *Reaper Man*. He is a sorcerer himself, who after his physical death continues as a Zombie because Death is reported missing. When Death checks back in to work, Windle can at last find his long-desired rest.

In Mary Shelley's *Frankenstein* (1818) the parts of various dead bodies are put together and are reanimated to form the monster. The resultant creature has no knowledge of his previous existence(s), but rather resembles a new born child. As to his bodily strength, he shows the characteristics of a zombie. The creature could be said to be a zombie which has escaped its master's control, i.e. it has a will of its own.

A special case might again be provided by Beckett in "Imagination Dead Imagine", where the bodies of a man and a woman lie immovably side by side, but are alive (in an animated state?), according to the narrator. It seems that "only" their minds are dead. This would constitute a complete reversal of the traditional pattern, which postulates the death of the body and the continuance of the soul.

Ghosts

Ghosts are related to, yet distinct from the Undead, since on occasion they can be perceived in the material world, but are not of it. They can also be said to acquire new bodily abilities, albeit not material ones, since they are not restricted by physical circumstances. They interact, however, with the world of the living, i.e. they have to manifest themselves somehow, often visually, but also aurally or through direct communication with the mind of the perceiver, often in a dream or in a trancelike state.

Ghosts are usually not very communicative as regards their mode of existence. Sometimes they converse with the living, usually in order to complain of some wrong that has been done to them or that they have done themselves, in consequence of which they are damned to wander the earth until they are redeemed. They often have to perform repetitive tasks, i.e. reenact the decisive moments before their demise or something similar.

Ambrose Bierce's "The Moonlit Road" combines various of these features: through the medium Bayrolles, Julia Hetman tells how she appeared as a ghost to her husband, who has presumably murdered her. By means of her appearance she has probably driven him crazy, but apparently she neither understands what happened to her nor what happened to her husband.

Technical Afterlives

Certain types of life after death require a physical basis, as we have already seen in the case of vampires and zombies. This does not have to be the actual body of the deceased, but can be a mechanical substitute. Here we are obviously not so much concerned with the soul, but rather with the mind, which need not, however, be fully continuous with its previous state.

In Joseph McElroy's *Plus* the brain of a fatally ill person has been removed and is now installed as the central computer of a space capsule orbiting the earth. Since the rest of the body has physically died, and since "Imp Plus" has only the dimmest recollection of what happened, this can be seen as an entirely new lease of a completely different life: "Imp Plus" evolves a new identity and even certain outgrowths of his brain, which make him ideally adopted to his new existence.

Researchers in Artificial Intelligence have suggested the possibility that consciousnes - in fact the whole personality - may exist independently of an organic body, because it can be seen as some kind of computer programme. Since this is posited not only for the creation of machine intelligence, but is said to be applicable to humans too, it is only a small step further to envisaging the possibility of transferring a given mind onto a machine. Apparently this is best done at or near the instant of death, when the exact state of the neural activities of the brain is read and copied onto another medium. Whenever this medium is activated, this state is then replicated and consciousness regained for as long as there is technical support. The rest of the time is spent in absolute nothingness.

There are two instances of this in William Gibson's Cyberspace-Trilogy, namely Dixie in *Neuromancer* and the Finn in *Mona Lisa Overdrive*. Neither of them seems to relish this state very much - Dixie actually asks Chase to erase his personality construct, i.e. to kill him for good, whereas the Finn leads a not very happy existence as a kind of public oracle.

The idea of "beaming", i.e. the teleporting of matter, especially of humans, is also based on the assumption that a complete description of the physical state is a sufficient basis for reduplication. This is not usually thought of as involving death, but as a matter of fact the "original" physical being is usually destroyed before it materialises in some other place. (This is a matter of convenience, otherwise there would be multiple identical beings.) Since there is no actual transfer of matter involved, this process can be said to imply physical death - even repeatedly. It is, however, not usually experienced as such by the participants, who may nevertheless be said to lead posthumous lives.

THE USES OF THE POSTHUMOUS NARRATIVE

The tradition of the posthumous narrative suggests that its main use lies in the giving of a new and unexpected perspective upon the events of the former life and the personality of the deceased. It can thus be closely related to satire on the one hand, on the other it can be used for didactic purposes, as a means of exhortation to rectify one's life. Both approaches are facilitated by a clear division between and awareness of the live and the dead state, which through contrast allows reflection and reassessment. The didactic purpose is more difficult to see, however, in those narratives where the protagonists lack this distinctive awareness and therefore are not able to make comparisons - the reader, on the contrary, may be quite aware of the dilemma.

This almost unbroken continuity between life and death is invariably shown to lead to unhappiness, because of a feeling of senselessness and of being lost: there is no past and no future, no wherefrom and no whereto, therefore we often encounter the image of the circle from which there is only the faintest - and usually delusive - hope of escape. Apparently there is nothing worse than being condemned to continue in invariably the same way forever - this is traditionally seen as the condition of hell. This could also be an explanation why stories of the Undead have proved so popular in the 20th century: in them, the daunting prospect of an unchanging life without the hope of an end can be studied.

The question is, of course, why the borderline between life and death has been so much blurred in the 20th century. The lack of a belief in a life after death can only be part of the answer, since neither Fielding nor Hawthorne can have believed that the afterlife would resemble their descriptions. It seems rather that death itself has vanished from the horizon, i.e. there is a lack of conviction that their will be an end to one's sublunary existence. Otherwise there would be a point of reference against which to judge one's life.

But if this is missing, there is nothing to distinguish life from, no negative to judge a positive, and therefore no possibility of a transcendent view. It is therefore not surprising that in many stories by Samuel Beckett, it is hard, if not impossible to tell whether the protagonists are dead or alive, because they are really neither. It seems, as if contemporary life were seen as almost indistinguishable from death. Paradoxically, since there is no belief in an ultimate redemption anymore, the afterlife becomes a playground for alternative lives. Fictional representations of the afterlife therefore do not only ask the question "What is death?", but also "What is life?". The latter, of course, is a question that is implicitly asked by every novel. At the same time, since every text is of necessity over and finished at some point, the novel also draws attention to the fact that it has its own affinities with death.

Chapter 6

Towards a Grammar of the Absurd

At the time when *Godot* was first done, it liberated something for anybody writing plays. It redefined the minima of theatrical validity. It was simple as that. He got away. He won by twenty-eight lengths, and he'd done it with so little—and I mean that as an enormous compliment. There we all were, busting a gut with great monologues and pyrotechnics, and this extraordinary genius just put this play together with enormous refinement, and then with two completely unprecedented and uncategorisable bursts of architecture in the middle—terrible metaphor—and there it was, theatre.

This is Tom Stoppard speaking in appreciation of Samuel Beckett, his ancestor of the absurd. Dialogue is the dramatists's major resource and the dramatic theorist's major problem. First-generation absurdists—Beckett, and then Pinter—did indeed usher in a new era for dramatic dialogue, rescuing the modern theatre from the tyranny of wordiness that even John Osborne's *Look Back in Anger* had failed to slough off. But little progress has been made in analysing the new language of the theatre.

Critics have not understood the nature of the absurdists' emancipation; and nowhere is the misunderstanding more flagrant than in the assumption that Beckett's dialogue moves in the same direction as Pinter's, that it tries to realise the same objective—greater realism. Pinter's stripped-down idiom is that of genuine speech faithfully reproduced, mimetic both of the free rhythms and punctuating silences of spontaneous discourse. Gone is the orchestrated language that created the sense of discussion or debate even in the dialogue of dramatists, like Ibsen, labelled 'naturalistic.' So free of embellishment and rhetoric is his dramatic speech that it has been paid the compliment of being thought banal by the unobservant: the dramatic contexts within which it operates ensures that it never is so.

But even alert critics, in assimilating Pinter's art to Beckett's, have failed to see that the linguistic effects created by Beckett work on antithetical principles. To liberate the modern theatre, Beckett first liberated himself from over-dependence on ordinary language, abandoning mimesis to the invention of a unique idiom, the very grammar of which is different from that of everyday speech. No-one speaks quite like Beckett's characters do, not because the playwright has got it wrong, but because he has given up the holy grail of realism altogether.

Critical myopia in this regard is a curious phenomenon, since the techniques of stagecraft developed by Beckett, as opposed to those of language, has never been mistaken for *trompe l'oeil* social accuracy. Arthur Miller has pointed out that the kind of questions an audience will ask of a character appearing on stage will depend on the degree to which his dress, speech and environment are seen to be realistic. Thus, questions which are appropriately asked of his own characters—who are they, what is their trade, calling or profession, what sort of upbringing might they have had, where do they live—are entirely ruled out of court by Beckett's way of presenting his characters to the audience. It is quite inappropriate to ask Miller's questions of characters embedded in sand, neck-deep in funerary urns or buried in dustbins. Such a restriction of theatrical resources as Beckett's plays increasingly countenance is a very conscious and important decision on the dramatist's part.

The withdrawal of the potential for expansive movement from plays like *Happy days*, *Play* and *Endgame* has the consequence that minute changes in position and minimal gestures will assume disproportionate importance. Another consequence of this attenuation will be a greater focussing of attention on the dialogue. In this article, I propose to examine some of the grammatical effects that obtrude themselves on the spectator's consciousness in the play that, to my mind, most profitably combines Beckett's linguistic and theatrical skills—*Endgame.*

In this play, Beckett invents constructions that reinforce both his view of experience and his staging techniques. The strangeness, power and profundity of his dialogue derives, I suggest, from the imposition of a grammar that imparts to the language an extra layer of significance.

The grammar itself becomes an image of the human predicament as the playwright conceives it; local linguistic effects directly reveal aspects of the experience at the heart of the play. Language in *Endgame* is self-advertising, arresting, continually drawing attention to its own curious properties, noticeable because in precise respects it departs from the 'language such as men do use.' Let us proceed to examples.

When Clov says: 'If I don't kill that rat, he'll die' we are arrested at first because the grammar has played a trick on us. The sentence poses as a genuine disjunctive of the form, 'If not - x, then y,' but it does not turn out to be so. There is no true juxtaposition of alternatives here—or is there? On closer inspection, it appears that the grammar and syntax have imposed on the passive verb 'die' an active role and this is quite appropriate to a Clov's eye-view of experience. To Clov, dying is the supreme expression of freedom possible in the austere, debilitated world he and the rat inhabit.

Suddenly, because of the way Clov frames the sentence, dying seems like a gloriously malevolent act of will on the rat's part, the more so because it deprives Clov of a chance to act—to kill him. Here, the very grammar of the sentence is a concrete embodiment of an existential statement. Just as every movement of Nagg's or Nell's *counts,* given the constraint of the bins, this sentence has created room to move, room to act or be acted upon in a world where being killed and dying seem to be the exclusive alternatives. Earlier in the play, we come across another example of this richness in surface texture:

Clov: You shouldn't speak to me like that.

Hamm: (*coldly*) Forgive me. (*Pause. Louder.*) I said, Forgive me. Here Beckett exploits the peculiar feature of the verb 'to forgive,' that it has a form resembling a genuine imperative, which is in fact, at the strongest, 'vocative.'

At the simplest level, Hamm is requesting forgiveness in a tone as brusque as the one that gave the original offence and this is amusingly paradoxical—'forgive me, or I'll beat your brains out.' You can't ask for forgiveness with menace. But in addition, he seems to be assimilating the locution 'forgive me' to the class of commands like 'shut the door!' which expect some performance for their satisfaction.

But what would constitute the performance, in virtue of which Hamm could be satisfied that he had been forgiven? Some act of ritual absolution, perhaps? God alone is entitled to use the word 'forgive' as a genuine imperative as in 'forgive thine enemies!' perhaps Hamm is playing God and trying to arrogate to himself some of the Divine authority. At all events, this is, like the previous example, a very suggestive use of grammatical ambiguity, seeming to point beyond itself to the deeper pre-occupations of Beckett's drama.

We might fomulate the deeper preoccupation of *Endgame,* tentatively, as follows: in a world no longer rendered purposeful by Christian conceptions of eschatology, time is experienced not as a linear development towards a goal, but as a yawning vacuum, a black hole without structure. Structure has to be imposed from without through routine and, for Beckett's characters, through the playing of games. The games Hamm and Clov play are futile, but they are all there is. The dramatic tension of the play derives from Clov's regularly threatening to stop playing—to upset the board—throwing Hamm back on his resources in inventing new games and devising new moves. Throughout the action, the advantage is constantly changing hands, and often, making a successful move depends on the adroit manipulation of language. In the following passage, Clov has again threatened separation, an action as decisive, if it could ever be performed, as is the killing of the child in *Who's Afraid of Virginia Woolf*:

Clov: I'll leave you.
Hamm: No!

Clov: What is there to keep me here?

Hamm: The dialogue. (*Pause.*) I've got on with my story. (*Pause.*) I've got on with it well. (*Pause. Irritably.*) Ask me where I've got to.

Clov: Oh, by the way, your story?

Hamm: (*surprised*). What story?

Clov: The one you've been telling yourself all your . . . days.

Hamm: Ah you mean my chronicle?

Clov: That's the one.

Pause.

Hamm: (*angrily*). Keep going, can't you, keep going!

Clov: You've got on with it, I hope.

Hamm: (*modestly*). Oh not very far, not very far. (*He sighs.*) There are days like that, one isn't inspired. (*Pause*). No forcing, no forcing, it's fatal. (*Pause.*) I've got on with it a little all the same. (*Pause.*) Technique, you know. (*Pause. Irritably*) I say I've got on with it a little all the same.

Clov: (*admiringly*). Well I never! In spite of everything you were able to get on with it!

Hamm: (*modestly*). Oh not very far, you know, not very far, but nevertheless, better than nothing.

Clov: Better than nothing! Is it possible?

In answer to Clov's challenge, Hamm introduces the set-piece topic of his story. Clov recognises that this move is legitimate and binding, yet he fails to give Hamm the mileage they both know this topic merits. Conversation in this play is a rule-governed activity. Hamm's irritation is entirely warranted because Clov is trying to cheat by refusing to ask all the old questions.

There are again in this exchange some arresting linguistic constructions. Beckett's characters often try words out for size, put on words as one would put on a new pair of shoes, to see if they feel comfortable in them. Clov's line: 'The one you've been telling yourself all your . . . days' has a momentum which demands the word 'life' to achieve itself fully: 'days' is a bathos, deliberately substituted because, of course, Hamm and Clov do not possess anything as meaningful as a 'life.' They possess only 'days'—empty, undifferentiated sheets of time. Following this line is Hamm's: 'Ah you mean my chronicle?' Suddenly the word 'chronicle' *fits*. It is right, and Hamm is happy with it.

'Chronicle' is superior to 'story' because the Greek word confers a superior status on Hamm's pursuit, but also because a chronicle, unlike a story, does not necessarily have an end and is the record of passing time. Hamm is issuing a timely warning to Clov that conversations like the one they are having, that they have had so many times in the past, will recur in the future. The word 'chronicle' is a show of power on Hamm's part, an astute move. Clov's last line is another brilliant example of Beckett's subversion of the pat phrase, his pressing of common speech into the service of a bleakly comic pessimism, as in:

Clov: Do you believe in the life to come?

Hamm: Mine was always that. (*Exit Clov.*) Got him that time!

By answering a question about the 'meta-future' with a statement in the past tense, Hamm excruciatingly emphasises the uniform greyness of all time-past, present or to come.

The seemingly innocent incident of the toy dog also gains thematic significance from its peculiar linguistic and logical structure:

Enter Clov holding by one of its three legs a black toy dog.

Clov: Your dogs are here.

He hands the dog to Hamm who feels it, fondles it

Hamm: He's white, isn't he?

Clov: Nearly.

Hamm: What do you mean, nearly? Is he white or isn't he?

Clov: He isn't.

Pause.

The question, 'He's white, isn't he?' allows Clov to equivocate, thus forcing Hamm into asking a second question which is too comprehensive to elicit the information he actually requires. There is too much 'overkill' in the question, 'Is he white or isn't he?'; what the blind Hamm needs to know is what colour the dog *is* rather than what colour he isn't, and the pause must be a moment for recapitulation as Hamm retraces his steps to find out where he made the *gaffe*.

In this exchange, we see very clearly the sinister potential the sighted Clov has for constructing a totally false picture of external reality with which he can amuse himself or torture Hamm. The grandiose 'Your dogs are here' is perhaps harmless enough, Clov posturing as butler to the English Milord. But towards the end of the play, there is something of a crux when Clov discerns a small boy in 'the without,' but Hamm refuses to allow him to investigate further:

Hamm: If he exists he'll die there or he'll come here. And if he doesn't . . .

Pause

Clov: You don't believe me? You think I'm inventing?

Pause

Hamm: It's the end, Clov, we've come to the end. I don't need you any more.

Perhaps Hamm is accepting defeat here, accepting that Clov's trump card is his ability to dominate Hamm's experience even to the extent of peopling his world with strangers, phantasms of Clov's own imagination. Earlier Clov demonstrated his capacity to withhold information (about the dogs) and now he demonstrates his capacity to falsify it. Whether there is or is not a small boy, whether Clov is or is not inventing, Hamm has no means of knowing.

Beckett's language demands from the audience a heightened form of attention. The way in to understanding a play like *Endgame* is the scrutiny of such oddly baroque constructions as Clov's description of the three-legged dog—'He lacks a leg.' Why does this sound so strange to us? What, precisely, is the effect of such an utterance? Language like this conveys no information about the 'character' or 'personality' of its employer and this is consonant with Beckett's purpose, since he deals in theatrical beings more Protean than characters. By contrast, any attempt to understand Pinter's language is liable to result in the conviction that the significance of his plays exists somewhere other than in the text. Theatre audiences of the sixties were often puzzled by stretches of dialogue like the following, subsequently deemed 'Pinteresque':

Stanley: So you're down here on holiday?

McCann: A short one. (*Stanley picks up a strip of paper. McCann moves in.*) Mind that. *Stanley*: What is it?

McCann: Mind it. Leave it.

Stanley: I've got a feeling we've met before.

McCann: No we haven't.

Stanley: Ever been anywhere near Maidenhead?

McCann: No.

Stanley: There's a Fuller's teashop. I used to have my tea there.

McCann: I don't know it.

Stanley: And a Boots Library. I seem to connect you with the High Street.

McCann: Yes?

Stanley: A charming town, don't you think?

McCann: I don't know it.

Such dialogue is disturbing because although it is mimetic of very familiar speech patterns, as Beckett's dialogue seldom is, the context within which it occurs differs from a 'normal' context in significant ways. At cocktail parties or in other situations where two people meet, it is common for them to attempt to mesh their experience together, to accommodate the other person into their lives in a 'Haven't I met you somewhere before?' conversational gambit. Normally, the two strangers will struggle helpfully and co-operatively to plaster over the cracks in their insufficient memories and arrive at consensus. ('Could it have been . . . ?' 'Yes . . . that's possible.') Seldom do we encounter such a trenchant denial as Stanley meets from McCann and this, coupled with his territorial attitude to his strips of paper, alerts us to the sense of a normal encounter having overstepped its bounds and generated unnatural tension.

Of course, in the context of the entire play, the motivation behind this exchange is easier to understand. Stanley is trying to establish a relationship with McCann by gaining purchase on his human sympathies, whereas McCann is rejecting this bid, rejecting Stanley and asserting his right to lobotomise him later on in the play. In this example, as in so much of the dialogue of the earlier Pinter plays, language is being used by the characters to establish the balance of power in a relationship, to negotiate respective status, to stake out a psychological or a physical territory. The spectator will be puzzled if he thinks the 'facts' under discussion are of primary importance; that is to say, if he thinks it important to establish whether or not the two men ever really did meet in Maidenhead. Such 'facts' often seem to be more fugitive in Pinter's plays than they actually are in the life of a person of average competence.

But language, in Pinter's plays, is seldom used for the straightforward purpose of giving information. Austin E. Quigley, in a recent book entitled *The Pinter Problem*, invokes a Wittgensteinian analysis of language to call attention to this aspect of Pinter's dialogue—that its referential function is minimal and that the meaning of an utterance more often depends on the use to which it is put by the speaker. Helpful as this is, I think the more familiar notion of 'sub-text' is equally explanatory. Conversations like the banal breakfast chatter of *The Birthday Party* and *A Slight Ache*, because they are successful theatre, call for sub-textual explanation. We can see them as attempts to manifest identity on the part of characters who, like Meg Boles, have few channels through which to do so.

When she serves up to Stanley a plate of what is manifestly fried bread, she says ludicrously, 'Well, I bet you don't know what it is,' to which Stanley replies 'fried bread.' Here, we might say that Stanley is resisting the claims of Meg's feminine mystique expressed through her cooking, claims which become overtly sexual as the action progresses. Solemn though this may sound, it could easily be conveyed in the theatre. Discussions between a director and actor will often make clear the real nature of such exchanges, or at least, the preferred interpretation of them, and there are many non-verbal methods of communicating this interpretation to the audience. Peter

Hall speaks of the need to suspect the language employed by Pinter's characters, to treat what they say as a series of ploys and to find out about the nature of the emotions they use verbal expression to conceal; and Hall's understanding derives not from Wittgenstein's philosophy, but from his theatrical experience.

Indeed, this is not so novel a use of dramatic language. In Chekhov's plays, it is equally important to see how the 'sub-text' betrays, undercuts and modifies the text and if his art were not so habitually likened to Ibsen's naturalistic drama, the sixties' audiences for Pinter's plays might have experienced a stronger sense of *déjà vu*. In a trivial sense, of course, it is true for all drama that the words a character speaks are governed by the way in which he speaks them and by what he does when he is speaking them, and, trivially, means no more than that drama is a performative art where a 'script' acquires its meaning only through interpretation and performance. But it is a condition of understanding Chekhov's art and Pinter's, that we suspect a character to have no belief in what he says and ulterior motives for saying it. In Rosmersholm, when Rebekka West confesses that she has driven Beate to suicide, we know that here, at last, is the truth. Neither Toozenbach nor Vershinin, philosophizinq together in *The Three Sisters*, are telling the truth or even believing that they are doing so.

Pinter's dialogue, then, preserves the surface of realism though this in itself is ultimately subversive because the conversation encourages a penumbra of accompanying expectations appropriate to realistic theatre that the plays often frustrate. In plays like *The Homecoming*, an uncannily accurate mimesis of ordinary conversation is formed to conceal and to belie the extreme structure of feeling that supports it. Beckett's art, in complete contrast, is in the best sense superficial. He has created a rich linguistic idiom as the ordinary currency of his plays, the characteristics of which is that the very diction and syntax is directly relevant to the experience at the heart of the drama. And the respects in which Beckett's idiom is notable are the respects in which it does *not occur* in naturally spoken English. One final example must suffice of Beckett's impressive ability to exploit the linguistic properties of his text in the creation of a grammar that is, in itself, a symbol of the human condition as experienced by the author:

Hamm: Give me a rug, I'm freezing.

Clov: There are no more rugs.

The normal linguistic expectation would be 'We have no more rugs,' though 'there are no more bananas' is quite legitimate, the distinction being that bananas are naturally occurring and their stock is not replenished in the same way as is the stock of rugs. Clov's defeated reply is a powerful reminder that in the world beyond, the machine is grinding to a halt, that even the stock of man-made products cannot now be replenished. Grammar is once again an image of the abyss.

THE COMPLETE SHORT PROSE, 1929-1989

Beckett's writing, with its aspects of perfection and vulnerability, inspires both intimacy and loyalty. It has the rhetorical power to make its readers feel that they want nothing less than fairness and good measure when it comes to response to the work, to feel offended by offense to the work, and to feel that this reaction must be common to readers of Beckett. This desire for justice is well satisfied in this volume. Beckett's short work has appeared and reappeared in journals and collections, often with various errors, so it is welcome that the more or less obvious errors and accidental alterations in the texts at least be corrected and a reputable edition of the work established. S. E. Gontarski is the right person for the job: as author of valuable scholarly work on Beckett, and editor of the Journal of Beckett Studies, he has cared for Beckett's work intimately. Gontarski's editorial decisions inspire confidence.

The volume's bibliography of Beckett's published short work is the most complete to date, and while this is a reading text and not an annotated scholarly edition, Gontarski's editorial decisions, recorded in "Notes on the Texts" at the end of the volume, appear sound and satisfying. Several wrongs are put right here. One, for example, is the claim that Beckett actually delivered "The Capital of the Ruins," an essay on the Irish Hospital at Saint Lo, as a radio address on Irish radio. Gontarski found that there is no record of this in the radio's archive, and Beckett reported to him no recollection of it in 1983. The text itself is also emended from earlier inaccurate versions, as is the text of "neither," a short piece that previously appeared in corrupt form in several places. These two textual interventions exemplify Gontarski's effort to correct mistakes reproduced, for instance, in Calder's 1990 volume, As the Story Was Told: Uncollected and Late Prose. There are also some previously unpublished materials here (including Edith Fournier's translation of "L'Image").

While this edition settles some matters, it unsettles others. Beckett's death provides an arbitrary but nearly transparent logic for a discussion of the wholeness of his writing; this editorial effort uses the categories of "short prose" and, less visibly, "the author" to argue for something complete in Beckett's work. Yet it does not include all of Beckett's short prose, and raises the question whether wholeness is the ruling criterion that scholarship often assumes it to be. This edition collects work that Beckett published as short (mostly the work assembled in the Collected Shorter Prose, 1945-1980), rather than short work he published. It does not make any effort to collect the nonfiction short prose—Beckett wrote a number of short essays and reviews—but uses the term to cover for the generic variance of Beckett's writing.

Two fiction items missing, for example, are Worstward Ho, a short fiction made into book form by Grove's large print and a separate cover, and Company, a volume similar in length to The Lost Ones (which is included). Does the generic tag attached to these works at some point determine their inclusion? The collection does not explain this important issue, which is already raised by the word "complete." This is a question of a sense of the continuum too, because one rhetorical function of the collection is to form a new reading of Beckett's short work. Gontarski argues in the Introduction that Beckett's work should be read serially as an "ontological exploration of being in narrative," of dispersal and return (an argument with which I have agreed some years ago). Evidently Worstward Ho is not to be taken as part of that overall trajectory, but the Fizzles are, even though the latter rework and comment on material from the novels of the 1940s, whereas the former develops different material closely linked to shorts All Strange Away and Imagination Dead Imagine.

It is difficult to formulate a vision of the wholeness of Beckett's work based solely on the short fiction, which cannot be so easily separated from the rest of the work. The notion of the whole, of whole work, is not supported by the collection; instead, the collection shows how compelling Beckett's rhetoric of wholeness can be—a rhetoric of beginning, of becoming, of ending. Beckett's work convinces the reader to think about completeness to the very degree that it, as epic fragments, denies it.

A related point made in the Introduction is that Beckett's short fiction belongs in the tradition of Irish storytelling. Some of it can be read convincingly this way, but almost any story has the dramatic quality Gontarski singles out. Though Beckett's work told in first person may be said to feature the voice more prominently—I don't find this argument appealing—part of the point of his writing overall surely is that there is a voice to any text, and textuality in any voice in literature, and that between them the two condemn us to the endless pilgrimage that is words:

> Quite audible then now for her and if other ears there with her in the dark for them and if ears low down in the wall at a for them a voice without meaning, hear that. (All Strange Away)

Because all of Beckett's work is intensely writerly, intensely written, it features, it emphasizes this quality of the word, and its loneliness.

Chapter 7

Editing Errors and the Changing Texts

It is no small irony that for a writer so punctilious about his texts — especially their performance — Samuel Beckett's work has been subject to so much inept editing and so many publication blunders that he could lament to his "official" biographer, James Knowlson, "My texts are in a terrible mess." The innumerable printing errors introduced into early editions of his work — the edition of Watt published jointly in France by Collection Merlin and Olympia Press (1953) and reprinted then both by John Calder in Great Britain (1963) and by Grove Press in the United States (1959) being perhaps the most egregious — have still never been fully corrected.

As recently as August 13, 1992, John Banville, Literary Editor of the Irish Times, could note in the New York Review of Books, "It is time now for all of Beckett's works . . . to be properly edited and published in definitive and accurate editions in order that future readers be allowed to see them for the unique testaments that they are" (20, emphasis added).

One could hardly agree more — but textual purity may simply be a longing for "paradise lost," since textual problems are more easily recognized and ridiculed than remedied. A recent spate of letters to the Times Literary, Supplement is a case in point. What should have been a cause for celebration, the publication of Beckett's long-suppressed first novel of 1932, Dream of Fair to Middling Women, has instead fueled the textual controversy and led to a clash of egos.

Although Beckett wrote only one Dream of Fair to

Middling Women, currently two separate and competing editions of it, with more than a few typographical differences between them, are in print.

In a letter to the Times Literary Supplement (16 July 1993), Eoin O'Brien, co-editor of Dream, dissociated himself from the second edition, although he remains listed as its editor: "Both the US (Arcade) and UK (Calder) 1993 editions of this work have been printed without taking into account the necessary corrections 1, and my co-editor, Edith Fournier, made to the proofs of the re-set text. It is of deep concern that Samuel Beckett's work be treated in this manner. We can be held accountable," he continues, "only for the first edition published in 1992 by Black Cat Press in Dublin and can accept no responsibility for the errors in the US and UK flawed editions". But even that 1992 Dublin edition of Dream is not without flaw and leaves itself open to question about editorial policy.

What justification there was for choosing one of Beckett's two endings to the exclusion of the other and why some silent editorial changes (which were not corrections of error) were made to the Dublin text remain unexplained. Let me cite a single example of the latter. In Beckett's typescript the narrator discusses the protagonist's (i.e., Belacqua's) translation of Rimbaud's Le bateau ivre into English as follows: "You know, of course, don't you, that he did him into the eye into English." For some reason editors O'Brien and Fournier decided that Beckett's original image wanted improving, and they published the following sentence as Beckett's: "You know, of course, don't you, that he did him pat into English." In the not too distant future I expect that Dream may have to be re-edited.

More recently, Beckett's French and American publishers, Jerome Lindon of Editions de Minuit and Barney Rosset, formerly of Grove Press and now of Blue Moon Books, have been at loggerheads over the publication of Beckett's last major unpublished work, the 1947 three-act play Eleutheria (the Greek word for freedom). After a series of threatened lawsuits by Lindon, functioning as literary executor, the work has been published in France by Minuit and in the United States, in a translation by Michael Brodsky, by Foxrock, Inc., an imprint devised by Rosset and his co-publishers, John Oakes and Dan Simon of Four Walls Eight Windows. That text is bound to be embroiled in additional controversy as well, if for no other reason than its being translated by someone other than Beckett.

Much of the frustration surrounding the accuracy of Beckett's texts is summarized by Gerry Dukes in a letter to the Times Literary Supplement (7 Jan. 1994) in which he attacks both publisher John Calder, who along with Richard Seaver apparently edited the second edition of Dream, and the Beckett estate: "Instead of dean texts, John Calder keeps providing misreadings, misprisions, misprints and distortions of the canon. The principal victim of these editorial and publishing eccentricities is the work of Samuel Beckett. Perhaps the Beckett estate and/or Beckett's literary executor should take a closer interest in an accurate publication of the work".

The nature of the textual problems with the Calder editions, of Beckett's short prose especially, is evident in the publishing history of the very short prose work, "neither," which was originally published in the Journal of Beckett Studies No. 4 (Spring 1979, vii) with line breaks suggestive of a poem. During the editing process a word was dropped from the eighty-seven-word work. The omission was evidently not immediately noticed, for the correction did not appear until issue No. 6, in the Autumn of 1980, where, in his "Editorial,"John Pilling noted, "It is very much regretted that the word `neared' was accidentally omitted from the end of the fourth line of the text neither printed in issue 4 at post page-proof stage beyond the control of the editors". When John Calder was about to reprint the work in the Collected Poems 1930-1978, Beckett resisted because he considered it a piece of prose, a story.

As Calder said in a letter to the Times Literary Supplement (24 Aug. 1990): I had "originally intended to put it ["neither"] in the Collected Poems. We did not do so, because Beckett at the last moment said that it was not a poem and should not be there" (895). Subsequently, it was omitted inadvertently from The Collected Shorter Prose 1945-1980, but printed in yet a more corrupt version in the posthumous As the Story Was Told: Uncollected and Later Prose.

This version not only included erroneous information (the story, identified in the Journal of Beckett Studies as "written by Samuel Beckett in September 1976 to be set to music by Morton Feldman," is described in As the Story Was Told as having been "written for composer Morton Feldman, 1962") but, instead of including the word missing from the Journal of Beckett Studies, reproduced a copy-editor's query marking the place of the missing word; line six, then, reads, "doors once? gently close, once turned" instead of "doors once neared gently close, once turned."

Beckett's plays fare only slightly better, often corrupted by the process of commercial publication, and so even the venerable house of Faber and Faber does not escape blame. In an essay entitled "Texts and Pre-texts of Samuel Beckett's Footfalls," I argue that,

Eager to make the play available for opening night, Faber and Faber secured a typescript from Beckett before he was finally satisfied with it and set their copy from what in the sequence of typescripts Beckett called Ts. 3 [of four typescripts].

To their credit Faber and Faber went on to correct their text, incorporating the revisions Beckett made for his 1976 world premiere production at the Royal Court Theatre into the text published in a collected edition entitled Ends and Odds, but as I point out, "This revised text . . . remains corrupt and is even inconsistent internally. Faber indeed changed the number of May's footsteps from seven to nine in the stage directions, for instance, but left her counting her steps one through seven in the dialogue". Evidently, neither Faber's in-house editors nor Beckett himself checked the revised and anthologized text of Footfalls very closely.

Even Beckett's most famous work, Waiting for Godot, is not immune from corruption. Godot exists in multiple versions in English because Faber originally published a bowdlerized version of it in 1956 to appease the Lord Chamberlain, with the result that the original English and American editions were not identical. Faber's note to its 1956 edition announced: "When Waiting for Godot was transferred from the Arts Theatre to the Criterion Theatre, a small number of textual deletions were made to satisfy the requirements of the Lord Chamberlain. The text printed here is that used in the Criterion production." In fact there are hundreds of variants between the Grove Press Godot of 1954 and Faber's 1956 edition.

Faber went on to "correct" its Godot in 1965, in an edition they called the "complete and unexpurgated text . . . authorized by Mr. Beckett as definitive," but it still differed substantially from the American text. To celebrate Beckett's eightieth birthday Faber collected all of Beckett's plays into a single volume, Samuel Beckett: The Complete Dramatic Works, in which, however, they inexplicably reprinted the 1956 bowdlerized text of Waiting for Godot.

Nor does Beckett's American publisher, Grove Press, escape blame. When in the midst of producing the American Beckett Festival of Radio Plays Everett Frost went to Beckett to discuss the project, he asked the author which text of Cascando he should produce. Beckett responded, "The printed version." He seemed shocked when Frost asked, "Which printed version?" After Beckett made a quick check of his texts, Frost asked "how far he might rely on Grove. 'Not very,' was the playwright's prompt but rueful reply."

Such publishing blunders aside, Banville's apparently simple plea for Beckett's work "to be properly edited and published in definitive and accurate editions," commendable as it is, is considerably less simple than it appears, complicated not only by the gremlins which inhabit the publishing industry but by Beckett's own practice as a theatrical director and by the critical and theoretical climate of our time, both of which make references to anything like a "definitive" text as suspect as references to any single performance as "definitive." Beckett himself tampered with the "definitive" Godot at least twice after Faber made its pronouncement.

As Beckett's direct work in the theater increased, he demonstrated a disregard for the sanctity of his plays as published — at least for his own productions. Beckett in the theater has himself destabilized Beckett on the page. Between 1953, when Waiting for Godot was first staged in Paris, and 1967, Samuel Beckett served a fourteen-year theatrical apprenticeship, moving from being a consultant in the staging of his dramatic works to taking full responsibility for their direction.

During his twenty-year directing career, 1967-1986, Beckett staged some seventeen productions of his work in three languages, English, French, and German. Each time he returned to his plays — most often to texts already in print — to prepare them for staging, he was dissatisfied. He found his plays wordy and incompletely conceived for the stage, and so he set about revising them as he staged them. Of Godot, for instance, he has said on more than one occasion, "I knew nothing about theater when I wrote it," and during rehearsals in Berlin in 1967 for Endspiel (Endgame) he conceded that the play was "not visualized".

By 1986 Beckett's own productions of his work suggested a repudiation of his published texts, even those dubbed by his publisher as "definitive." Beckett's oeuvre generally exists in multiple versions because he revised as he translated, so that each self-translation became a textual transformation. The translation became not a literary equivalent but essentially a new and parallel text, one which did not necessarily supersede the original. After his work as a theatrical director, multiple versions or texts existed even within a single language. Without access to Beckett's notes and revisions, critics and directors were forced into a position of building interpretations and mounting productions not so much on corrupt or incomplete texts, such as almost all British versions of Waiting for Godot, but on those the author himself found unsatisfactory, unfinished.

As Beckett grew increasingly dissatisfied with his plays as published, he decided in 1986, after years of suggesting that theatrical directors not stage the published scripts but follow instead his directorial revisions, to authorize publication of his theatrical notebooks and what he called "corrected texts" for his plays, that is, texts which incorporated the revisions he made as a director, along with the notebooks in which the rationale of those revisions was worked out. This was an extraordinary decision on Beckett's part, essentially repudiating his dramatic canon as published and available to the public, and offering instead a much more fluid and multiple series of performing texts.

The execution of that project, recently completed as the four-volume series called The Theatrical Notebooks of Samuel Beckett, was, however, fraught with complications, since each volume finally contained a single, "corrected" text for each of the plays Beckett staged. Such a solution which bows to the conventions of commerce is somewhat misleading since it runs counter to Beckett's own practice as a theatrical director and to the critical climate of our time, much of which Beckett himself embraced. In another, more tranquil, less skeptical era, one less ideologically charged than our own, the job of editing or correcting Beckett's works might have been achievable without a great deal of theoretical soul-searching, a simple matter of replacing those texts with which Beckett was dissatisfied — those which he himself revised for production — with the rewritten texts, and then correcting obvious typographical errors, oversights, and inconsistencies in the remainder of his work.

Within the theoretical discourse of our age, however, an enterprise of "correcting" literary texts, or, as Stanley Fish calls them, literary documents, to emphasize that they are the physical objects of interpretation (or phenomenological intention or performance, which I treat as a "reading"), is bound to generate theoretical and ideological debate. Traditional theories of editing threaten to resurrect the specter of a single "correct" text, for one, and so the authority of the text and the author over the reader, a position which Beckett himself has both embraced and repudiated.

The problem of textual authority or validity is further compounded in the theater by the collaborative nature of the theatrical enterprise itself and the inconsistent quality of the collaborators, problems about which Beckett was quite aware and which he took into account in his own directing. In the theater we may, on the whole, be more willing to accept the playscript as an incomplete artwork, something less than the final stage of a work's creation, a document which needs to be real-ized on stage through a set of intermediaries; that admission suggests that theatrical texts are themselves extraliterary, if by literature we mean at very least a completed and consistent work of art.

In Beckett's case the value of the performance is enhanced, given authority, by the fact that the author himself has directed his play. But the relation between performance — even authorized performance — and published text remains as problematic with Beckett directing as with any other director.

Quite clearly, as a director approaching his work afresh after at times a ten-year hiatus, Beckett continued reshaping his work, but many of his changes were not necessarily evolutionary, that is, necessarily improvements, but reflected particular circumstances. Beckett's revisions from production to production were not always consistent, a clear progressus. Two productions of the same work directed by Beckett — even in the same language — were not necessarily identical.

If they were, there would have been little point doing the second. Beckett has often designed a text and production for a particular set of actors playing on a particular playing space under a particular set of circumstances. In a letter to Polish critic Marek Kedzierski (15 Nov. 1981), for example, Beckett has admitted, "Herewith corrected copy of Fin de partie. The cuts and simplifications are the result of my work on the play as director and function of the players at my disposal. To another director they may not seem desirable."

Even Beckett's own revised or "corrected" texts, then, seem something less than stable, absolute, or definitive, but instead subject to the subsequent intervention of future directors, that is, future readers. In Beckett's post-publication revision of Play, the note called "Repeat" ends with the phrase, "and so on if and as desired" (emphasis added). Presumably the indecision allows for future directorial flexibility, but whose desire then are we finally staging? The challenge for the textual editor working in the postmodern textual climate that Beckett himself has encouraged is to reconcile the traditional demands for a single final version of a text, one version bound between boards, and the theory of the incomplete or mutable text; that is, how does one reconcile the demand for a single text closest to the author's final textual intention and the postmodern notion of the multiplicity of texts? Such questions of textual plurality at least foreground much of the current theoretical debate about the nature of texts, textuality, and finally meaning, particularly in the theater.

Even the phase "corrected" if not "definitive" texts threatens to revivify the epistemological paradigm that meaning is somehow contained immutably within and restricted to a text, impervious to the inconsistencies of language and the vicissitudes of culture, a notion particularly dubious in the theater. Further, the idea of "correct" texts suggests a linear, evolutionary model of literary history where later versions are by definition improvements of or progress beyond the former and so supersede them. In the case of Beckett's theatrical texts (and even his translations) — that is, those cases where multiple and parallel texts exist — such assumptions are dubious.

The problems of textual validity and stability are further complicated in Beckett's case by his own fundamental authorial and so textual ambivalence. On the one hand, Beckett has abandoned the author's traditional role as textual authority, the final arbiter of meaning, by steadfastly refusing interpretation of his own works. In a letter to his American publisher, Barney Rosset, Beckett, for instance, expressed his own diminished authority soon after the writing of Godot: "had a highly unsatisfactory interview with SIR Ralph Richardson who wanted the low-down on Pozzo, his home address and curriculum vitae, and seemed to make the forthcoming of this and similar information the condition of his condescending to illustrate the part of Pozzo.

Too tired to give satisfaction. I told him that all I knew about Pozzo was in the text, that if I had known more I would have put it in the text, and that this was true also of the other characters which I trust puts an end to that star." To critic Colin

Duckworth Beckett announced, "I produce an object. What people make of it is not my concern.... I'd be quite incapable of writing a critical introduction to my work" (En Attendant xxiv). Asked by his assistant at the rehearsals of Endspiel (Endgame), "Are you of the opinion that the author should have a solution for the riddle at hand?"

Beckett replied curtly, "Not the author of this play" (Haerdter). In a letter of 26 October 1957 to his long-time American director Alan Schneider he admitted, "Sorry I was not of more help about the play [Endgame] but the less I speak about my work the better". And in rehearsals for Endgame in London in 1980, Rick Clutchey, who was playing Hamm under Beckett's direction, asked Beckett directly if the little boy in Hamm's narrative was actually the young Clov. "Don't know if the little boy is the young Clov, Rick," Beckett responded, "simply don't know" (in presence of S.E.G.).

On the other hand, Beckett has exercised so much authorial control over the production of his plays, even taking legal action against some forms of textual deviation, most recently posthumously through his estate against the Fiona Shaw / Deborah Warner production of Footfalls in London's West End, that he has maintained more authorial control over his work and performances than any other writer in history — with the possible exception of James Joyce, who seems to have manipulated the early criticism of Ulysses and Finnegans Wake fairly directly.

Yet despite correcting a variety of proofs for various editions, Beckett allowed obvious textual inconsistencies to stand, namely in the text of Come and Go, whose English version has four lines missing at the opening and two at the closing. With Come and Go the textual variants were the result of simultaneous translation. Beckett added some six lines to the 121 words of the English version while translating the work into French and after sending John Calder a typescript for publication. All British editions were subsequently based on the incomplete Calder text while the French and German editions contain the six lines added in translation.

The American edition used first the later typescript which

included the six lines, but then for convenience photo-offset the British edition for subsequent publications and so lost the six lines. Those six lines, incidentally, have been added by the editor to the text published in Volume IV of the Theatrical Notebooks. Beckett was still undecided about the final text of Endgame in 1987, forty years after writing it. Going over the "final" text, for the final time before its final publication in the Endgame volume of the Theatrical Notebooks, Beckett was still undecided whether or not, when Clov hits Hamm with the toy dog, Hamm should retain the dog or let it fall.

In the climate of post-structuralism the goal of retrieving something like an "original," "definitive," or "uncorrupted" text has been essentially discredited, since it assumes that an ideal text exists somewhere outside the process of reading it, or in the case of theater outside its "real-ization" on the stage. Such a critical climate has undermined the editor's traditional function of recovering and presenting something like an "original," "uncorrupted," or "corrected" text in its originary, prelapsarian purity. This age of dislocation and plurality of meaning invites a concomitant plurality of texts, and textual editors may finally have to adjust their aims to embrace that plurality or multiplicity and settle for the more modest goal of the "best recoverable text" or set of texts.

On the other hand, the problem of whose words exactly we are reading, hearing, performing, and finally interpreting, the historical author's, his scribe's, some typesetter's, an editor's, or an over-zealous theatrical director's, is a question all too often slighted by post-structural theorists. On the one hand, if the literary text is created by the reader, and so differs from reader to reader, why bother with a quest for the uniquely authorial or "uncorrupted" document? One might simply suggest fatalistically that textual deviations, alterations, or corruptions are inevitable, another cultural force at work on any text, and in many cases it is that same cultural imperative which generated that text through a particular historical author in the first place. The simple answer to the question "Why bother?" is, however, that although there are innumerable kinds of hats, and noses come in an incalculable variety of sizes and shapes, a hat is not a shoe, and a nose is not a knee. How an author or editor fills the space on a page is at least as important as how the reader will fill the "literary space" left by the author; that is, what exactly the reader will turn into a text in her reading remains of utmost importance. Catherine Belsey, for one, poses the dichotomy of meaning and textuality as follows:

While on the one hand meaning is never single, eternally inscribed in the words on the page, on the other hand readings do not spring unilaterally out of the subjectivities (or the ideologies) of readers. The text is not an empty space, filled with meaning from outside itself, any more than it is the transcription of an authorial intention, filled with meaning from outside language.

As a signifying practice, writing always offers raw material for the production of meaning, the signified in its plurality, on the understanding, of course, that the signified is distinct from the intention of the author (pure concept) or the referent (a world already constituted and re-presented).

Despite such ideological sensitivity and authorial ambiguity, the question of accurate or even complete texts, those that represent as much of the author's creative process as possible, remains a pressing theoretical and practical issue, one given renewed energy (if not method) by the publication of Hans Walter Gabler's 1984 "synoptic" edition of Ulysses, the 1986 Vintage "Corrected Text" that followed from it, John Kidd's assault (more on the methodology than on the ideology) of the project, and now the proliferation of Ulysses. Gabler's Ulysses (and calling it that proclaims its difference from, say, Joyce's Ulysses, that is, from any single edition Joyce ever wrote or read), for all its many faults in design and execution, has at least refocused attention on these issues, and his "synoptic text" offers one possible solution to the problems of a postmodern theory of textuality and textual transmission by acknowledging the plurality of texts. As Jerome McGann notes:

By giving priority of importance to the "synoptic" text over the "reading" text Gabler forces us to think of Ulysses as something other than a given object of interpretation on the one hand (which is the traditional New Critical view), or as an invention of interpretation on the other (which is the common post-structural view).

In Beckett's case, the problems of establishing a single, final theatrical oeuvre are further compounded because of Beckett's own associations, however loose they were and however suspicious he was of them, with creative and critical movements which held the traditional concepts of textual stability and literary meaning in contempt, the surrealists in particular, but also their offspring in la nouvelle critique. One version of a theory of an unstable (because incomplete) text is offered in a brilliant (if still neglected) work of literary theory, The Space of Literature by Maurice Blanchot. In it he argues that the work of art can never be absolutely finished. It is itself an infinity which depends on an Other, and it gains a semblance of completion only when it is read or performed. That reading (or performance), however, is only one of a multiplicity of possible readings, and hence texts.

Blanchot's view of texts and textuality is one which Beckett in many respects shared. The infinite or impossible or perpetual or incomplete or open text has been characteristic of Beckett's work at least since Dream of Fair to Middling Women, published only recently, and, among those works published in Beckett's lifetime, Watt, which celebrates its own lack of completion. The impossible and interminable, the always incomplete text is at least a metaphor which Beckett has embraced and folded into what passes for plot in his ground-breaking trilogy of novels begun in French just after World War II, Molloy, Malone Dies, and The Unnamable, and the fourth volume in that series, the thirteen texts which followed the novels, called Texts for Nothing. That metaphor of the infinite, incomplete, perpetually unfolding, self-reflexive text is as useful a paradigm for reading Samuel Beckett's creative process as any other. We know from studying the manuscripts of his work, for instance, that Beckett was a tireless reviser. That observation might, of course, be made for any number of authors — James Joyce and William Butler Yeats among them.

In Beckett's case the process of revision, and hence creation, continued — consciously and deliberately — well beyond publication, which was, therefore, not always the statement of a work's "completion," a concept which seems alien to Beckett's oeuvre as a whole. Once Beckett intervened in the process of performance, had become his own Other in a series of theatrical self-collaborations, and began directing his own work in 1986, he took those directorial opportunities to reread and so rewrite apparently completed texts yet again. Conceptually for Beckett, the process of creation, of literary composition, did not end with publication. Initial publication might then be only an intermediary step in the work's evolution.

But should such self-collaboration, Beckett's reading Beckett, particularly in the theater, be treated differently from that of any other reader's or director's readings? Should it be given author-ity and hence priority? As a director then is Beckett only another reader of his work, coming to his text as an Other and so acting as a reader whose insights might have no more validity than any other reader's? They may or may not, but they are at least worth reading and knowing, even if they are allotted no more weight, no more author-ity than any other reasonably intelligent critic's readings. Even the most ardent post-structuralist must concede that not all readings are equally insightful. This is why we read Derrida and other critics and theorists at all. What is clear from Beckett's post-publication revisions of his texts, his Theatrical Notebooks, and finally his stagings of his own plays, is that Beckett is an extraordinarily adept reader of Beckett. His Theatrical Notebooks, for instance, contain a remarkable wealth of information, speculation, and structural outlines of his work, all of which open the text rather than close it.

Despite Beckett's disclaimers to be incapable of writing a critical introduction to his own work, as a director he has come close to doing precisely that. Beckett's Theatrical Notebooks disclosed details of his work heretofore unseen by other critics. His direction is marked by a surprising amount of realistic subtext, for instance. As usual Beckett insisted in his direction of Endspiel on not intellectualizing his text in rehearsals. He noted early on, "I don't want to talk about my play, it has to be taken purely dramatically, to take shape on the stage.... Here the only interest of the play is as dramatic material." Beckett's admonition is not surprising. It is one that many a director has delivered to his actors early in rehearsals.

In the theater, one plays action not ideas. What is surprising, however, is that Beckett also suggested a realistic presentation: "The play is to be acted as though there were a fourth wall where the footlights are." While on occasion Beckett would say, "Here it oughtn't to be played logically," more often he would provide "realistic" motivation. For "Have you bled," he told Clov, "you see something in his face, that's why you're asking." Examining the parasite in his trousers provides Clov with the occasion for "What about that pee?" Hamm's "Since it's calling you" should be choked out to trigger Clov's "Is your throat sore?" And Clov's opening speech is motivated by some barely perceptible change that he perceives while inspecting his environment. In the Riverside notebook Beckett writes: "C perplexed. All seemingly in order, yet a change."

Pattern is crucial to Beckett's art, and patterning dominates his theatrical notes and productions: motion is repeated to echo other motion, posture to echo other posture, gestures to echo other gestures, sounds to echo other sounds. The principal of analogy is fundamental, and much of that analogy is detailed in the theatrical notebooks. In the Riverside notebook for Endgame Beckett says, for instance, "analogy N's knocks on lid, H's on wall"; "Analogy Clov-dog when trying to make it stand"; "Analogy voice and attitude [of Hamm during his narration] with N's tailor story" (Theatrical II 216). The action is filled with circles, arcs, and crosses, from Hamm's rounds to Clov's thinking walk. The linguistic analogue to such patterning is the revision of phrases to echo each other. Even when the phrasing is not parallel, Beckett established an echo, as in the Schiller Theater notebook, where he suggests that "Why this farce" should have the "same quality as `Let's stop playing'".

Beckett's own direction of Endgame seems a fulfillment of the structure he originally outlined for Roger Blin's Fin de partie in 1957. "He had ideas about the play," Thin noted, "that made it a little difficult to act. At first, he looked on his play as a kind of musical score. When a word occurred or was repeated, when Hamm called Clov, Clov should always come in the same way every time, like a musical phrase coming from the same instrument with the same volume.". Ten years later Beckett realized this musical conception of the play. "The play is full of echoes," he told his German cast, "they all answer each other."

Even though they are written in German, the two notebooks that Beckett prepared for his 1978 Schiller Theater production of Spiel (Play) are equally revealing. They demonstrate Beckett's near obsession with language (German in this case), structure, and formal detail — all three of which are, of course, inextricably entwined. Beckett's notebooks not only comprise a motif index to his plays, they constitute as well a remarkably detailed external record of the artist's internal processes and struggles. They document Beckett's continued aesthetic and stylistic development. At the head of a series of notes he prepared for Donald McWhinnie's 1976 Royal Court production of That Time Beckett wrote what amounts to a one-sentence theatrical manifesto, the most succinct and explicit statement of his late aesthetics that we have: "To the objection that visual component too small, out of all proportion with aural, answer: make it smaller, on the principle that less is more."

As Beckett adapted the aesthetics of architects that "less is more" (Ludwig Mies Van Der Rohe) and that "ornament is a crime" (Adolf Loos), as he developed what he often called his own "mania for minimalism," or what he punningly named a "Process of elimination" in the What Where notebook (Theatrical II 437), he also seized directorial opportunities to recreate his work according to principles more in keeping with sculpture, painting, or even architecture than with traditional drama, and to test the results directly on the stage.

The Eh, Joe notebook which Beckett prepared for the

second of his German productions outlines succinctly the central thematic and theatrical conflicts of this his first teleplay. While Joe may be "Out of sight, [and so consequently out of] reach," for example, he would not feel safe even without the assailing voice because of his "Fear of Dark." Beckett outlined the ten scenes of the play as follows:

- Out of sight, reach. Fear of dark.
- Rupture formula — "Best to come"
- Voices in head — behind the eyes. Mental thugee.
- Present voice last, then his own to still, then silence till God's, unstillable
- Clues for voice and hearer. Worse when nearly home. What if final whisper unstillable;
- God to him 1
- Deficient in kindness, strength, intelligence, looks, cleanliness, normality.
- Green one. 'Best to come' 2. Duly laid
- Same as 4.
- Voice falling to whisper. (Theatrical IV 263)

In the notebook for Tritte (Footfalls) Beckett makes explicit the relationships among the embedded characters of that play in his discussion of voices. In the dialogue within the monologues (parts II and III), for example, the Mother's "What do you mean, May, not enough" of part II should be echoed by the voice of Mrs. W's in part III, "What do you mean, Amy, to put it mildly," according to Beckett. "Same style for both relationships," he notes. The Kommen und Gehen (Come and Go) notebook details Beckett's preoccupation with pattern in theater space. Kommen und Gehen (finally directed by Walter Asmus, not Beckett) was on the programme with Spiel (Play) at the Schiller Theater Werkstatt in October of 1978. While Beckett rethought the da capo ending of Spiel, he considered adding a similar repetition to Kommen und Gehen. Although he outlined the pattern of what would amount to a second act to the play in his directorial notebook, he finally dismissed the possibility as "Mathematically desirable [but] logically impossible".

Not all aesthetic and theatrical and finally textual issues, however, were resolved during productions. Having worked closely with Anthony Page on the 1973 Royal Court Theatre production of Not I and having directed it himself in 1975 at the Theatre d'Orsay, Beckett still remained ambivalent about the final visual image of the play.

The best advice that he could finally offer directors of Not I was to omit the Auditor. As he wrote to a pair of directors on 16 November 1986, "I should have written . . . to advise you simply to omit the Auditor. He is very difficult to stage (light — position) and may well be of more harm than good. For me the play needs him but I can do without him. I have never seen him function effectively." Beckett's final comment presumably includes the English production he supervised closely, the 1973 Royal Court production with Billie Whitelaw, directed by Anthony Page. For the 1978 French productions with Madeleine Renaud, which he directed himself, Beckett omitted the Auditor altogether, as did the B.B.C. film production of the Billie Whitelaw performance. To date no script for the play suggests that the elimination of the Auditor is a directorial option.

One solution then to the problems of postmodern textual multiplicity is that offered by Beckett's English-language publishers Faber and Faber and Grove Press in the current series entitled The Theatrical Notebooks of Samuel Beckett. That series contains the theatrical notebooks Beckett kept for a particular work, published in facsimile, transcription, translation (where necessary), and annotations along with the revised texts. The revised texts which accompany the theatrical notebooks and are often justified by them are also fully annotated so that each of Beckett's changes will be at least noted and often discussed.

The result is something like a postmodern performance text, with an emphasis on process and transformation, which traces and documents Beckett's post-publication creative process. The Theatrical Notebooks series offers, then, not a definitive or uncorrupted or static text, the telos of the creative process, but rather a processive text, a multiplicity or plurality of texts whose endpoint is only Beckett's latest rereading of

Beckett. The revised text may place the original published text under erasure by superimposing a later stage of creative development over it but without necessarily obliterating it.

By presenting the textual and production possibilities of Beckett's texts, then, a postmodern dramatic text emerges, one which features Beckett's post-publication creative process and one which opens up reading and performance possibilities. It is admittedly an unstable text, but the instability exists within set textual limits. As a generic text the revised texts of Beckett's plays bear similarities not to Hans Gabler's "reading text," the one finally published as the Vintage "corrected" Ulysses, but to his "synoptic" text with all its variants, although in Beckett's case the generic text features post-publication changes exclusively.

For his "ideal" text, Gabler abandoned the traditional textual goal of retrieving the author's final intentions and focused on the process of composition, the authorial function. As Jerome McGann notes, "In fact, all texts are unstable to the extent that they are all processive and (in Gabler's terms) 'continuous.' At the same time, all are fixed within certain real, determinable limits as they assume certain specific form". Traditional critics tend to overlook the former, post-structuralists the latter. Faber and Faber will indeed publish Beckett's revised and corrected texts separately and without the theatrical apparatus I have been describing, but that's a business decision, not a theoretical one. The critically (and theoretically) significant texts are the "synoptic" versions published in the Theatrical Notebooks series.

Chapter 8

Keats, Sartre, Beckett

[. . .] life is a thing of beauty, Gaber, and a joy for ever. He brought his face nearer mine. A joy for ever, he said, a thing of beauty, Moran, and a joy for ever. (Beckett, *Molloy*)

Monsieur, at one time I ventured to think that the beautiful was only a question of taste. Are there not different rules for each epoch? (Sartre, *Nausea*)

In the context of deciding what kind of weather was better fitted to his taste, Beckett's absurdist quest-hero Molloy decides that he has no taste, that he had lost it long ago. To be sure, modernism never wholly let go of the aesthetic legacy of taste, but by 1947 when Beckett was working on the first in his series of three novels, *Molloy, Malone Dies*, and *The Unnamable*, it had already experienced this legacy in the form of an existentialist nausea. For Molloy, as well as for Sartre's existential man in *Nausea* (1938), there could be no escape from the imperative to exercise taste, although there could be no actually doing so either. Both were born on the wrong side of Romanticism as to taste, for that is where taste as a means of aesthetic self-making begins to fail. Perhaps nowhere do we see this more clearly than in Keats's late fragmentary epic, *Hyperion* and *The Fall of Hyperion*, where the metaphor of taste gives way to into an all-pervasive sickness seated in the stomach.

While the starving speaker of *The Fall of Hyperion* fails to relish the stale banquet he is offered at the outset of the poem, the defeated gods of *Hyperion* suffer an existential queasiness that plays itself out in bodies that are "crampt and screw'd". Even the eponymous hero Hyperion experiences a "nauseous feel" from the repulsive smells he is forced to consume. Critics since Walter Jackson Bate have noticed the proleptically existential tone of the *Hyperion* poems, the fact that they "anticipate much that we associate with existentialism (no other major nineteenth-century poem does this to the same extent)". Here, I would like to pursue the possibility, evinced by Keats, that existentialism itself—and its dominant paradigms of nausea and disgust—constitute the philosophical aftermath of aesthetic taste.

The gesture is toward an extended literary history of the aesthetic in which the metaphor of taste does serious work in the philosophical field of subjectivity. Because the reach of such a gesture is potentially unbounded, the following pages will limit themselves to a consideration of the Romantic legacy of taste (particularly Keatsian taste) in key moments of Sartre's *Nausea* and Beckett's *Molloy* (1955). In the opening scene of *Nausea,* when Sartre's existential man stands on the shore feasting his eyes on the traditionally sublime landscape of the sea, he suddenly finds himself cloyed and disgusted, unable to stomach the raw existence that obtrudes upon him in the form of a nauseating stone.

I read Beckett as revising this figurative trauma of taste by transforming Sartre's nauseating stone (*galet*) into a collection of absurdist "sucking stones" (*pierres a sucer*) that the vagabond Molloy collects from the shore and periodically sucks in a bravado display of connoisseurship. In this light, the existential stone takes on figurative significance in a tradition of iconic taste-objects extending back through the Century of Taste to Addison's tea-leaves in *Spectator* paper 409 ("On Taste") as testing ground for the so-called Man of Taste to prove his fine palate.

In the end, however, Beckett's absurdist epicure finds that the more he sucks, the more he transforms the idealized subject of taste, turning him inside-out by way of his digestive tract. According to Beckett's revisionary aesthetic of disgust, which I discuss in the final two sections of this essay, the subject becomes constituted according to a "general economy" in which waste and taste lose all distinction. In order to understand how taste gets remade in *Molloy*, I wish to first consider the souring of taste in *Hyperion* as a paramount instance of what will become a modernist disgust. While literary texts prior to *Hyperion* (for example, Shakespeare's *Titus Andronicus*), have also been read as protoexistentialist, my particular concern with Keats's late epic poetry lies in its role as mediator between the two major intellectual fields of taste and existentialist nausea.

Christopher Ricks, in his foundational study of Keatsian taste and distaste, proposes that Sartre has produced "the best criticism of Keats ever written not about him". When reversed, this trenchant insight also holds true: Keats has produced the best criticism of Sartre ever written not about him. In particular, the nausea portrayed by Keats in *Hyperion* suggests that this key emblem of Sartre's phenomenology originates in the eighteenth-century discourse of taste. This is not to say that Keats's nausea is equivalent to Sartre's fictional portrayal of nausea in his novel by that title, or that Sartre's nausea is equivalent to Molloy's disgust as modernist efforts to digest Romanticism. Rather, I wish to pursue how the nausea Keats describes follows philosophically from taste, and how this nausea hypostatizes certain elements of the existentialist condition. Let us keep in mind the figurative deployment of "taste" and "relish" by the Keatsian poet who "lives in gusto," an oral formulation whereby the poet *tastes* and *relishes* the world it perceives: "its relish of the dark side of things [. . .] its taste for the bright one" (*Letters* 1: 387).

This poet is also described as a "camelion poet," a figure of endlessly negative capability who inhabits a world of "gusto"—a term derived from taste (*gustus*) and defined by William Hazlitt as an effect whereby the eye acquires "a taste or appetite for what it sees". As Keats knew from reading *Hamlet*, chameleons were not only capable of changing colors, but of dieting on airy nothings, or "the chameleon's dish [. . .] the air". As such, the chameleon was an ideal figure to enact the kind of ethereal feasting that Keats used to allegorize the process of aesthetic consumption and production. The poet gorges on beauty and gives it back as expression, or, in Keats's words, "sees Beauty on the wing, pounces upon it and gorges it to the producing his essential verse". Everything in this closed cycle of consumption circulates through the mouth as the place of both taste and expression, a more tasteful mode of emission than occurs at the other end of the digestive tract (in other words, excretion).

In the *Hyperion* poems, however, the same poet who "lives in gusto" enters a realm where taste devolves into disgust. When he first appears in Book I of *Hyperion,* Hyperion is attempting to taste the sweet smell of incense (we will return to this synaesthesia in a moment) that drifts up to him from the world below. Yet, his pleasure is blocked, and instead we are told that when he *would taste* the spicy wreaths Of incense, breath'd aloft from sacred hills, Instead of sweets, his ample palate took Savour of poisonous brass and metal sick: (I: 186-89; emphasis added) In this scene of frustrated pleasure, the "poisonous brass and metal sick" interferes with Hyperion's effort to taste as defined above.

In fact, as Keats's manuscript of the poem makes clear, the final line of this passage did not originally begin with "Savour," or taste proper. It began instead with "A nausea" (*Manuscript Poems* 13). As Jonathan Bate narrates this revision, "Keats struggled with the final line in an attempt to convey the sickly sweet smell of incense. 'A nausea,' he begins. 'A nauseous feel,' he then tries, but 'feel' is heavily crossed out". Whether Keats could not bring himself to admit explicitly the feeling of nausea, or whether he abandoned "Nausea" in favour of "Savour" (albeit a sickening savor), the holograph suggests how closely these two concepts were bound up together in the creation of the scene. Although I suspect that it is not the "sickly sweet" taste of the incense, as Bate suggests, but the repulsive concoction of "metal sick" that nauseates Hyperion, the lines register a trauma of taste: Hyperion's physiological failure to taste and express beauty by means of his "ample palate."

Technically, he is attempting to taste the sweet *smell* of incense. In medical discourse of the eighteenth and early nineteenth centuries, taste and smell were linked as "chemical" as opposed to "mechanical" senses. However, smell was distinguished from taste as being more receptive to disgust than to pleasure. Kant ponders the implications of this distinction in his *Anthropology from a Pragmatic Point of View*, where he observes that "when confronted with many dishes and bottles, one can choose that which suits his pleasure without forcing others to participate in that pleasure"; on the other hand, he observes: "Smell is, so to speak, taste at a distance, and other people are forced to share a scent whether they want to or not". Smell in its sensual invasiveness leaves little room for idealization.

This obtrusive quality of smell disturbs Kant again in the *Critique of Aesthetic Judgment*, where he considers the problem of a scented handkerchief. Even the sweet smell of perfume can be a source of disgust, he argues, especially in a crowd where it is forced upon us: "the man who pulls out his perfumed handkerchief from his pocket gives a treat to all around whether they like it or not, and compels them, if they want to breathe at all, to be parties to the enjoyment, and so the habit has gone out of fashion". By the same token, he claims that objects "awaken nausea less through what is repulsive to eye and tongue than through the stench associated with it [. . .] this sense can pick up more objects of aversion than pleasure". Given the emphasis on smell in Keats's text, when Hyperion consumes incense and "metal sick" through his "ample palate," he finds himself particularly vulnerable, not to pleasure so much as disgust.

Like Hyperion, the speaker of *The Fall of Hyperion* is immediately confronted with the task of attempting to taste. And here too the matter he is offered augurs nausea far more than delight. The picked-over banquet he discovers at the outset of the poem strikes him as rubbish, or "refuse of a meal/ By angel tasted, or our mother Eve" (I.130-31). Everything seems parched and stale for this already sickened speaker, to whom the grape stalks appear not half full, but "half bare" (I.133). Far from bursting joy's grape against his palate fine like the speaker of Keats's "Ode on Melancholy," he can hardly stomach the sight of the grapes. Readers such as W. J. Bate,

Harold Bloom, and Marjorie Levinson interpret this scene as an allegory of poetic belatedness, or the difficulty of assimilating literary tradition into original expression. Yet when viewed as a key moment in a literary history of aesthetic taste, the unpalatable meal in *The Fall of Hyperion* prefigures the more full-scale souring of taste into nausea that marks existentialism's point of departure. As the speaker digs in to the remnants of the unappetizing, and potentially nauseating, meal, he, like Hyperion, experiences a "nauseous feel."

At the time Keats was working on these poems, his own physical condition entailed digestive complications from an advanced state of tuberculosis, and the poet's nausea in the *Hyperion* poems has its relation to an all-too-real physiological nausea experienced upon the pulses. In his letters, Keats complained miserably of his prescribed diet of "pseudo-victuals," and his physician, James Clarke, properly guessed that "The chief part of his disease [. . . was] seated in his Stomach" (*Letters* 2: 271; Rollins 1: 172). Painfully describing Keats's final days, Joseph Severn was moved to exclaim: "his Stomach—not a single thing will digest—the torture he suffers all and every night—and the best part of the day—is dreadful in the extreme—the distended stomach keeps him in perpetual hunger or craving" (Rollins 177).

Neither hunger nor a fevered condition was conducive to Keats's effort to distinguish himself through "matters of taste." On the eve of his *annus mirabilis* (31 December 1818), he declared that he had "not one opinion upon any matter except in matters of taste" (*Letters* 2: 19). Hunger was counterproductive to the experience of taste, and when viewed in light of Keats's ongoing efforts at aesthetic self-creation through taste, the queasiness and "nauseous feel" of his late poetry signal more than his own deteriorating physicality. They are symptomatic of the greater philosophical and cultural sickening of the Enlightenment subject of taste.

Keats's metaphorical encounters with taste may help us to think through more carefully the ways in which Sartre's portrayal of nausea, as both a fictional event of high modernism and a phenomenological symptom of subject-making, results from the oral schema defining the idealist subject of taste. In *Nausea* Sartre's protagonist, Antoine Roquentin, confronts a world that will no longer be assimilated by the idealist-turned-existentialist self. Sartre associated a digestive imagery with the Kantian mode of apperception, which he applied to the neo-Kantianism in vogue in France at the time: "We have all read Brunschvicg, Lalande and Meyerson, we have all believed that the [Kantian] Mind-Spider drew things into its web, covered them with white goo and slowly swallowed them, reducing them to its own substance" (qtd. in Stoekl 7). In *Nausea* this all-consuming idealist selfhood, which readily assimilates the world of objective reality, comes in for fictional critique.

Such critique is part of Sartre's more overarching challenge to Romantic idealism, leveled in the years leading up to the novel in *La Transcendence de l'ego* (1936), where Sartre disputed Kant's notion of a "transcendent ego," and *L'Imagination* (1936), in which he separated perception from imagination as modes of consciousness-consumption. His novelistic depiction of nausea, in turn, is an explicit response to the idealist understanding of taste. Derrida has shown how in Kant's third critique the aesthetic subject is organized around the *Os*, or all-consuming mouth. According to the restricted cycle of consumption that defines aesthetic taste, everything passes through the mouth: the socially acceptable end of the digestive tract and gateway to aesthetic subjectivity. A classic example of the consuming orality that characterizes the post-Kantian subject of taste is the Wordsworthian mind that feeds upon infinity in the final book of *The Prelude*. Romantic scholars such as Geoffrey Hartman and Alan Liu recognize the philosophical correlative of this scene to be the all-devouring Hegelian subject from the *Phenomenology of Spirit* (1807).

Earlier in his *Philosophy of Nature*, Hegel describes this subject in physiological terms as an organism which relates to the external world through the medium of its assimilating skin. This interface with objective reality is conceived as an expanded orifice, which when it "turns back on itself towards the organism's interior in addition to being a general orifice, it is now a single orifice, the mouth, and organic nature is seized and ingested as an individual thing" (2: 372). In an extensive study of Hegel's digestive imagery, Werner Hamacher has shown how Hegel's "sucking mouth, enjoys more than one specific location in the system of spirit, for this [. . .] is what systematizes body and spirit, what joins them together and articulates their unity". As body and spirit are unified through the circular economy of the "sucking mouth," the resulting totality becomes an idealist culmination of the Kantian subject of taste. I wish to suggest that Molloy's "sucking stones" demonstrate the absurdity of the aesthetically sucking mouth. But in order to do so, let us first consider the Sartrean stone from *Nausea* as the modernist taste-object *tout court*.

Groping for words to express the feeling provoked by the touch (etymologically, taste) of the stone in the opening scene of the novel, Sartre's existentialist man describes it as a "sweetish sickness" (*d'écoeurement douceâtre*). "Now I see," he observes, "I recall better what I felt the other day at the seashore when I held the pebble. It was a sort of sweetish sickness. How unpleasant it was! It came from the stone, I'm sure of it, it passed from the stone to my hand. Yes, that's it, that's just it—a sort of nausea in the hands". A similar sickly-sweetish sensation keeps Hyperion from experiencing pleasure, and there too the "sweetish sickness" is akin to "a nausea." Sartre's existential man explicitly recognizes this "sweetish sickness" as "the disgust of existing [. . .]. My saliva is sugary, my body warm: I feel neutral".

The stone that prompts Roquentin's initial wave of nausea presents itself as an unconsumable lump of external reality. As he gags on the unpalatable taste-object, he becomes uncomfortably aware of the salivary interface between self and world—his organ of taste turns literal. Roquentin becomes a self-conscious literalization of the aesthetic organism who tastes and relishes the world, and he begins to perceive the mouths of others (an increasing obsession throughout the novel) as not only a means of expression, but an opening to a disgusting, even monstrous reality. In one typical nightmare vision, he imagines himself as he "goes to the mirror, opens his mouth: and his tongue is an enormous, live centipede, rubbing its legs together and scraping his palate. He'd like to spit it out, but the centipede is part of him and he will have to tear it out with his own hands".

In place of a proper self-effacement in the activities of tasting and expressing (for which the tongue achieves privileged status in the idealist subject of taste), the tongue of Sartre's existential man obtrudes itself as an unwelcome reality. Everywhere he looks he sees smiles revealing the horror of rotting teeth, mouths opening as dark passages into a digestive tract, which traditionally runs in the opposite direction from taste. Simultaneously the eyes, which since classical times have represented the ideal mode of aesthetic intake, become occluded with their own materiality: "His eyes are glassy, I see a dark pink mass rolling in his mouth". For Sartre's existential quest-hero seeking a way out of contingent existence, the eyes are no longer the window to the soul, nor are the tongue a path to aesthetic existence. Rather, as his bodily "white goo"—saliva as an analogue for semen (another appetitive discharge)—intrudes upon the act of aesthetic perception, the one sure route left to freedom, it sickens the self-forming subject of taste. In *Nausea* the organ of taste itself is slimy, and it telling that when Ricks cites Sartre as the final word on Keatsian taste, he quotes from Sartre's extended meditation upon *le visqueux*—both slime and the slimy—in *Being and Nothingness* (1943).

For Sartre, the slimy resists the standard categorizations of solidity and liquidity, maintaining itself in a disgusting physical condition somewhere between the two: "Slime is the agony of water. It presents itself as a phenomenon in the process of becoming; it does not have the permanence within change that water has but on the contrary represents an accomplished break in a change of state. This fixed instability in the slimy discourages possession". The slimy presents an existence that will not qualify it for (as Bataille would say) the world of things, and so it cannot be perceived as object. It will not circulate through the restricted economy of aesthetic perception, to be converted into expression, and the inevitable result is nausea. As a mucous substance that collects in the mouth, Sartre's phenomenological concept of *le visqueux* enters the metaphorical world of *Nausea,* where, disgusted by his own slimy tongue, Roquentin struggles to maintain the consistency necessary to exist as a subject in the world of things. When he finds himself devolving into a gelatinous pool of fat, he struggles to pull himself together, to feel his "body harden and the nausea vanish." Yet as the act of aesthetic perception yields to the aftertaste of existence, the existential man is blocked from tasting his way into a higher ideal of selfhood.

Roquentin's name relates him to the stone—or rock (*roc*)—and just as *le visqueux* coats his organ of taste, it coats the untasteable stone. While scholars have recognized the iconic status of the stone within existentialism, it is significant that Roquentin's nausea began with the touch of a stone that had grown slimy from extended contact with the sea. According to the *Oxford English Dictionary,* the original meaning of slime is "Alluvial ooze; viscous matter deposited on stones, etc." Often, the stone is thought of as a smooth round object of contingent existence, but when Roquentin describes it, he describes its slimy underside: "I saw something which disgusted me, but I no longer know whether it was the sea or the stone. The stone was flat and dry, especially on one side, damp and muddy on the other. I held it by the edges with my fingers wide apart so as not to get them dirty". This metaphysically disturbing underside of the stone is damp and muddy (*humide et boueux*), or, in a vocabulary that will become more significant for Sartre, slimy.

Roquentin himself holds it gingerly with his fingers in order to avoid contact with its repulsive coating—a dark underside that has yet to come to light in critical accounts. According to Sartre, the paramount fear provoked by the slimy is that of "being sucked into the body of the slimy substance," and despite his best efforts to avoid contagion, the slimy stone (*roc*) sticks to Sartre's existential man. As if recalling his experience in *Nausea,* he writes in *Being and Nothingness*: "I cannot *slide* on the slime, all its suction cups hold me back; it can not slide over me, it clings to me like a leech". Roquentin finds it impossible to let go of the slimy stone throughout the remainder of the novel. As he reflects upon his experience, what stands out is his inability to throw, or otherwise detach the stone, or "pebble," from himself: "I was going to throw that pebble, I looked at it and then it all began: I felt that it existed. Then after that there were other Nauseas; from time to time objects start existing in your hand".

As Sartre's latter-day Man of Taste stands by the sea holding the "pebble" in his hand, unable to free himself from it, he becomes acutely aware of its mucous touch. For in a novel founded on an oral schema whereby everything passes through the mouth, all perception is metaphorized as consumption. After his initial nauseating contact with the stone, Roquentin's orifices of aesthetic perception all become blocked. Everywhere he looks, existence rises up to choke him: "I'm suffocating: existence penetrates me everywhere, through the eyes, the nose, the mouth". Aesthetic taste is founded on a clean cycle of consumption whereby the subject tastes and expresses, and nausea inevitably occurs when an object of external reality refuses to pass smoothly from substance into expression, obtruding itself in-itself. Such objects, stubbornly resisting being broken down and assimilated into a subjective system of meaning, get stuck and disrupt the circular economy of taste. In *Nausea* the encounter with the stone recurs in the form of other taste-objects that get stuck, as it were, in the gullet. The climax occurs when Sartre's existential man finds himself gagging on the sight of an immense black chestnut-tree root: "the black stump did not move, it stayed there, in my eyes, as a lump of food sticks in the windpipe. I could neither accept nor refuse it".

The fact that the root gets stuck in his "eyes," just as food gets stuck in the windpipe, causing one to gag or spit it out it, suggests the degree to which it is being visually consumed as taste-object. Dominick LaCapra refers to this scene as "one of the more lapidary philosophical interludes in the text," cleverly associating it with the opening scene. Roquentin's experience with the root registers on a grand scale the existential sickness prompted by the stone: his nausea is a phenomenological reminder of his own existence, his saliva a physiological barrier between himself and the world of aesthetically consumable reality. Like Keats's nauseated epic hero and Sartre's protagonist, Beckett's Molloy experiences an existential sickness which hinges on an anxious relation to taste.

The earliest critical responses to the novel intuited that his bodily activities entailed powerful metaphysical statements. Maurice Blanchot argues that Molloy brings about the death of the author through a brutal self-deconstruction, while Bataille extends this eschatological vision to encompass the end of subjectivity as such. I agree that Molloy is misunderstood if his appetites and aversions are read as merely contingent, mired in the body, stripped of philosophical import. The consistently abstract use of the term "taste" in the novel suggests that his pleasures and perversions (experienced by means of *his* ample palate) remain accountable to the civilizing project of taste. At the point that he would declare his independence from taste ("I had neither taste nor humour, I lost them early on"), the narrative perspective pulls back, in a rare moment abandoning the first person, to portray him not as tasteless, or free from the imperative to exercise taste, but as an inside-out version of the chameleon poet, tasteless in a way that Keats would never have shown: "Chameleon in spite of himself, there you have Molloy, viewed from a certain angle".

As descended from Keats's idealized creature of taste, Beckett's "Chameleon in spite of himself" would also live in gusto. Yet Molloy is not capable of feeding on the ethereal food of beauty and turning all substance into expression. He is obsessed not with the "relish of the dark side of things" but the dark side of relish—the physiological realities of ingestion, digestion, and excretion—and his gusto are ultimately in the service of disgust. Should a relation between these two seemingly antithetical chameleons, Keats's ethereal poet and Beckett's rudely appetitive, even scatological, anti-hero seem hard to swallow, one need only recall the climactic line from *Molloy*, "life is a thing of beauty [. . .] and a joy for ever." This line, derived from Keats, occurs at the point in the novel when Molloy's alter-ego, Moran, finally learns the nonsensical reason for his nonsensical quest.

In reaction to his stunned disbelief, the line is again repeated: "A joy for ever, he said, a thing of beauty, Moran, and a joy for ever". Keats himself set the terms for the reception of this maxim in his preface to *Endymion*, when he offered up the poem as more cloying than tasteful, productive of disgust rather than pleasure. As a result, the poem along with its opening line ("A thing of beauty is a joy for ever") became associated with what Keats had called that "mawkishness, and all the thousand bitters" that readers "must necessarily taste" in going over the romance. For nineteenth-century readers, the poem came to represent, as Keats's friend John Woodhouse put it, "that sugar & butter sentiment that cloys & disgusts". Moran is unable to swallow Keats's line on beauty, which in addition to being ridiculously out of place, is freighted with the same nauseous associations as its Romantic prototype. If beauty and its aesthetic pleasures are failing Molloy and Moran, the dual protagonists of *Molloy*, it is in large part due to the fact that they continue to hold themselves accountable to the paradigm of tasteful subjectivity. At the outset of the novel, Molloy defensively remarks, if I have always behaved like a pig, the fault lies not with me but with my superiors, who corrected me only on points of detail instead of showing me the essence of the system, after the manner of the great English schools, and the guiding principles of good manners, and how to proceed, without going wrong, from the former to the latter, and how to trace back to its ultimate source a given comportment.

Molloy recognizes that he is a product of a cultural system whose principles elude him (as they in fact eluded all the Enlightenment philosophers of taste). Yet, unlike eighteenth-century taste theorists, who recognized the difficulty of establishing rules for what was supposed to be an inherent faculty while proceeding to pin down its slippery principles nonetheless, Molloy responds to the inaccessibility of the system by turning his back upon it. He disclaims all responsibility to the ideal of tasteful selfhood, plunging headlong into the antithetical realm of the appetitive. His bold and randomly directed desires, whether physical or psychological, are such that he claims to "swallow everything, greedily". Yet his excessive appetite is overdetermined by the modernist nature of the text, and his desire constitutes more than a merely physical desire directed at food. Molloy postdates the extended worrying over human identity that generated the various paradigms of sensibility, sentiment, and taste which were deployed throughout the eighteenth century, and thus his appetites are also directed *against* all his efforts to taste.

Not only is Molloy separated from the Century of Taste by Romanticism, but he is even further removed from the pre-Enlightenment vision of the human being as a creature driven by appetite. Hobbes's materialist vision of appetitive man in *Leviathan* (1651) helped to motivate the entire Enlightenment culture of taste and its favourite fiction of selfhood, the Man of Taste. For Hobbes, human beings were organized not around the mouth (the site of tasting and expressing), but the stomach, spurred by a drive which "when it is toward something which causes it, is called Appetite, or Desire; the later, being the generall name; and the other, often-times restrayned to signifie the Desire of Food, namely *Hunger* and *Thirst*. And when the Endeavour is fromward something, it is generally called Aversion". This Hobbesian creature of "Appetite" and "Aversion," located on the other side of the Century of Taste from Molloy, does not confront the same cultural and metaphysical anxieties of the palate that the latter inherits from Romanticism. As a result, when Molloy describes his eating habits, they are revealed as contradictory—they are calculated to confound the various distinctions between taste and appetite, aesthetic pleasure and bodily enjoyment, which define the eighteenth-century discourse of taste.

Molloy, for instance, eats little and casually, as if he were guided more by distinction than appetite. Yet he describes this toothless eating (a version of sucking) as uncontrolled: I ate like a thrush. But the little I did eat I devoured with a voracity usually attributed to heavy eaters, and wrongly, for heavy eaters as a rule eat ponderously and with method, that follows from the very notion of heavy eating. Whereas I flung myself at the mess, gulped down the half or the quarter of it in two mouthfuls without chewing (with what would I have chewed?), then pushed it from me with loathing.

Impossibly vacillating between two oppositional modes, hunger and aesthetic disinterestedness, Molloy at once gives in to his appetite and maintains the disinterestedness necessary to taste. As Kant makes plain in his third critique, hunger disqualifies a person from taste: "Hunger is the best sauce; and people with a healthy appetite relish everything, so long as it is something they can eat.

Such delight, consequently, gives no indication of taste having anything to say to the choice. Only when men have got all they want can we tell who among the crowd has taste or not". Since Molloy is perpetually hungry, he maintains an uneasy relationship to his own status as connoisseur. His paradoxical displays of appetite always entail a presumed touch of indifference. According to this same logic, Malone, who is likewise toothless and who has also struggled all his life against the menace of starvation, exercises a decided indifference (or discrimination, the distinction again unclear) toward the institutional soup he is offered: "I eat it one time out of two, out of three, on an average. When my chamber-pot is full I put it on the table, beside the dish" (*Malone Dies* 7).

The chamber-pot beside the dish suggests general-economic confusion in which Beckett implicates aesthetic taste, and the possibility that a coprophagic scenario will come to replace the connoisseur's taste-test. Yet like Sartre's existential quest-hero, randomly seeking a way out of a nauseous existence, Beckett's vagabond protagonist is compelled to imagine himself as something more than a creature of appetite. His desire *not* to eat in part can be seen as a frantic reaction to the hunger that disqualifies him from taste. Shortly after the above bravado display of culinary disinterestedness, Molloy describes himself as "bent double over a heap of muck, in the hope of finding something to disgust me for ever with eating". In this light, any description of Beckett's protagonist as Rabelaisian proves instructive in its insufficiency. Rabelais's giant who "shat, pissed, vomited, belched, farted, yawned, spat, coughed, sighed, sneezed, and blew his nose abundantly" experiences a far greater freedom than Beckett's anti-hero from the cultural constraints of taste.

The former has been described by Mikhail Bakhtin as a porous creature whose orifices, clotted with waste, represent unregulated exchange between self and world. If this exchange can be considered triumphant, as Bakhtin argues, productive both of sociality and commensality, it is owing to the fact that it occurs prior to the time when the Enlightenment had imposed the lasting distinction between bodily enjoyment and aesthetic pleasure. Insofar as the physiological pleasures described by Rabelais had not yet been conscripted into the sociopolitical project of taste, in other words, they cannot be compared to Molloy's. Molloy himself is aware of this distinction, and his displays of greedy gorging, absurdly mixed up with his finicky preferences, suggest the dialectic relation to taste in which his appetites are always already involved.

Despite his driving appetite, Molloy cultivates a refined palate through his habit of sucking stones. Much like Sartre's indigestible stone, these "sucking-stones" are absurdist taste-objects which bring the tension between taste and appetite into relief. From the first, Molloy acknowledges that his habit of sucking stones is a defence against hunger: "I thought of the food I had refused. I took a pebble from my pocket and sucked it. It was smooth, from having been sucked so long, by me, and beaten by the storm.

A little pebble in your mouth, round and smooth, appeases, soothes, makes you forget your hunger, forget your thirst". These stones, first introduced as pebbles (*caillou*) and later renamed "sucking-stones" (*pierres a sucer*), divert Molloy from a hunger that would disqualify him from taste. Stones would seem a poor substitute for food, yet Molloy is extremely picky about his stones preferring to suck nothing than an unsatisfactory stone. When he loses his original sucking-stone, he refuses to allow a servant to fetch him another from the garden: "I deemed it wiser to say nothing about it, all the more so as he would have been capable, after an hour's argument, of going and fetching me from the garden a completely unsuckable stone".

Molloy is, after all, a connoisseur of stones, and to be a connoisseur of anything one must maintain a disinterested attitude. Even though he does achieve or perform (one never knows quite which) the disinterestedness necessary to exercise taste, Molloy boasts of his lack of distinction: "And now I come to think of it, my attempts at taste were scarcely more fortunate, I smelt and tasted without knowing exactly what, nor whether it was good, nor whether it was bad, and seldom twice running the same thing". At the same time, where there is no taste, there is only taste for Molloy. Just as he fails to distinguish between tastes and smells that do exist, he makes fine distinctions among stones that (he admits) have no taste. Shortly after his haughty dismissal of the unsuckable stone, he embarks on an extended meditation about his sucking-stones. This episode, in part a critique of an Enlightenment faith in ratiocination, establishes these sucking-stones as a specific conundrum of taste.

The question that preoccupies him in this scene is how to suck sixteen stones, which he carries in his pockets, in such a way as never to suck the same stone twice in a row. Any possibility that he might suck his stones out of order threatens to destroy all aesthetic delight. He proceeds to devise a complicated system of circulating the stones throughout his four pockets, which as another one of Beckett's permutation games, serves as an allegory for the restricted circulation of taste. He decides, "as I sucked a given stone, to move on the fifteen others, each to the next pocket, a delicate business admittedly, but within my power, and to call always on the same pocket when I felt like a suck. This would have freed me from all anxiety". The "anxiety" Molloy speaks of here is the *angst* of a connoisseur devoted to a pleasure that theoretically cannot exist. From this perspective, taste winds up in a place its own principles would never allow: the scene of a hunger which is no hunger, the paradoxical pleasure of sucking tasteless stones.

A radical contingency governs Molloy's most exacting discrimination, and at the height of the crisis he is forced to admit: "deep down it was all the same to me whether I sucked a different stone each time or always the same stone, until the end of time. For they all tasted exactly the same." The only solution for this absurdly sucking mouth is to somehow break it of the habit. Just as he had formerly abandoned the "guiding principles of good manners," Molloy concludes his experiment of taste with sudden indifference: "And the solution to which I rallied in the end was to throw away all the stones but one, which I kept now in one pocket, now in another, and which of course I soon lost, or threw away, or gave away, or swallowed". The only solution to the futile attempt to taste is, in the end, to swallow. Consuming that which he prefers only to suck, or process according to the restricted economy of taste, Molloy sucks taste back into the body. In doing so, he returns this iconic existentialist taste-object back to the unconscious realm of enjoyment.

Eventually, the wider economy in which Molloy's sucking involves him turns the mouth, *qua* portal to aesthetic subjectivity, into the other physiological end of the digestive tract. Whereas aesthetic taste (in Derrida's words) "prohibits the substitution of any non-oral *anal*ogue," such substitution is precisely what *Molloy*'s absurdist, inside-out mode of consumption manages to do. When Moran sees a face that "vaguely resembled" his own, he focuses on the "thin red mouth that looked as if it was raw from trying to shit its tongue". Such physiognomy stands as an embodied critique of the all-consuming idealist subject, which gives priority to the mouth in the role of philosophical becoming. Novalis nicely sums up this oral, self-constituting model of selfhood when he writes that "If an organ serves another then it is, as it were, its tongue—its throat, its mouth. The instrument that serves spirit most willingly and is most readily capable of manifold modifications, is above all its linguistic instrument" (qtd. in Krell 38). Against this idealist model, Molloy drags the organ of taste through the dark channels of the digestive tract and out the other end, turning the aesthetic subject of taste upside-down and inside-out. Simultaneously, he invests the one orifice that traditionally has nothing to do with taste with a subjective (and subject-making) capacity: "We underestimate this little hole, it seems to me, we call it the arse-hole and affect to despise it. But is it not rather the true portal of our being and the celebrated mouth no more than the kitchen-door".

Demoting the "celebrated mouth" to a kitchen door (an escape route as well as means of ingress for servants, raw meat, trash, and other distasteful elements), Molloy refigures the "arse-hole" as "the true portal of our being." He finds it no paradox to speak—literally and metaphorically—of his "First taste of the shit". And rather than expressing himself into spirit, Beckett's perverse "Chameleon in spite of himself" speaks of excreting (or "shitting out") his organ of speech. His physiognomy is adapted to the absurdist subject who no longer "lives in gusto," but who inhabits in a world of disgust. Like their Romantic prototype in *The Fall of Hyperion*, Molloy and Moran are both sickened, rapidly decomposing creatures involved in senseless quests. Moran's description of his counterpart Molloy could apply equally well to the Keatsian poet: "He hastened incessantly on, as if in despair, towards extremely close objectives".

Yet whereas in Keats's poem the speaker wastes away after several frustrated efforts to taste, Moran (the protagonist of the second half of *Molloy*) finds himself "succumbing to other affections, that is not the word, intestinal for the most part," and vows: "I would get there on all fours shitting out my entrails and chanting maledictions". As he gropes his way forward in despair, he ends up trailing not clouds of glory but entrails and the rest of his physical interiority. We increasingly become privy to the details of his digestive problems as his exterior becomes caked with his own physiological excess, his breeches having "rotted, from constant contact with my incontinences". And whereas Keats's speaker is propelled forward in order not to starve, or have his flesh "parch for lack of nutriment" (*Fall* I.110), both Molloy and Moran treat their hunger with indifference. Moran for one recognizes his hunger to result from an inability to digest: "For several days I had eaten nothing. I could probably have found blackberries and mushrooms, but I had no wish for them [. . .]. And though suffering a little from wind and cramps in the stomach I felt extraordinarily content, content with myself, almost elated, enchanted with my performance".

Moran is rotting, falling apart like the chameleon-poet of *The Fall of Hyperion*, but he remakes himself according to a general-economic schema which (to borrow Raphael's pun from *Paradise Lost*) turns all nourishment to wind. His performance is a perverse form of expression on the part of his absurd, reformulated *Os*. In reimagining the idealist subject of taste, a creature capable of turning everything into ideality or expression rather than excretion, Beckett goes further than Sartre to transform taste into a modernist aesthetic. Although Sartre reorients the subject in a world of nausea, he has often been accused of returning to the same idealism his novel had seemed written to oppose. At the end of *Nausea*, his existentialist man seeks "to drive existence out of [himself], to rid the passing moments of their fat, to twist them, dry them, purify myself, harden myself, to give back at last the sharp, precise sound of a saxophone note". His existentialist quest (really nothing more than a senseless wandering around the provincial French town of Bouville) ends on the distinct possibility of finding a way out of the contingent existence that was choking him through all his orifices of aesthetic perception. Allan Stoekl speaks for those who find themselves dissatisfied with the conclusion when he claims that "Roquentin, then, may be not only a jerk, but the final savior of neo-Kantianism".

For many readers, Roquentin's status as existential man is compromised by this final urge to raise himself out of his existence into a higher subjectivity. At the height of his nausea, he declares that "If you existed, you had to exist all the way, as far as mouldiness, bloatedness, obscenity were concerned".

But whereas Roquentin finally turns back from the obscenity of full-blown existence, Molloy goes all the way, winding up in the ditch of his own excreted materiality.

Beckett's eponymous quest-hero finally attains an identity as the expelled. From the beginning of his senseless wanderings, he had been preoccupied with his mother, or "her who brought me into the world, through the hole in her arse if my memory is correct". We are never told where he set out from, and he himself does not know where he is going, but if he has any goal at all it is to find his way back to this ur-site: the maternal arse-hole. Similarly, the first-person narrator of *The Unnameable,* presumably a deteriorated version of Molloy, delights in imagining himself as an excrementum: "I like to fancy, even if it is not true, that it was in mother's entrails I spent the last days of my long voyage, and set out on the next". Like the narrator of Beckett's "The Expelled" (1967), Molloy is a scatological creature self-identified through the "other" end of the digestive tract.

Both are products of creation-via-purgation, and like Molloy after his formative expulsion, the title character of "The Expelled" also claims to have "dragged on with burning and stinking between my little thighs, or sticking to my bottom, the result of my incontinence" (*Stories and Texts* 14). Rather than seeking his way back through the usual channels to the proverbial womb, he directs himself toward the site of his original expulsion. The Expelled explicitly refers to this expulsion as a "fall," drawing upon the esoteric notion of creation as a fall into materiality.

I would submit that Molloy's expulsion from his mother can also be understood as a metaphysical fall into matter. Just as "The Expelled" winds up in the gutter (a place of refuse, drainage and waste), Molloy winds up in a ditch. Malone perhaps puts it best of all when he says: "In any case here I am back in the shit" (*Malone Dies* 98). A certain strain of Beckett criticism locates him in a tradition of Irish satire extending back through the Century of Taste to Jonathan Swift, and the ditch at the end of *Molloy* bears too close a resemblance to the metaphysical ditch at the end of Swift's *A Discourse Concerning the Mechanical Operation of the Spirit* to go unremarked in conclusion here. Bloom for one proposes that "Swift, had he read and tolerated Schopenhauer, might have turned into Beckett". Swift's scatological satire was directed in part against the developing Enlightenment culture of taste, and the volume that contained his *Mechanical Operation of Spirit* also contained *A Tale of a Tub; Written for the Universal Improvement of Mankind* (1704). In the preface to both Swift explicitly distances himself from Anthony Ashley Cooper, third Earl of Shaftesbury, the prototype for the eighteenth-century Man of Taste. The premise of his intentionally distasteful *Discourse* is that all subjective pretensions to spirit can be reduced to the mechanical operations of the body, whose various expressions and emissions are shown to have a material basis. In the final paragraph, Swift's narrator remarks: "Too intense a contemplation is not the business of flesh and blood; it must by the necessary course of things, in a little time let go its hold and *fall into matter* [. . .] a perfect moral to the story of that philosopher who, while his thoughts and eyes were fixed upon the *constellations,* found himself seduced by his *lower parts* into a *ditch*. When Molloy falls into a ditch, he falls metaphorically out of the world of spirit (for the sucking Molloy, aesthetic subjectivity) and into an excremental place where the "*lower parts*" find relief. As he relates: "The forest ended in a ditch, I don't know why, and it was in this ditch that I became aware of what had happened to me. I suppose it was the fall into the ditch that opened my eyes, for why would they have opened otherwise?" (122-23).

Metaphorically, we might read Molloy's "fall into the ditch" as what Swift refers to as a philosophical "fall into matter." Molloy is Beckett's remade creature of taste, and his fall is also a fall out of himself and into his own excreted materiality, or the absurdity of general-economic existence. The orifice which orients this space is no longer the Kantian *Os*, but what Derrida would call its unthinkable analogue. Ironically, it is Molloy's self-expression through this *Os*—an absurdist inversion of the ideally sucking mouth—that finally opens his eyes.

Chapter 9

The Last Modernist

Biographies often begin with a date of birth, the date on which the subject's experiences can be said to begin. In the case of Samuel Beckett there are two difficulties about adopting this simple procedure. One is his claim to have been born on Good Friday, 13 April 1906. The other is his repeated insistence that he had memories of life in his mother's womb. The idea that he had been born on Good Friday, the day of the Saviour's crucifixion, pleased him, more especially since Good Friday happened in 1906 to have been Friday the thirteenth.

What better birth-date could there be for someone so conscious of the suffering which underlies human existence; and conscious also that misfortune, in comic or tragic guise, awaited every venture and departure? In a late work, Company, which is highly autobiographical, the coincidence of his birth-date with the day of the Saviour's death is emphasized. 'You were born on an Easter Friday after long labour...' And: 'You first saw the light and cried at the close of the day when in darkness Christ at the ninth hour cried and died.' Not only was Beckett pleased with the Christ connection involved in having been born on a Good Friday, but he was never averse to introducing analogies and comparisons between Christ's life-story and those of his degraded characters.

It is a little unfortunate therefore that his birth certificate shows him to have been born on the 13 May 1906, which was a Sunday. The birth was not registered until a month later, on 13 June. Since it was Irish custom to allow a clear four weeks to elapse between birth and registration, this fact would if anything tend to confirm the May rather than the April birth-date, but of course there is always the possibility of error — even an error of immediate recollection on his father's part, or a slip of the tongue or the pen, neither of which was rare where registration was concerned. Since Beckett was on the whole truthful about such matters and on at least one occasion claimed to have the authority of his mother for the Good Friday birth-date, the balance of probability is in its favour, but it is a pity nevertheless that there should be any doubt about it.

The other difficulty about beginning on Friday the thirteenth is Beckett's claim to have had memories which preceded this date. He told more than one person that he had such memories; and in an interview given when he was sixty-four he said, 'Even before the foetus can draw breath it is in a state of barrenness and of pain. I have a clear memory of my own foetal existence. It was an existence where no voice, no possible movement could free me from the agony and darkness I was subjected to.'

On an earlier occasion he had told Peggy Guggenheim that he had, in her words, 'retained a terrible memory of life in his mother's womb. He was constantly suffering from this and had awful crises, when he felt he was suffocating.' And with his close friend Geoffrey Thompson, a psychiatrist who tried to help him with subsequent difficulties, he also discussed his pre-natal memories and the feelings of entrapment and suffocation they brought with them.

But not only did he have these generalized memories; he had, he said, a particular memory of being at the dinner table in his mother's womb shortly before birth. There were guests present and the conversation was, perhaps needless to say, of the utmost banality.

In any case Samuel Beckett, son of William — known as Bill in family circles, but generally to friends and associates as Willie — and his wife Maria — known as May — was born at nightfall, in the family home at Foxrock, a prosperous suburb on the outskirts of Dublin. At the time of his birth Bill and May Beckett had been married almost five years. A first child, Frank, had been born within eleven months of their marriage;

the second, Samuel, was not conceived for three more years. The place of May's accouchement was the bedroom in which the conception had most likely taken place, a big room with a bow window facing the Dublin mountains. It was a difficult labour, the pains lasting all day; and as soon as it began in the morning Bill absented himself, going for a tramp in the mountains with a packet of sandwiches and a flask of whiskey. He returned to find his wife still in labour, and being, like most fathers of the time, neither welcome nor anxious to hear or see anything of the delivery, he took himself off to the garage, where he sat in darkness in the driver's seat of his high De Dion Bouton until a maid came to tell him it was all over and that his wife had been happily delivered of a son.

In later life Beckett was fond of the verse in the Book of Job, verse 3, chapter 3, 'Let the day perish in which I was born and the night in which it was said, there is a man child conceived.' Mr Tyler in the radio play All That Fall apologizes for cursing, in the presence of a lady, God and man and 'the wet Saturday afternoon' of his conception, while Neary, in the novel Murphy, curses first the day he was born, 'and then, in a bold flashback, the night he was conceived'.

Whereas Bill and May's first son, Frank, had been healthy and placid, Samuel was a sickly, thin baby who cried constantly. The Becketts were prosperous people and the house in which the birth took place reflected that prosperity, as did its situation in Foxrock, then a very exclusive suburb of Dublin. Willie Beckett's father, also William, was a building contractor and what nowadays would be called a speculator who had acquired both money and house property in Dublin on a considerable scale.

Among the contracts awarded to his firm were those for the new National Library and National Museum, flanking the Royal Dublin Society's headquarters in Leinster House in Kildare Street, which subsequently became the home of the Dail or Irish parliament. These had been begun in 1885 and finished in 1891. There was fierce competition for the contract and some of William Beckett's enemies were pleased when it was established that the Mountcharles sandstone employed had been wrongly used: face-bedded instead of end-bedded, so that it began to crumble almost immediately, though this was never clearly established as the builder's mistake and may well have been the architect's.

The Becketts vaguely supposed themselves to be descended from Huguenot refugees who had come to Ireland from France after the revocation of the Edict of Nantes in 1685, fleeing their homeland to escape persecution as Protestants and settling in a country where persecution of Catholics was just about to begin on a systematic scale. The Huguenots had supplied Ireland with much of its industrial and business energy, bringing with them a knowledge of the linen and poplin trades as well as of banking; and they fitted in easily enough in a country which was in process of transition after the Williamite Wars a place where much was in the melting-pot and most business activity represented a new departure.

Within a generation or two the Huguenots generally were as happy to forget their French origins as many other members of the land-owning and business classes were to forget their English; and by the early twentieth century no trace or definite knowledge of a former French connection remained. Samuel Beckett's adoption of France as his homeland would have nothing to do with the French origins of his family: and in fact there is doubt that the Becketts really were Huguenots.

The name does not occur in early listings of Huguenot refugees and is not commonly regarded by historians of the Huguenot influx as a likely Huguenot one. The suggestion has therefore also been made that the Irish Becketts were of Norman origin, and those who like aristocratic lineages for their heroes have even claimed that Samuel Beckett's family were descended from the family of Thomas a Becket, the turbulent priest who was Henry II's Archbishop of Canterbury.

What makes the Huguenot connection the more likely is that originally the Becketts were silk- and poplin-weavers, a form of manufacture in which Huguenots certainly engaged, and in fact William Beckett senior's father, Samuel's great-grandfather, James Beckett, had been in the silk-weaving business. By the time his son entered the building trade, Irish silk-weaving, which had once been important, was dying out. In 1869 William the builder had married Fannie or Frances Crothers — Crowther in one family record, but certainly Crothers — daughter of a Dublin merchant, Thomas Crothers, who was also of course a Protestant. A talented and sensitive woman, perhaps more talented and sensitive than William Beckett had bargained for, to some extent she broke the mould of philistine business success and introduced other elements into the make-up of the Becketts.

She was an accomplished musician, who played the harmonium and composed settings for poems which she thought sufficiently solemn and religious-sounding, such as Tennyson's 'Crossing the Bar'. In later life she took to the drink and Dublin gossip was pleased to report on her eccentricities, including the fact that she would lock herself in her room, presumably with supplies of alcohol, for days on end. What in the course of time her grandson, Samuel, would remember best about her was the parrot who always perched on her shoulder and flew into a jealous rage when anyone kissed her.

Fannie and William Beckett had four sons, of whom one, Howard went into the family contracting business, J. and W. Beckett of South King Street; and two, Gerald and James, studied medicine and became doctors. A daughter, also Frances, but known because the boys called her that as Cissie, would have a somewhat less orthodox career, as a painter, member of Dublin's bohemia and wife to an unsuccessful Jewish art dealer. The fourth son, in fact the eldest and christened William after his father, was destined to be the father of Samuel Beckett.

William senior and Frances lived in a house called Earlsfield which was Number 7 Prince William Terrace in the fashionable district of Ballsbridge, and it was there that William junior was born in July 1871. He grew into a burly, athletic youth of a not very studious disposition and left school early to become apprenticed to a member of the trade or profession of quantity surveying. Quantity surveyors were employed to estimate the amount of material likely to be used in any particular building contract, and had begun to appear in the early nineteenth century, when they were known as 'measurers'. Originally anybody could set up who had the right connections and thought he could get the work, but by the late nineteenth century entry was being increasingly if loosely regulated by-an apprenticeship and examination system. Willie Beckett was apprenticed to the firm of J. and E. Pannister where he served the requisite five years, after which a partnership was purchased for him in a firm which had offices in Clare Street, near the back gate of Trinity College.

Besides the fact that estimating could prove a lucrative extension of the activities of an already well-established building concern, William Beckett senior, like many successful business people at the time, was anxious that his eldest son should become a member of one or other of the professions. This was a tendency everywhere, but it was especially the case in snobbish Dublin, which was keenly conscious of social gradations. Since William junior showed no interest in a prolonged period of academic study, quantity surveying was a good halfway house. His success, it was felt, would be almost automatically ensured by his connection with the firm of T. and W. Beckett, while at the same time it would be a step up in the world, since quantity surveying took rank as a profession, not a trade. The line between it, civil engineering and architecture was still rather blurred. Quantity surveyors were free to describe themselves as one or the other and frequently did.

Willie Beckett may not have been academically minded, but neither was he a dullard. He had a good, shrewd business brain and he was soon a success in his profession. He was also a socially minded, good-natured, seemingly uncomplicated young man, fond of masculine pursuits, including the game of rugby and the drinking and horse-play that went with it. All the Becketts were athletic and interested in athletics and Willie's brother Jim, one of the two who became doctors, was a famous swimmer and a member of the Irish international swimming team about which later verses would be written:

Dockrell, Taggart, Beckett, where
Now are the men I worshipped there?

In manner Willie Beckett was an extrovert, who appeared glad to see people and was prepared to make the best of them. He was, like his brothers, naturally athletic and besides being a rugby player he was a golfer, a tennis player, a great walker and a year-round swimmer. In the course of time he became a member of several men's clubs, including the exclusive Kildare Street. Until he was over thirty he lived at Earlsfield, a mansion substantial enough to house a British embassy in later years, an active young man already inclining to stoutness.

It was an uncomplicated life: the office or the building site during the day, nights at the club with a game of billiards after dinner, summer evenings on the golf course and in the club-house bar. But to go with all this masculine activity and joviality there was church-going with his parents at weekends before Sunday dinner at Earlsfield, often followed by a tramp through the Dublin mountains.

Then he fell in love; and unfortunately with a Catholic — the seventeen-year-old daughter of William Martin Murphy, the most successful Catholic businessman in Dublin, owner of newspapers, the tramway company and much else, whom he had met at the Fitzwilliam Lawn Tennis Club, one of the few places where Catholics and Protestants could meet socially. There was talk of marriage and both sides were appalled, the Catholic Murphys even more than the Protestant Becketts. The girl was forbidden to see any more of him and was forced to make a solemn renunciation at her mother's death-bed, the death itself occurring at just the right moment to induce a sense of guilt and transgression. Then, apparently almost before she had time to breathe, let alone weep, she was married off to a distinguished Dublin surgeon, Sir Arthur Chance, a widower with children who happened to be a knight as well as a Catholic and was not only much older than her, but considerably older than Bill Beckett as well: in short, a good match.

Shortly afterwards Willie went down with pneumonia. He appears to have been out of sorts for some time after being parted from his love, with ailments difficult to diagnose and probably evidence of a shock to the psyche greater than was to be expected from his extrovert demeanour; in fact, a breakdown. But the pneumonia was an indisputable reality and he wound up in the Adelaide Hospital, where he was nursed by a tall, thin-faced, serious girl called Maria, or May, Roe, who was exactly the same age as himself.

The Roes had been in Ireland since 1641, before the Cromwellian invasion, and had once been considerable landowners in County Tipperary, with villages named after them, such as Roesborough and Roe's — now corrupted to Rose — Green. The Tipperary Roes had a reputation for wildness which sometimes overlapped with one for oddity but by the early nineteenth century a branch of the family was centered in Leixlip, a small town or village not far from Dublin in County Kildare, and was producing principally clergymen. In the mid-part of the century May's father, Samuel Robinson Roe, son of a clergyman also called Samuel, had possessed a property near Mountmellick in Queen's County, now County Laois. He was also, however, a miller and grain merchant and in 1864 had moved to another property, Cooldrinagh in Leixlip, and another mill in nearby Celbridge. Besides owning the mill he still had land with tenants on it and had therefore not forfeited his right to be called a gentleman; but when he died he left his family in seriously reduced circumstances.

Whatever sort of gentleman he may have been, Samuel Robinson Roe was certainly not much of a businessman. He was, as people benevolently say in Ireland, fond of a drop, which means that he was a heavy drinker and he died relatively young. Whatever his failings, however, the religious atmosphere in his household was strong, and was not lessened by his marriage to Anne or Nanny Belas, for the Belases, who were solicitors in Andrew Street in Dublin, were very evangelical. In the days of his prosperity Samuel Roe had rather fancied himself as a speculator and financier discounting bills and buying up mortgages, but when the mill, which failed to thrive, ate up his capital, including his land, his resourcefulness appears to have been exhausted at the same time. The strong will and character that May Roe exhibited throughout her life seems to have come from her mother, a neat little woman of high — or should one say low? — Evangelical principle, which she passed on to her daughter.

The Roes had a number of children; and when Samuel Robinson Roe died his daughter May was only fifteen. Since they had not been well provided for, it was desirable that she should find an occupation and eventually she had, to use a phrase of the day, 'gone nursing'. The burden on relatives of a large family had to be alleviated in any way possible. What made nursing an acceptable option was the advent in Ireland in the late 1880s of the 'lady probationer', the daughter of gentlefolk who entered a hospital for training as a nurse. After this it became quite a fashion for such young ladies to do so. The Adelaide Nursing School was especially popular among Protestants with some social pretensions, but it was also a good place as far as actual training for the profession was concerned, the Adelaide having been among the first hospitals in these islands to institute any sort of training system at all, in 1858, when a colleague of Florence Nightingale's set it up.

The financial rewards of nursing were not very great, varying between 12 [pounds sterling] and 30 [pounds sterling] a year when the training period was over, but a nurse might be expected to have good marital opportunities, especially if she had the right social background herself. Samuel Robinson Roe's relatives may well have considered nursing to be as good an option as any other. Whether May had any real vocation for it is a different question. There was not much in her subsequent attitudes which suggested a natural nurse, though she was efficient enough at binding up her children's smaller physical wounds.

While it was not a matter of remark that a young man of Willie Beckett's age and type should still be a bachelor at thirty, a girl of that age who was still unmarried was regarded as in danger of being left on the shelf. When she met Willie, or, as she shortly began to call him Bill, Beckett, May was doubtless under some pressure, whether great or small, overt or otherwise, to find a husband. Bill for his part was on the rebound. He had suffered a severe emotional reverse; and, besides he too would have had urged upon him the necessity of 'settling down'. No doubt all this contributed to whatever process of falling in love or falling for each other there was; but on the surface at least they were a somewhat ill-matched pair. Bill was a comfortable fellow, pleasure loving and emotionally undeveloped; she was moody, questioning and exacting. She was also witty, even sarcastic, and she had a vivacious side, being subject to states of comparative elation as well as depression; so he may have seen her as high-spirited as well as serious.

She had been educated at the Moravian Mission School, Gracehill, outside Ballymena, County Antrim, which does not mean that either the Roes or the Belases were necessarily of the Moravian persuasion. Gracehill had been the first boarding school for girls in Ireland. The Moravians were known as good, thorough-going educators. Low Church Protestantism — which virtually all Irish Protestantism was — would have little difficulty with their non-doctrinal approach. And in any case their doctrines, such as they are, conform to the mayor Protestant confessions. At school she had frequently been in trouble for indiscretions and breaches of discipline, the sort of high spirits that verge on hysteria; and there had been a threat of expulsion for talking to a boy over the rear wall, an episode to which as a married woman she made occasional reference and of which she seemed rather proud. Probably the extreme high sprits which she occasionally displayed were evidence of a tendency to mood-swings, what a later age would call manic-depressive tendencies, before calling them bi-polar personality traits, but of course that would not have been evident then.

Whatever the degree of attraction between them, the courtship was swift and conclusive. Bill Beckett and May Roe were married according to the rites of the Church of Ireland on 31 August 1901. Bill's degree of prosperity as a young man of thirty is indicated by the fact that he immediately set about building a substantial new home in the most fashionable suburb of Dublin. Obviously he was good at his job, but he also had family connections; and in truth it was not easy for a Protestant with a good start to fail in business or the professions at the time. At the turn of the century the grip of the Protestant element on business and professional activity in Dublin was still very strong, though for a long while now they had been conscious of a challenge from upwardly mobile Catholics.

This supremacy was largely maintained through the Freemasons and other mutual aid societies. An approach from one mason to another was a recognized way of landing a contract or getting a job or even a bank loan and it was utilized to the full. The Catholics too had their mutual aid societies, such as the Knights of Columbanus, but the masons, with headquarters in a splendid building in Molesworth Street, not far from Bill Beckett's office, still reigned supreme. Both Bill Beckett and his father were masons; and Bill made use of his membership of the order to an extent which his old master Pannister considered to be scandalous, refusing to speak to him because of it.

Like the aristocracy, the Protestant business community of the towns and cities looked down on Catholics as, in general, rather feckless, lazy and dishonest. A sort of right to ownership and control of business as a prerogative of greater thrift and industry, never mind the favour of Providence, was widely assumed. Except perhaps perforce as employers, and to some extent as manufacturers or shopkeepers, they took care to have very little contact with Catholics; and the aim of many Protestant business people as employers was as far as possible to recruit their clerical staff and work force from among their co-religionists.

There were then many thousands of lower-middle-class Protestants from among whom to recruit and even a relatively smaller number of working class, of which number John Casey, or Sean O'Casey, was one. Socially too they kept their distance as far as possible. It was a boast among the denizens of Foxrock, the suburb in which the newly married couple were about to live, that one could pass one's day without speaking to any Catholic other than the railway company's employees. As Vivian Mercier has put it:

The males and some of the females of the typical

Protestant family took the train every weekday to office, school or university in Dublin. In all these places they were likely to be associating almost exclusively with fellow Protestants. The females who stayed at home spent their leisure time with other Protestant ladies, though their maids and gardeners were usually Catholic. If one preferred to think of oneself as English there was really no reason not to.

But to call this class Anglo-Irish and to lump it in with the Protestant land-owning aristocracy — the class to which Yeats affected to belong and to which J. M. Synge and Lady Gregory actually did — is to create considerable confusions. Of course, the two sometimes overlapped: Bernard Shaw's father was, rather in the pattern of Samuel Roe, an unsuccessful Dublin corn merchant who had a bit of land with tenants on it — as John Butler Yeats, a member of the Protestant professional middle class, also had — and therefore had pretensions to gentility. But in general the line between people in trade and those deriving their income from land or a profession was very clearly drawn, as it was at that time in other countries; and though Willie Beckett's professional or quasi-professional qualification and May's descent from land-owners freed them from the opprobrium attached to being in trade, it was the business class to which the Becketts really belonged.

Anglo-Irish is a misnomer also because in fact the Protestant Dublin middle classes probably looked to England less often and with less social anxieties than did their landed co-religionists. They did not, for the most part, send their offspring to English schools or take their daughters to London for the season, still less disport themselves at Cowes or Ascot. They did not take it for granted that their cadets would obtain commissions in the British army. Though their loyalty to the Crown and the Union Jack was automatic and unquestioning, their sources of income had not been threatened by the sort of legislation which had brutally loosened the aristocracy's grip on the land — and therefore on Ireland itself — since the 1880s and so their interest in British politics was less fevered and personal. They were content to vote Unionist and hope for the best. The other ways in which they differed were the ways in which a bourgeoisie differs from an aristocracy everywhere, but with some exacerbations which were peculiar to the Irish situation.

Even among aristocracies, the Anglo-Irish was notoriously improvident and devil-may-care in its outlook. Its tradition of rakehelly violence, celebrated in the novels of Charles Lever and Samuel Lover — just as its improvidence is bemoaned in those of Maria Edgeworth — went back to the seventeenth century; and though tamed somewhat by Victorianism, was still being celebrated by W. B. Yeats in the 1930s. Whatever the past history of the Roes, it was far from the outlook of the Becketts and their kind; and far too from the outlook of their offspring, Samuel Beckett, either as a man or as a writer.

As befitted a bourgeoisie the outlook of the Protestant middle class was far more scrupulous, honest and industrious, less eccentric and also less centred on the Vice Regal Court in Dublin Castle with its multifarious snobberies and its petty pretensions. The middle class was snobbish enough, the principal internal manifestation of its attitude being the line drawn between professional people and those in trade, one of the reasons why Bill Beckett called himself a civil engineer in Foxrock when he went to live there. But it was more in touch with reality.

And there was another reason why the term Anglo-Irish for members of the Protestant middle class is misleading. By comparison with Anglicanism the Church of Ireland was a Low Church and had been since Cromwell. But the incumbents of city parishes were expected to be even lower in their practices and their disdain for ritual than their country colleagues and were more jealously examined for traces of Romanism in their ritual or dogma. O'Casey has brilliantly described the violence and obloquy that was visited on the incumbent of an East Wall parish who was adjudged too Anglican in his practices. For the middle class the Bible was the supreme guide and test of religious belief; and in many middle-class homes it was the only reading matter encouraged.

Bill and May Beckett's first home was a substantial late

Georgian, rented house in Pembroke Road, fairly near Earlsfield. Three years later they moved to Foxrock, which for most members of the Protestant Dublin middle class represented the pinnacle of social and commercial success.

Where he built, inland towards the mountains, new houses were appearing, but nearer the Stillorgan road the merchant princes of Dublin had earlier bought some of the substantial mansions to be found there, each behind its demesne wall with a stretch of driveway croquet lawns and frequently tennis-courts, some of them houses of considerable architectural distinction. As Foxrock spread west towards the mountains it retained its exclusive character, the new houses being sizeable and standing in fairly extensive grounds. At a slightly later period, when suburbia was growing fast, the great Dublin comedian Jimmy O'Dea would describe the more central districts of Rathmines and Rathgar as a purgatory for souls awaiting the heaven of Foxrock'.

The house, which was proudly featured in a supplement to the Irish Builder on its completion in 1903, is sizeable but commonplace, with elements of the mock Tudor in its mullioned windows and projecting gables. When it was sold again in the 1970s, its mock Tudor elements were made a virtue: 'This is a charming Tudor style family residence well set back from the road at the corner of Kerrymount Avenue and standing amid totally secluded mature gardens laid out in lawns, tennis court and croquet lawn.' After pointing to the 'extremely high standard of finish' and the 'spacious proportions' of the main rooms, the advertisement concluded: 'Churches and schools are conveniently situated and there are excellent shops situated in Foxrock Village which is five minutes' walk from the property. 'Cooldrinagh' is approached by a sweeping gravelled driveway.'

Except that the implied length of the driveway is something of an exaggeration, it is true enough; and of course Foxrock with its little railway station was even more of a village when Samuel Beckett was born. Inside, the house gave an impression of bourgeois solidity and comfort, with mahogany panelling in the hallway and on the staircase, heavy mahogany furniture and thick velvet curtains. It was a time when most people in most social classes preferred evidences of expense, durability and workmanship to aesthetic considerations — or rather, they equated these things with the beautiful: and the Becketts were no exception. Except for the master bedroom with its big bow window on the first floor the house was rather dark. There were two other bedrooms on that first floor and two more rooms on the top or attic which could be used as servants' or children's bedrooms or playrooms.

Downstairs were a drawing room and a dining room. Like the bedrooms, these had bell pulls to which, supposedly at least, a servant would respond. Outside the grounds were, as the advertisement said, spacious enough to accommodate a tennis-court and a croquet lawn, as well as a vegetable garden, flower beds and wilderness areas with larch and pine trees. Besides all these there were outhouses, including a hen-house, a garage and a stable in which, later on, May would keep a donkey. There was also a little wooden summer-house or gazebo with stained-glass windows which is described in the story Company.

The house was called Cooldrinagh after the house which the Roes had owned in Leixlip. Some commentators have identified it with the description of Mr Knott's house in the novel Watt; and certainly it resembles it in its general situation; but Mr Knott's house is much larger, and its American bar, oratory and dairy are taken from the biggest house in the locality, in fact the original 'big house' which was there before Foxrock became a suburb, the neo-Gothic Glencairn — home, when Samuel Beckett was growing up, to the exotic American, the Boss Croker. Cooldrinagh is, however, the model for Moran's house in Molloy, even to the lemon verbena to whose scent he refers, a flower which, by the time Sam was a toddler, already grew in profusion round the hall door, giving forth 'a fragrance in which the least of his childish joys and sorrows were and would for ever be embalmed'.

Chapter 10

Translation of Mercier et Camier

Most of the writers who have turned their attention to the strange phenomenon of Beckett's selftranslation have concentrated upon the extraordinary facility he displays in this, by all accounts, unenjoyable task. There has been some disagreement about such matters as the relative proportions of obscenity or humour in the French and English versions of his work, but most critics have stressed Beckett's uncanny ability to reproduce the effects of the originals in his translations, reinventing puns, and compensating with new material for anything which resists translation. Most critics therefore feel that it is safe to assume for Beckett an *oeuvre* consisting of a number of pairs of new-identical twins.

Close examination of Beckett's self-translation reveals this idea to be mistaken. Certainly, there is very close (though rarely complete) correspondence between the French and English versions where Beckett has set about the translation immediately upon—or even, in some cases, before—completion of the original. But in cases where there is a time-lag between the two versions there is considerable evidence in the translations of changes in Beckett's outlook, stylistic priorities and attitude towards his originals. The amount of variation is particularly great in the French versions of *Murphy* and *Watt* and the English version of *Mercier et Camier*; and the translations of the novels of the Trilogy, which also experienced some delay in being translated, show more variants than such texts as *Company* or *Ill Seen Ill Said*. A. R. Jones has shown how the alterations in the French *Murphy* register Beckett's philosophical dissatisfaction with the first of his fictional self-embodiments, and the English *Mercier and Camier* has a large number of revisions of the same kind.

Many of these are due, no doubt, not only to the fact that there was a long gap between writing and translation, but also to the delay before Beckett would allow even the French version to be published. (*Mercier et Camier* was written in 1946 but not published until 1970. The English translation occupied Beckett intermittently from 1970 to 1974 and appeared in 1974.

Examination of the revisions of *Mercier et Camier* reveals more than just a badly-curbed impatience on Beckett's part, however; Beckett's awareness of the philosophical implications of the act of self-translation means that he can use the exercise to explore the problems raised by the successive reconstruction of the self in language and fiction, problems which are already a central concern in his work. The most obvious difference between the two texts of *Mercier and Camier* results from the amount of material that Beckett omits in the English. The omitted material varies from the odd line or phrase to two or three pages at a time, and amounts at a conservative estimate to a loss of about 12% of the material in the French version.

These losses are compensated for only by the addition of a few phrases here and there. A large proportion of the omissions seems to result from Beckett's impatience with passages which he considered ineffective or repetitious. Thus, two pages of dialogue are lost early in the first chapter in which Mercier and Camier try to make sense of the commands of the park ranger, and Beckett shows a tendency throughout to compress or drop altogether the more laborious passages of bewildered wrangling between the two. It might be claimed that the English version of the novel is crisper and more forceful than the French as a result of these excisions. I am not altogether sure about that myself; but what is more important are that Beckett's excisions seem to have a thematic as well as a cosmetic purpose, and that, as such, they have important consequences for the reader.

Already, in the French version, Mercier and Camier are strangely cut off from the world of ordinary people and objects, hardly communicating and finding it easier to discard than to retain possessions. Beckett intensifies this divorce in his translation by the frequent omission of details which might link Mercier and Camier to the ordinary world. At the beginning of the book, we are told that "Things were getting ponderously under way", but the specification "et notamment les véhicules lourds, tels camions, charrettes et transports en commun" is lost.

Similarly, the omission of passages in which Mercier and Camier plan the retrieval of their luggage, or plot their course forward serves to focus attention upon the couple's poverty of purpose no less than of equipment. And at one point, Beckett omits a reference to Camier paying for his drink, a change which seems wanton and incomprehensible unless seen in the context of other moves made in the translation to detach Mercier and Camier from ordinary physical affairs. There are two other ways in which Beckett tries, if not exactly to spiritualize, then to "discarnate" his two heroes.

The French version of the book has a number of references to food and drink and episodes of comic by-play involving them, and Beckett takes care when he can to remove these. The conversation in chapter 2, for example, about what the two have eaten, and the altercation following Mercier's request for a "massepain" are completely left out. The relish with which the barman in the pair's first port of call describes the food he has available is much diminished—we are told that he "raffled off a list", but not that he has "beaucoup de bonnes choses". Camier's request for a "petite collation" is omitted, as is Mercier's demand "Donnez-nous a manger" (Minuit, 67, Calder, 44) and throughout the book Beckett makes similar changes. Some of these involve only shifts of emphasis, but are the more convincing because of this—as when, in the French, Camier reassures the vomiting Mercier "Ca te fera du bien" (Minuit, 105), but reinforces the prejudice against food in the English by saying "You'll feel better without it" (Calder, 65). In a series of related revisions, Beckett also seeks to diminish the prominence of sexuality in the book.

Though enough survives to make it clear what kinds of services are available in Helen's hotel, a couple of substantial omissions reduce Camier's involvement with them. In the French chapter 7 (chapter 5 in the English), Camier disappears a second time up the stairs and keeps his comrade waiting around even longer than he has done previously, before reappearing with the sheepish apology "C'est toujours un peu plus long la deuxième fois" (Minuit, 125, omitted Calder, 75) and, towards the end of their journey in chapter 7 (chapter 10 in the French), an interchange is left out in which Mercier upbraids Camier for his lasciviousness (Minuit 171-2, Calder, 100).

Ruby Cohn has observed that Camier seems to be the slave of his senses much more than the intellectual Mercier, and has suggested that, like Vladimir and Estragon in *Waiting for Godot,* they dramatize the relationship of body and soul. But, in fact, this distinction between the two is deliberately much less apparent in the English version, which, of course, did not exist at the time that Ruby Cohn was writing.

There are signs, too, of Beckett's attempts to make the friendship of Mercier and Camier much more fragile in the English version. The two seem less solicitous for each other's health after the omission of passages where Camier asks how Mercier is feeling (Minuit, 42, 92, Calder, 28, 58), or where Mercier shows a kindly interest in the state of Camier's cyst (Minuit, 172, Calder, 1 00). No doubt, the same motive impels another omission when, in the English, we are told that Mercier and Camier 'raised their glasses and drank', but not, as in the French, that h was 'à la santé l'un de l'autre' (Minuit, 140, Calder, 83). It is probably in order to make the relationship of the two colder and more remote that Beckett also omits the following from the final English version; in it we see the rapport which remains in some of the exchanges between Vladimir and Estragon in *Godot,* but which the grimmer vision of the older Beckett cannot accommodate: I personally to be quite frank see nothing whatever anymore, neither the road, nor my feet, nor my legs, nor my chest (admittedly hollow).

A wisp of beard, perhaps, to be quite honest, a snow-white wisp. We might have passed before the Scala, a night of gala, and I none the wiser. It's a wreck you are towing, my dear

Carder, with your customary loving-kindness. And I went a wool gathering, said Camier.

It's unpardonable. You have every excuse, said Mercier, every excuse, with no exception. Don't let go my hand whatever you do. The gymnastics of despair, by all means, to your heart's content, they help, while they last, but don't let go my hand. For Camier had been suddenly seized by a sort of convulsion. Poor Camier, said Mercier, you're done in, don't deny it. I'll show you if I'm done in, said Camier. Your little arse is hurting you, said Mercier, and your little penis.

No turning back from now on, said Camier, come what may. (translation of Minuit, 177-8, omitted, Calder, 102) Beckett even seeks to diminish the bonds of memory between the two; when they discuss their pasts, the narrator remarks in the French version that "Ils ne se connaissaient pas alors, mais depuis qu'ils se connaissaient, ils en avaient parlé, de cette époque, trop parlé, par bribes, suivant leur coutume" (Minuit, 13).

Beckett translated this in his second draft as "They had not known each other then, but ever since they knew each other they had spoken of those days, immoderately, sporadically, after their fashion"; but even the habit of shared recall is denied them in Beckett's final version, where he omits all but the bald comment that, in those days, they "did not know each other" (Calder, 11). There are many other kinds of changes made in the translation of *Mercier et Camier,* and, as we might expect most of these are the symptoms of Beckett's deepening pessimism and bitterness; the Beckett who set to work in 1970 on the translation of what John Fletcher describes as a "warm and funny book" had escaped the celebrated impasse reached after *L'Innommable* and had begun to produce the calm, scrupulous, but uncompromisingly bleak texts which characterized the 1960s and 1970s—*Le Dépeupleur, Bing, Imagination Morte Imaginez.*

Thus, the voices which speak to Mercier and Camier in the English version of the book have become as unreliable as they are for the Unnamable; "la petite voix implorante ... qui nous parle parfois de vies antérieures" of which Camier speaks

(Minuit, 94), becomes "the faint imploring voice ... that drivels to us on and off of former lives" (Calder, 59), and the voice "qui veut me faire croire que je ne suis pas encore mort" (Minuit, 94) is, for Mercier, "the one that tries to cod me I'm not yet dead" (Calder, 59). Christopher Ricks pointed in an early review of *Mercier and Camier* to some other comic intensifications and diminishment; Camier "had felt even worse" for "il ne sentait pas trop mal"(Calder, 110, Minuit, 191), and Mercier's cry of "Speak up ... I'm not deaf" for "Je n'entends rien" (Calder, 85, Minuit, 143). In a similar way, it is the "plus fort" of the two who gives the "plus faible" to drink in chapter 2 of the French, but the "less weak of the two" who gives "the weaker" in the English (Minuit, 33, Calder, 23) and it is not of "leurs déboires... leurs espoirs" that the couple speak to Helen, but of "their hopes both shattered and forlorn" (Minuit, 114, Calder, 70).

Revisions such as the ones discussed so far do not radically alter the direction or purpose of the book, of course, though they are certainly disconcerting. Even in the French we see Mercier's and Camier's quest gradually foundering, as they are stripped of their possessions and come to lose their sense of their relationship and identity. In this, the book looks forward to the concentrated studies of decay and renunciation to be undertaken in Beckett's later fiction and drama, and his revisions clearly accelerate the process of decay of the characters and narrative of *Mercier et Camier*. The dwindling of energy, purpose and certainty which Beckett emphasize in his translation resembles particularly the entropic running-down which is represented in those two-act plays like *Waiting for Godot, Happy Days, Play* and, more recently, *Quad,* in which the second act is a repetition and a contraction of the first act.

There are interesting resemblances between the self-repetition involved in these plays, especially *Happy Days* and *Play,* where the actual words of the first act are repeated, and the self-repetition involved in translation. In both cases, the repetition is the same as and yet different from the original utterance, an addition to it and yet also a diminution of it. The relationship between the original and the translation, is, like the relationship between the first act and the second act which repeats it, a problematic one. This is because the translated text has two levels of reference or signification; its signified is both the story that it tells, with its actual characters and events, and also the previous version of that story represented by the original text.

The translated text alludes all the time to its dependence upon this earlier text. In the case of Beckett's self-translations, there are interesting forms of "interference" which can be set up between the two levels, as the second text not only tamely reproduces the original but comments upon it and upon the act of translation. Much of this commentary is given to the narrator of the book, who seems in the English version a great deal more intolerant and even disdainful of the characters of the book and the book itself than in the French (though the French narrator is also prone to fits of exasperation with them). At one point in *Mercier et Camier* the narrator, true to his opening promise that he was with his heroes "all the time," reflects on the necessity for reader and narrator to cleave closely to them: Suivons-les attentivement, Mercier et Camier, ne nous en éloignons jamais plus que de la hauteur d'un escalier, ou de l'épaisseur d'un mur. Qu'aucun souci d'ordonnance, ou d'harmonie, ne nous en détourne jamais pour l'instant. (Minuit, 96)

The English narrator has no such scruples about this, apparently, for, taking a hint from the uncertainty of "jamais, pour l'instant," the whole passage is omitted (Calder, 60). Beckett's translation of the passage was actually retained until his final typed draft, but already reflects the narrator's growing distance from his characters, with the sly hint in its penultimate phrase of the unworthiness of his subjects: Let us now follow them closely, Mercier and Camier, never lose them by more than the height of a stairs, or a wall's breadth, never again let our love of ordinance, or of harmony, divert us to worthier objects, for the time being. The attitude of the narrator to his characters and the narrative itself become more problematic in the English version of *Mercier and Camier*.

In fact, the narrator does not come merely to despise his

characters, and the revisions of the English version give evidence of a complex mingling of sympathy and criticism. At the end of the French version there is a passage in which the taste and culture of the two heroes are admired: Dommage que Dumas Père ne puisse nous voir, dit Watt. Ou l'un des évangélistes, dit Camier. Mercier et Camier, c'était tout de même une autre qualité. (Minuit, 195) Of course, the final comment is sourly ironic, but there is a kind of affectionate admiration there too, which is magnified by its context in the elegiac last section of the book.

In the English version this admiration is more mixed, however, for the oblique and conceding "tout de meme" becomes, more explicitly, "for all their faults" (Calder, 112). At times, the friction between the new, more critical narrator and his French predecessor is brought out into the open. The new narrator has the advantage of being able to see the book whole from start to finish, and so can hint at oddities and mistakes in the design, as when, reporting the plans which Mercier and Camier are making for their journey, the narrator remarks "No mention of the sack" (Minuït, 27).

This is an addition made in the translation, and a comment upon the French version, which, indeed, makes no mention of a sack (Minuit, 27), until later, when there is an agitated discussion as to the value and purpose of the sack and its contents—though Beckett omits this discussion in the English version! The comment which the English narrator makes is directed at the French narrative, and has no meaning except by reference to this other, absent version of the text. This is a small but telling exam᠆le of the kind of logical paradox which the act of self-translation is liable to generate, paradoxes which reflect Beckett's sense of the "issueless predicament" that is experience and narration.

We can find the English narrator commenting elsewhere in the book on the shortcomings of his French predecessor; at one point the English narrator seems to draw attention to the shortcomings of the French narrator in providing circumstantial detail, when Camier says to Mercier, "I was on the point of not keeping our appointment" and the English narrator sniffs "So they had an appointment" (Calder, 91, Minuit, 153).

At other times the excessive fastidiousness of diction is mocked; Mr. Gall informs Mercier and Camier that his inn is *gemütlich*, "in a tone of tentative complicity, whatever that sounds like" (Calder, 43). There is a double joke here, however, because, though this looks like a rebuke to a previous version of the text, the French in fact reads, unexceptionably, "d'une voix basse et comme tâtonnante" (Minuit, 66). The overelaborate "tentative complicity" is only added in the second draft of the English translation, with the sneering aside only appearing in the third draft. The comment refers us to a previous, but absent text (the manuscript draft) in the same way as the comment about the sack, and, in doing so, seems to open up the prospect of even more, hitherto undetected, previous "versions" or translations of a text, each of which may add a layer of self-reflection to it. So the "final" text comes to seem less like a end-point than just a stage in a continuing process of self-division and self-modification.

Where the English narrator of *Mercier and Camier* makes the most telling interventions, however, is in the ordering and editing of his material. Ways have frequently to be found in the translation of knitting together passages where substantial amounts of material (often dialogue) have been omitted, and ways of shortening passages which have come to seem tediously long to Beckett. An example of how this is done is an extended passage in the French in which Mercier and Camier give detailed accounts of their states of health, which is shrunk down in the English to the dry comment that "Before going any further they asked and told each other how they felt" (Minuit, 92, Calder, 58).

There are a number of ellipses like this in the English, and it is striking that they are rarely neutral; rather they convey the narrator's disapproval or disdain of the original, and therefore provide, not an elegant concealment of the ellipsis, but an elaborate allusion to it. At one point, for example, a passage of conversation about Mercier's desire for a "massepain" is omitted, but the translation alludes to the absence by telling us wearily that "an altercation ensued, too foolish to be recorded, so foolish was it" (Minuit, 46, Calder, 30). Other examples of the translator alluding to his own revisions can be found in passages where the direct speech of the French is rendered in indirect speech in the English: Quand ils eurent fini de courir, Camier [sic] dit: Nous allons arriver chez Hélène dans un bel état, mouillés Jusqu'aux os. Nous nous déshabillerons aussitot, dit Camier. Nous mettrons nos vêtements à sécher, devant le feu, ou dans l'armoire à linge o_ passent les tuyaux d'eau chaude. (Minuit, 37)

When they had done running Mercier deplored the nice state, soaked to the buff, in which they would arrive at Helen's, to which in reply Camier described how they would immediately strip and put their things to dry, before the fire, or in the hot-cupboard with the boiler and hot water pipes. (Calder, 25-6) Here, the indirect construction clearly results in no economy at all. In fact, the construction seems to exhibit its own redundancy, and the devices of style indirect libre "The nice state, soaked to the buff") to clash with the bureaucratic formality of "described" and "deplored," and the specifications "in which," and "to which in reply" so that the editor's presence is not obscured but make fussily obtrusive. And again we are given the impression that what is being described for us here is not an event from the narrator's memory, or anything that has ever happened in the real world, but a passage from a previous text, with which the present text is in conflict, even as it colludes with it.

Of course, this sort of thing is by no means a new departure in Beckett's writing. From the very beginning he had been fond of representing the vexed relationship between an author, or editor, and his texts, and in a novel like *Watt* seems deliberately to create a narrator who is out of control of his material. Similarly, there are plenty of indications in the French *Mercier et Camier* that the narrator's testimony is unreliable. The poker-faced "résumés" which are placed after every pair of chapters do not succeed in hiding beneath their blandness the caprice which governs the choice and emphasis of material. In the résumé of chapter 7, for example (chapter 5 in the

English), nothing is said of one of the most interesting episodes in the book, Mercier's encounter with an old man who looks like the narrator of "The Calmative," while the extraordinary passage of meditation following this encounter is shrunk ruthlessly down to the designation "Cerveau de Mercier" (Minuit, 163, Calder, 95).

In the résumé of the next chapter, there is an outright distortion, when the murder of the police-constable becomes the prim "Mort de l'agent" (Minuit, 164; the English goes further in omitting this item altogether, 96). Hugh Kenner has rightly seen these summaries as anticipation of Krapp's entries in his ledger of tapes; like the non-committal entry "Farewell to Love," the dry résumés seem like attempts to control and neutralize the unruliness of the preceding material. Indeed, we might also see these as anticipations of Beckett's own attempts to shrink down his fiction in the search for a hardness and abstraction to replace the molten intensity of the earlier "battle of the soliloquy." And since the résumés are repetitions which are at the same time revisions, they are rather like intermittent self-translations within the original French text. This is an example of the way that self translation can highlight instabilities within language and narration, for the French is shown to be different from itself in something of the same way that it is different from the English text which follows and revises it.

Repetition itself has, of course, an important function in Beckett's work. Usually its function is to embody the drive to make an end, often by "unsaying" what has already been said once. But if the compulsion to repeat has the need to close off at its basis, then it also has, as an unlookedfor consequence, the need to carry on repeating as long as the tiniest anxiety remains that the original may not have been satisfactorily unsaid. Already, in the French *Mercier et Camier*, Beckett seems to be demonstrating, by the imperfect correspondence between narration and summary, that the desire for consummation through repetition is always liable to be baulked. As we might expect, the summaries provided in the English version continue to differ from the text they summarize; Beckett omits more material from the summaries, sometimes, it is true because material has vanished from the main chapters, but also, apparently, as the result of changes of mind as to the relative importance of various incidents.

Thus, the reference to the "Colère d'un barman" (Minuit, 54), is changed to "The bicycle" (Calder, 35) and the reference to the "départ des fermiers" (Minuit, 112) is resolved (Calder, 68), as are references to Mercier's arrival in the bar, the wind, and the death of the policeman. It might be claimed that all the changes that I have been discussing could not possibly be evident either to a French or English reader, for whom the text would be single and self-sufficient. But, as we have seen, the effect and purpose of these changes and omissions is not merely to revise and repress, but also to draw attention to those processes. And, what is more, the revision and repression are always imperfect in Beckett's translations, since he never changes his originals to bring them into line with his second thoughts.

The original is therefore always left as witness to the gaps and differences of the translation. The problem really comes from the fact that the two versions of the text, though they are incompatible with one another in various ways, are both "definitive," too. Oddly, the effect of this is to reduce the autonomy of each version of the text. Each becomes merely a version of the other, and is apprehensible as itself only by virtue of its differences from the other text. Indeed, another of the striking effects of Beckett's self-translation is that it abolishes the priority of original and copy, since the English text is not only a "mutilation" of the original, but also, in some senses, an improvement upon it, so that the French might be considered as in some respects as an inferior, derived version of the English.

To put it in the terms suggested by Derrida, the translation is a "supplement" or sequel to the original text which, while appearing to guarantee the integrity of the original, actually subverts that integrity by opening up areas of absence, or "lack" in it. As we have seen, this lack of priority is instanced within each text itself, with the oddly unreliable résumés, which give us translations into a different idiom of events that have already been narrated, but do not give us the means of deciding which version to prefer. The structure is one of double-bind, because there is no way of breaking out of the vicious circle of the relationship of the two texts without reproducing it. This is borne out by my own practical difficulty in referring to the novel in this essay. I have the feeling all the time that I ought to be able to refer to a text which lies somehow behind, or prior to both versions, but there is no way of referring to this text except in its manifestation either as *"Mercier et Camier"* or *"Mercier and Camier."*

For the book only exists in versions of itself, and there is no Platonic Ur-text which will account for and resolve the contradictions between them. The text consists in its inconsistency, and is only itself by being congenitally not-itself. The issue of Beckett's self-translation is closely related to his actual style and language in his work. One of the most interesting things about Beckett's turn to French is the way that it connects with the decided shift in his style, after 1946, from the baroque elaboration of the earlier work to the conversational directness which characterize the Trilogy. However, by 1970, when Beckett began to translate *Mercier et Camier,* his style had moved into a third phase, one of calm, exact austerity; in *Bing, Le Dépeupleur, Imagination Morte lmaginez,* and *All Strange Away* Beckett's energies have been devoted to the stylistic control of the resonances of language, rather than the multiplication of associations and implications.

With the simultaneous shriveling of narrative content, style has become more and more important as the bearer of meaning in Beckett's work, and he has become ever more scrupulous and exacting in his translations, seeking to exert the same rigorous control over both versions of a text. One might expect to find signs of this new stylistic austerity in the translation of *Mercier et Camier,* but, remarkably, this does not seem in general to be the case, apart from the obvious excision of material which he finds to be flabby or unnecessary. In fact, the general tendency in Beckett's translation of this work is to emphasize the similarly between *Mercier et Camier* and his early works, *More Pricks Than Kicks, Murphy,* and *Watt,* rather than to try to draw it into line with his later stylistic practice.

Time and again, Beckett takes the opportunity of increasing the range of obscure allusions, introducing archaism, compressing, polishing and even distorting the language of the original. Where the French version is pitched more or less in the solid middle ground of ordinary colloquial language (though with a few quirky departures from it), the idioms of the English are drawn from much more wide-spread and often incompatible sources, ranging from philosophical jargon to the fierce obscenity of the street. Beckett often shows a preference in the English for inkhorn Latinisms, which can seem very awkward when compared to their French equivalents: Il tenait du dédale, le petit square, on y circulait avec gêne, et il fallait bien le connaître pour en pouvoir sortir à la première tentative. (Minuit, 11)

It had something of the maze, irksome to perambulate, difficult of egress, for one not in its secrets. (Calder, 9) The early drafts show Beckett working towards the ironic and self-defeating elevation of this sentence. His first translation of the end of its last phrase was "difficult to leave, for one not knowing it well" which is closer to the original, but also flatter and less effective. A similar comic elevation of language is brought about by the translation of the description of Mercier's and Camier's frequent collapses on the road; "ils s'effondraient tous les deux en même temps, comme un seul homme, sans s'être concertés et dans une parfaite indépendance l'un de l'autre" (Minuit, 179-80); in the English, Mercier and Camier collapse "simultaneously, as one man, without preconcertation and in perfect interindependency" (Calder, 102).

Although the French version of *Mercier and Camier* is sometimes itself very elaborate and very funny, it seems nowhere to match the range of comic discontinuity between registers and idioms to be found in the English. The piece of description which begins chapter7 (chapter l0 in the French) shows this clearly: throwaway asides ("a thousand feet above sea-level, two thousand if you prefer," Calder, 97) alternate with self-conscious poeticism like "the sea ... pale plinth as pale as the pale wall of the sky" (Calder, 97), the alliterative density of which contrasts with the more conventional and explicit syntax of the French—"elle n'a guère plus de couleur que le ciel qui n'en a guère, elle est comme une cimaise" (Minuit, 165). At times, Beckett approaches lampoon: "des deux ports, ils avancent bras minuscules dans la mer vitreuse, on les sait a plat mais on les voit levés" (Minuit, 166) becomes "tiny arms in the glassy sea outflung, known flat, seen raised" (Calder, 98).

It is difficult to decide whether Beckett has adopted this compression in order to charge up the sublimity of his description or actually to debunk it. The latter seems to be suggested by the draft versions of this passage which show Beckett working towards parodic intensification, with "the tiny arms stretched out in the glassy sea" as first attempts. The ugly grinding of gears in the cadence of "known flat, seen raised" seems deliberate, too, with the substitution in Beckett's second draft of "known flat" for the smoother "known level." It is often as though Beckett is trying deliberately to hamstring his language in the translation, as though, like Molloy speaking the name of his mother, he wished to abolish his words in the act of uttering them. Beckett shows in the translation a fondness for mixed metaphors which reveal the artificiality and inadequacy of language, as when Mercier is left "on fuming tenterhooks" (Calder, 31) where the French has the less concrete "guet rageur" (Minuit, 48).

And where there is awkwardness in the original, Beckett will often highlight rather than amend this in the translation; the description of Mr. Graves' voice has a certain jingling oddity in the French—"sa voix basse et grasse de patriarche pastoral débutant'"(Minuit, 73)—but the clotted English version—"his incipient pastoral patriarch's tick bass"(Calder, 47)—is deliberately and desperately strange. Similarly, the language of characters in the English version of the book is much quirkier and less realistic than in the French. Perhaps the most extraordinary language in the book is that ascribed to Mr. Madden. This already has strange features in the French version, including the frequent use of the aorist tense, normally confined in French, of course, to written language. But the violent agitation of Mr. Madden's language is much more marked in the English version, with collision of extreme formality of diction with casualness and crudity. Indeed, it is very often difficult in the English to make out what the furious Mr. Madden is saying: The truth is I had that too in my bleeding blood. . . Oh I gave it to them! *Potopompos scroton evohe.*

Like that, hot and strong. . . . Step out of here, I said, with a stout heart and your bollocks in your boots and come again tomorrow, tell the missus to go chase apes in hell. There were delicate moments. . . Brats the offscourings of fornication and God Almighty a cheap scent in a jakes. . . . (Calder, 39-40) Il faut dire que j'avais de qui tenir. . . . Potopompos scroton évohé, que je leur disais. . . Sortez d'ici, que je leur disais, la queue basse et la tête haute, et revenez demain. La bourgeoise, au pilon, qu'elle se démerde. Des fois je me faisais attraper. . . . Les enfants, queje leur disais, c'est la scorie de l'amour. Dieu aussi, il en prenait pour son grade. (Minuit, 59-60) Watt is another character who picks up the contagion of the narrators verbal oddity, and his language mingles angry obscenity with Elizabethan courtliness; instead of "les agents, les" he speaks of "dogberries and kips", but, a little later, can declare "Bugger like!" and "Fuck like!" (Calder, 114-118—the French is as virulent, but less obscene— "La vie au Poteau!" and "La vie aux chiòttes!"). Mercier and Camier themselves speak a language in the English which is much less realistic and more contentedly mandarin than that of their French counterparts. Camier's "Soyons francs" becomes "a truce to dissembling" (Minuit, 24, Calder, 16), while Mercier's remark about the dogs—"Abrutis par l'amour ils n'y avaient pas pensé"—becomes "Less rut-besotted they would have thought of it themselves".

The convolution of their language can be very sustained in the English: Do I ask, said Mercier, how exactly you came to break the umbrella?. . . I combed innumerable sites, questioned innumerable parties, made allowance for the invisibility of things, the metamorphoses of time, the foible of folk in general, and of me in particular, for and fibbery. . . . Do you not inkle, like me, how you might adjust yourself to this preposterous penalty and placidly await the executioner, come to ratify you? (Calder, 89) Est-ce que je demande comment tu as fait, exactement, pour casser le parapluie? dit Mercier. . . . Moi j'ai inspecté un grand nombre d'endroits, j'ai interrogé de nombreuses personnes, j'ai fait la part de l'invisibilité des choses, des transformations qu'opère le temps, du penchant des gens, dont moi, à la fable et au mensonge. . . . N'entrevois-tu pas, comme moi, le moyen de t'accommoder de cette absurde peine, d'attendre le bourreau avec placidité, comme l'entérinement d'un état de fait? (Minuit, 149-50)

The pomposity of Mercier's diction ("innumerable parties"), combined with the superbly fatuous alliteration ("foible of folk in general ... for and fibbery") and anxious neologism ("fibbery," "inkle") hardly conceals the underlying desperation which gives the language Its nervous inventiveness. Mercier's language, in the English, at least, is stretched to breaking point, and threatens to collapse at any moment into more noise. The fragility of language is suggested, too, by the hair-raising jokes that Beckett plays in the translation of *Mercier et Camier* by allowing the leakage of one language into another. Just as some critics have seen the evidence of Anglicism in Beckett's early French writing, so *Mercier and Camier* is studded with imperfectlydigested Gallicisms—Mercier tells Camier that he has looked for the umbrella "longly" ("longuement"—Calder, 89, Minuit, 149), and later says to the manager of a bar, "Your whisky likes us" (this looks like a bungled translation of "il nous plait," but the French has the equally odd—"Votre whisky est succulent," Minuit, 201, which Beckett translated literally in his second draft.)

These may, of course, represent Beckett's grim revenge on himself for the embarrassing Anglicisms to be found in his early French work. But, at the same time, these intentional slips form part of an elaborate network of allusions to the absent French text, allusions which remind us of the dependence of the two texts one upon another. One feature of Beckett's work since the Trilogy has been the tendency to try to damp down lyricism and poeticism in the language, and to narrow its evocative range.

Indeed, Beckett has given instructions to this effect to translators of his work into other languages, so we should not be surprised to find the same tendency at times in the translation of *Mercier et Camier*.

Certainly, there is evidence in both versions of the weary lyricism developed in *L'Innommable* and *Textes Pour Rien*, with the marvellous sustaining and variation of rhythm by the use of successions of commas: Les voilà donc sur la route, sensiblement rafraîchis quand même, et chacun sait l'autre proche, le sent, le croit, le craint, l'espère,le nie et n'y peut rien. De temps en temps ils s'arrêtent, l'oreille dressée vers le bruit des pas, des pas reconnaissables entre tous les pas, et ils sont nombreux, qui vont doucement foulant les chemins de la terre, jour et nuit. (Minuit, 183)

There they are then back on the road, appreciably recruited in spite of all, and each knows the other is at hand, feels, believes, fears, hopes, denies he is at hand, and can do nothing about it.

Now and then they halt, all ears for the footfalls, footfalls distinguishable from all the other footfalls, and they are legion, softly failing on the face of the earth, more or less softly, day and night. (Calder, 104) Beckett's translation of the wonderful widening series of vowels in "le sent, le croit, le craint, l'espère, le nie et n'y peut rien" stutters rather, but he has surely improved in the English upon the final words of the passage, with its controlled diminuendo, echoing the end of Joyce's "The Dead" (this assisted by the change in the second draft of the translation of "ears cocked" to the gentler "all ears" and the literal "many" to the evocative "legion.") But there is also evidence in the translation of *Mercier et Camier* of attempts to diminish the prominence of this lyrical strain, or to break it up with harsher, more sardonic writing.

At the end of chapter 5 (chapter 7 in the French) there is a long meditation on the horrors of time which, in the French version, concludes: La main de Mercier lâcha le barreau de la grille auquel l'avait cloué ces renvois, supportés avec courage, d'époques révolues, comme on dit. Oui, il les avait supportés avec courage, car il savait qu'ils cesseraient à la fin dans une lente chute vers le murmure et puis le silence, ce silence qui est aussi un murmure, mais inarticulé. La porte se ferme, ou la trappe, dans l'oubliette ce sont toujours les mêmes propos, mais dans la prison proprement dit le calme est revenu. (Minuit, 130-1) The translation in Beckett's second draft shows him already trying to sour the language of the French, especially in the case of "ces renvois," "époques révolues" and "les mêmes propos": Mercier's hand let go the railing round which {these eructions— deleted} this attack of wind had fastened it, bravely borne from the sewers of the past so called and gone.

Yes, bravely, for he knew they would die down in the end, slowly down to murmur and then that silence which is murmur still but wordless. The door shuts, or the trapdoor, in the dungeon it's still the same old {blather— deleted} moan, but the prison proper is quiet again.

In the end, though, Beckett's impatience seems to have been too much, for all that remains of the passage in the final version is the sentence "Mercier's hand released the railing to which this attack of wind had fastened it" (Calder, 77). It seems, therefore, that the act of translation is a means, for Beckett, of distancing himself from the original *Mercier et Camier*, even though, in another obvious sense, it is translation which reacquaints him with his previous work. Like many of his characters, Beckett reaches into his own past but finds there no confirmation of the singleness and continuity of his identity but rather evidence of otherness, of the divided nature of experience and memory.

The act of translation, like the act of memory, recalls the past in order that it may be rejected; Beckett, in translating *Mercier et Camier*, deliberately makes the text different from himself, remaking it in the manner of his earlier works, like *More Pricks Than Kicks*, *Murphy*, and *Watt*, rather than in the manner of any of the works that he was composing in the late 1960s and early 1970s.

It is perhaps significant that Beckett had spent some considerable time revising the translation made by Ludovic and Agnes Janvier of *Watt* before embarking on *Mercier and Camier*, this may be a further indication of Beckett's sense that to have done with, or unsay the past it is necessary somehow to repeat it. It may account, too, for the peculiar intensity of the style of *Mercier and Camier*, compounded as it is of equal parts of fascination and loathing, which seems the result of a curiously double impulse to repudiate the earlier work, even as it is being repossessed.

This is very close to the narrative principle within Beckett's works themselves, especially *The Unnamable*, where previous narrative incarnations (including those of *Mercier and Camier*) are relentlessly recapitulated in order that they may be annihilated; and there is a close correspondence between the exploration within Beckett's work of the metamorphoses and multiplications of personality and his own practice of self-reconstruction in translation.

The relationships between Molloy, Moran, Malone and the Unnamable are oddly like those between the successive translations of a text—it is no accident that Molloy has an Irish name while Moran's is French, or that Malone has a spare pencil somewhere in the bed "made in France, a long cylinder hardly broached" (Trilogy, p. 223)—just as the relationships of many of Beckett's couples, including Sam and Watt, and Mercier and Camier, remind us of the strange similarityin-difference obtaining between his twin texts. But the compulsion to repeat leads continually to the recognition that repetition is endless.

We should remember that Beckett does not confine himself to two languages, for he takes an interest in the German and Italian translations of his work, and has, of course, directed plays in German as well as in French and English. (Beckett's direction of his own plays presents itself too as an interesting example of self-repetition or self-translation, for each now production is in a sense different from the text which it repeats, even as Beckett strives to make it definitive.)

But, in the echo-chamber of Beckett's *oeuvre*, nothing can

be unsaid, except by being perpetually reiterated, and therefore no character, no story can ever be brought to conclusion, as Henry seems to acknowledge in *Embers*: "stories. I never finished any of them, I never finished anything, everything always went on for ever."

Beckett's translations dramatize the gnawing sense that "le language n'est qu'une fiction, une traduction sans original" where both the identity of texts and relationships of priority between them are annulled, leaving us only with multiplying alternative versions of the self, its memories, its fictions and its language.

Chapter 11

Shifting Ground

This is the English version of an essay published in German as 'Auf schwankendem Boden', in the catalogue of the exhibition *Samuel Beckett, Bruce Nauman*. At one point in Beckett's *Waiting for Godot*, all four main characters, Vladimir and Estragon, Pozzy and Lucky, collapse into a struggling heap on the ground.

For some minutes, the action threatens to stall altogether, with none of the characters able to get back on their feet. Nauman's work too often approaches this zero condition, through the enactment of falling or lying, or rolling, or collapse. Both Beckett's and Nauman's work is held or called by the ground. In both artists gravity exerts its pull everywhere, though not always visibly. As with all human beings, the groundward tug effects or exerts (as an accidental byproduct) shapeliness, grace and balance, even as it deforms those things, pulling them into disorganisation, flatness or comic indistinction.

There are countervailing forms of motion or aspiration. An early sign of the impulse to escape or deny the ground in Beckett's work appears at the end of his novel *Murphy*, where the wheelchair-bound Mr. Kelly imagines flying his kite out of sight, and beyond the reach of his ruined, wheelchair-bound body. The same aspiration is to be found in *Happy Days*, in which Winnie, buried up to her waist in a mound of earth, speaks of her sensation of being pulled or sucked up into the air. But the ground continues to organise the work, even in its absence. Mr. Kelly is detained in his wheelchair, Winnie is cinched, then noosed tightly in her ground.

The ground is temporal, for both Nauman and Beckett. It is temporal first of all in the sense that it is closely associated with the here and the now. In Beckett's *Footfalls*, we watch an old woman, dressed in a tattered wrap, pacing up and down a track, while a voice off tells us of a young girl who paced with a similar intentness and desperation, and eventually asked her mother to take up the carpet, explaining: 'the motion alone is not enough. I must hear the feet, however faint they fall.' Hearing the feet establishes the young girl's sense of being there, in the sensation of the faint impact on the ground and its answering resistance. In Nauman's work, the ground is similarly a place of last resort, the lowest common denominator, both a continuous threat, and also a place of trust, a generalised securing or orientation of the sense of place.

A human body moves between many different experiences of different floors and plots of ground, but is nevertheless orientated always just to one ground, just to 'the ground', spreading, various, but everywhere singular. As the 'hypostasis', that which lies beneath, or 'understands' all being and beings living on earth, even and especially creatures of the air like birds, and of the midair, like spiders, the ground has its say in every action and experience. The ground is limit itself; the hereness, or present condition that underwrites every elsewhere, the actual of every possible. It is time thickened and slowed into space, a stay against the passage of time. It is that towards which all movement tends. The dimension of downness, or underness can never be fully in mind, or in view, but is always at work.

It is perhaps for this reason that falling features so markedly in the work both of Nauman and Beckett. Falling, the involuntary or voluntary reversion to the ground, is a coinciding with the necessity which the ground represents. One of Nauman's earliest performance pieces of 1970 (unrecorded, but recalled by Meredith Monk in an interview) involved him accompanying Monk's vocal performance by a repeated series of actions in which he lined himself up exactly with the edge of a stage, fell off at intervals, then climbed back on the stage and did it again. This primal action of falling and rising itself seems to underlie many of the other seemingly primal actions, for example of walking, lying, bouncing, that Nauman has undertaken in his work. Describing his ideal of an art that 'was just there all at once', without preparation or expectation, Nauman does not reach for metaphors of expansion or progress or eminence, but reverts spontaneously to the ideas of impact and collapse. Such an art is 'like getting hit in the back of the neck. You never see it coming; it just knocks you down.' For both Beckett and Nauman, art does not lift you up; it stretches you out, and lays you low.

But the ground is temporal in another, more complex sense. The passing of time always dematerialises the ground. Walking over the ground lengthens the body into duration. A central principle of Beckett's and Nauman's work is that of balance, and a central shared problem is that of how to bring the space and place of the ground into balance with what is enacted in time across its face, how, in other words, to give temporal existence a shape.

Neither Beckett nor Nauman can quite trust the ground. There is in both an impulse to walk through or walk out space, as though space would fade unless repeatedly made to start forth by the tread of the foot. Rather than the ground merely preceding and permitting the application of the foot, it comes to depend upon it. Rather than the ground providing a resting-place for the foot, as in Beckett's poem 'Echo's Bones', where the ground is 'Asylum under my tread all this day', the foot, or the body in motion, must bring about its own solace or asylum in the repetition of its movements back and forth or round and round.

The ground means permanence, and the here and now, it can also shift, as we make shift upon it. We have no idea whether the woman we see in the 'real time' of performance in *Footfalls* is the young girl spoken of by the voice 'V', now aged, or her mother, or another, and we have no idea what the 'now' is and who the 'I' is when we hear a voice, which does not come from the figure we see, saying 'I walk here now.' The ground is impalpable as well as actual; the ground becomes an ideal and ordeal of the foot. The placing of the feet attempts to give the ground an answering solidity, but the more often the ground is traversed, the less it coincides with the single, authoritative here-and-now of the footfall.

In the French version of Beckett's play, the footstep, *pas*, is a not-step too, *pas*. Pacing out the same piece of ground over and over again, like the woman does in *Footfalls*, or the hurrying, robed characters do in Beckett's TV play *Quad*, draws the ground up into the figure, and its action of walking. Stop walking for an instant, and the fear is that the ground will sheer away, and one be left in agonised mid-air, between one step and the next. In *Quad*, as in a number of Nauman's pieces involving repeated walking round a track or carrying out of a controlled set of movements, the place is brought into being by the action, space precipitated out of time.

Both Nauman and Beckett have attempted to resist or complicate the downward pull of the earth, denying gravity in the exploration of different forms of disembodiment or virtuality, especially in the substitution of electronic or audiovisual experience for the here and now performance space of the theatre or the gallery. Nauman's early work included a number of combined installation and performance pieces in which he, or the viewer would walk through a narrowing space, sometimes in the form of a corridor.

Nauman has spoken of his interest in these pieces of the body's sense of constriction, of the encroachment of limit. The same fascination with narrowing and enclosure is to be found in some sculptures of the late seventies and early eighties, such as *3 Dead End Adjacent Tunnels, Not Connected* (1979), *Dead End Tunnel Folded Into Four Arms With Common Walls* (1980), *Smoke Rings: Two Concentric Tunnels Skewed, Non-Communicating* (1980).

For Nauman as for Beckett, who produced during the 1960s and 1970s a family of related 'cylinder pieces', including *Ping, The Lost Ones, Imagine Dead Imagine* and *All Strange Away*, dealing with the enclosure of human beings, there is a reassurance in constriction: a claustrophilia rather than a claustrophobia. Or rather, in both cases, there is the possibility of coming to rest against a surface that holds as well as obstructs, defines shape in denying movement. But, from early on, Nauman was already adding to these primary experiences of constriction and concussion elements that embarrassed or dispersed their quality of the here-and-now.

In a series of works from the early 1970s, Nauman combined video with sculpture in a series of what he called 'surveillance corridors', in which a viewer in a closed space or corridor saw of themselves was distorted or detached or desynchronised in various ways. The viewer of or visitor to the work is thus both inside and outside it; the here and now is cut into by the there and then.

In these pieces, the screen provides an alternative to the ground. A screen, which usually hangs on a wall, and operates in the plane of the wall, is congruous with the traditional picture plane of the painting and the gallery. But, in Nauman's work, the screen is often defined not in its relation to the imaginary, suspended space of the wall, but in its complex relation to the ground.

Nauman used double exposure in some of his photographic work of the 1960s and 1970s in order to allow a play between the idea of the ground and the photographic surface. In *Failing to Levitate in the Studio* (1966) and *Tony Sinking Into the Floor, Face Up and Face Down*, the doubling of the image of the human figure in each case allows us to see it in two places, above and below the ground at once, unsupported by anything except the skin or screen of the photographic plate.

It is conventional to imagine the victims of suffering or oppression bowed, or brought down to the ground. Nauman and Beckett, by contrast, have found and formed in their work the pain of the mid-air. The exposure of the nameless creature manipulated by the Director in Beckett's *Catastrophe* is highlighted by the fact that he is raised on a plinth. There is no hilarity or exhilaration for Nauman in the inhabitation of the air and he has made the mid-air signify pain, threat and coercion.

In the neon sculpture *Hanged Man* (1985), a sequence of lights marks out the shape of a viciously daubed stick-figure made to dance grotesquely and given a ridiculous erection as it dangles from a gallows.

The gallows itself rests on nothing, and the piece is nothing but its own endlessly reenacted sequence, as though, in reference to the children's guessing game 'Hangman', it were trying to get the viewer to guess some agonisingly missing word, which would bring things to a halt. *Shit In Your Hat - Head on a Chair* (1990) also puts together two kinds of impalpability or groundlessness. On a screen, a female mime responds obediently to a series of humiliating instructions given by an offstage voice: in front of the screen, a chair on which a green severed head has been placed, dangles, leaning a little backwards and to the side.

What is occurring on screen ritually enacts abasement - the shit in the hat and the hat placed on the head, a simple embodiment of the replacement of the high by the low, the head by the arse. But the chair, which both does and does not participate in the action depicted on the screen, is a painful refusal of the possibility of subsiding to the ground.

The meaning of the clown for Nauman, like the meaning of the tramp in Beckett, is its imminence to the ground. The clown is at every moment threatened with collapse. Nauman literalises this condition in his *Clown Torture* of 1987, in which a series of actors dressed as different kinds of clown were filmed as they attempted to tell an endless loop story, like the song sung at the beginning of the second act of *Waiting for Godot*, in an imaginary seated posture, standing on one leg, with the other crossed over it.

The clown's body had to hold itself up, be its own chair. The tension of the piece derives from the knowledge that none of the clowns will be able to sustain this position, and will eventually topple to the floor. Time is here not a medium, but a weight and an ordeal; it does not so much pass, as press. The ordeal is made worse by the awareness of being watched, a condition dramatised in the hilariously solemn sketch *Clown With Video Surveillance* of 1986, in which a traditionally-garbed circus clown squats on a lavatory, in a cubicle which is also a picture hanging on the wall, while a roughly-sketched video camera protruding from another picture apparently hanging from the wall of the cubicle records his every move. The clown is not permitted even the security of his abasement, the recording of his actions painfully suspending the clown between this time and place and the other times and places of surveillance and playback. cutting into this scene with the suggestion of another time and another place.

Both Beckett and Nauman have found a compulsion in the act of walking. Early in Beckett's career, there is to be found the miniature pedestrian career of his character Watt in the novel of the same name:

Watt's way of advancing due east, for example, was to turn his bust as far as possible towards the north and at the same time to fling out his right leg as far as possible towards the south, and then to turn his bust as far as possible towards the south and at the same time to fling out his left leg as far as possible towards the north, and then again to turn his bust as far as possible towards the north and to fling out his right leg as far as possible towards the south....

The act of walking is here an ongoing, chaotic compromise between the dimensions of up and down, left and right. It is only Watt's clownish imbalance that keeps him on the move. In fact, there is an element which Beckett fails to specify in this seemingly precise and exhaustive set of instructions, which, if followed rigorously, would leave the subject merely rocking stiff-legged from side to side. In order for Watt to move, to become a 'headlong tardigrade', there must be an inaugural leaning, or movement of falling forward. Watt must be and remain off balance, pulled forward towards the ground, for the action of walking to begin and continue. This unbalancing may perhaps be identified with the principle that Michel Serres borrows from Lucretius of the *clinamen*, the theory of the origin of the world in a first tiny deviation, or asymmetry in the orderly rain of atoms, which makes the world possible at all, even as it makes it impossible ever for the world to add up or come to consummation.

Nauman pays homage both to Watt's way of walking and to the similarly awkward, unbalanced gait of Molloy in his

Slow Angle Walk (Beckett Walk) of 1968. In this piece, Nauman videotaped himself walking slowly and with awkward precision around a track marked out on the studio floor. As he walks, arms behind him, he lifts his leading leg high before him and, as it lands, lifts his following leg high in the air behind. The unbalancing of the walk is doubled by the fact that Nauman taped the movements with the camera on its side, so that he appears to be walking up a wall, gravityless. As in many other pieces from this period in which Nauman uses the interaction of video and live movement to interfere with orientation, such as *Stamping in the Studio* (1968), *Revolving Upside Down* (1968), *Pacing Upside Down* (1968) and *Bouncing in the Corner, no 2: Upside Down* (1969), the camera is drawn into the play of relative positions and substitutions, creating a sense of mutually shifting grounds.

The concentrated, careful, sometimes even tender attention to awkwardness is a feature of the work of both artists. Clumsiness speaks of the infiltration of falling in human action. The English word 'clumsy' is derived from a Northern dialect word *klumse,* which means benumbed by cold. The clumsy one is weighed down by his cold or numb body, by a body that he does not fill or coincide with sufficiently to command. His body is faster and slower than itself at once. His body is of a piece with the ground, but has not yet acquired the grace of the ground. Awkwardness, clumsiness, rendered with this kind of care can acquire its own kind of grace, lightness and fluency, as in Nauman's beautiful rendering of a slow motion slip on a banana skin in one portion of his video installation *Falls, Pratfalls and Sleights of Hand* (1993). Here, the experience of seeing the pratfall repeated slowly and set against renderings of hands performing various kinds of play with eggs and cards is to run together the different forms of movement, to create an impossible imaginary new syntax of bodily movement.

The pull of the ground, the compulsion of down, is always at work in Beckett's world. It is perhaps partly what makes it a 'world' at all, that it is so strongly orientated by gravity, that it is so weighed down by itself. The work itself keeps striking out anew, in what promise to be new directions, but which are always drawn back in to the orbit. By the end of his long career, Beckett's work has built for itself its own ground. In Beckett's *Company*, the one to whom, on his back in the dark, a voice is supposed to come and speak of a past, cannot be certain of anything, not even the pressure of the ground on his hind parts. The work, like so much of Beckett's writing, is composed out of pure supposition. Even the confirming pressure of the ground has vanished in *Worstward Ho*, in which the ground is removed from every hypothesis the instant it is posed. But to 'suppose' is literally to place beneath. As Descartes could doubt everything but the fact that he was doubting, so Beckett can suppose anything but that he is not supposing. The work creates its own artificial gravity system. Becoming its own world, it comes down to itself.

One of the striking differences between Nauman's and Beckett's work is the horror of repetition in the former. Notoriously, Nauman reinvents his art, reinvents his way of being an artist, with almost every work, as though art had to be the opposite of repetition, as though art could be recognised only when unrecognisable as itself. His are the workings of the death instinct as explicated by Freud in *Beyond the Pleasure Principle*, the instinct to disconnect, to atomise, anatomise and particularise, to make a work composed of sunderings and breakings off, which will resist gathering into substance, and will refuse to be weighed down by its own self-resemblance.

Of course, there are islands or passages of self-similarity in Nauman's work - the recurrence of certain subjects, like the tunnels and channels of 1979-80, the use of certain materials, such as neon tubing, and motifs, as in the clown pieces, the hanging pieces and actions, as in the video pieces, and the distinctive styles and signatures of the video work. But, taken as a whole, Nauman's work is allergic to the idea of wholeness. It is not an *oeuvre* but a *désoeuvrement*; every work a working loose from what has come before and threatened to solidify into a whole. It does not anywhere or anyhow come to rest; the most that can be said is that it hangs together.

Chapter 12

Three Beckett Plays

Two of the three plays performed in the Summer of 1983 in New York were receiving their English language premiere, the other, written and titled for the Beckett seminar at Ohio State University in 1981, was being seen for the first time in a public theatre. Alan Schneider, was once again in charge of putting on stage the author's special vision of the world as he wants it done. David Warrilow, who led the cast during the early weeks, sadly had to withdraw, but the force of the three plays did not diminish with a change of cast, and he eventually returned to it. *Ohio Impromptu* is unchanged from its Ohio premiere, but suffered a little from a smaller stage. The sculptural quality of a Beckett play always lends itself better to distance, width and surrounding blackness. It is the first Beckett play to present a Doppelganger on stage, another Beckett pair, but this time seen as mirror images; it belongs to Beckett's ghost period, where phantoms that echo the haunting quality of memory and nostalgia in his work are seen or described on stage.

Meaning is less important than atmosphere: *Ohio Impromptu* catches, in those tones of calm resignation that has characterised the Beckett of recent years, the sense of loss of a loved one, seen both from within and without, not only the memory of a face and a presence, but also a memory of that memory. The reader reads to his own image, is visited by that image, reads about that image that is his own memory of being visited. Some passages that have special poignancy for the listener are repeated on request. Seldom has the atmosphere of personal loss as it must be suffered by millions daily, been so perfectly captured in dramatic and literary terms. As with *Company*, the author again returns to a theme he has portrays many times, that loneliness and nostalgia are too personal, after a certain age, to be shared with any being other than oneself. Beckett writes in metaphor, but seldom as directly as in *Catastrophe*, the second play in this group. He accepted a commission from the Theatre Festival at Avignon to write a play for a special evening to draw attention to the plight of Vaclav Havel, the Czech dissident playwright, who had then been in jail for some years.

Without in anyway moving closer to naturalistic theatre, he has nevertheless caught in a way that must be clear to any audience the essence of Havel's situation and of any victim in the hands of total authoritarian power. As always with Beckett's most frightening situations, it contains much humour, and the audience laughs, before it draws in its breath as it begins to catch the point, much as it usually does in *Happy Days*. *Catastrophe* portrays a man in a studio or theatre being made-up and prepared for a "performance" in which he becomes a living statue portraying, from the director's point of view, the quiescent, unprotesting victim, a symbol of the ideal citizen of a totalitarian regime; to us he portrays helpless misery, but in spite of his helplessness, defiance shines—there can be no better word for it—from his suffering eyes. *Catastrophe* is not only about a political situation and the place of the artist in it. The victim or "protagonist" is also representative of all actors, having to portray what writers write for them in the way directors tell them to do it (Beckett is not unaware of his own relationship with actors, particularly those who in the past have resisted his stage directions).

The director in the play catches two prototypes, that of the political commissar and of the all-powerful personality director like Peter Brook, Vitez or Chereau, who bend a performance to their own interpretation, where often the victim is the author himself; there are many "in" theatrical jokes. The director's assistant coolly carries out her instructions, and it matters little if we are in a concentration camp or a film studio: all humane considerations are ruled out to achieve the ultimate work of art. The twopronged metaphor is incredibly effective for all its surface simplicity. In time, as with all of Beckett's work, more strands and allusions will be discovered. *What Where* arrived at the last minute when the first two plays were already in rehearsal. Written in French for the Graz Festival, 1983, it must have been hastily translated by the author to finish off Alan Schneider's evening, and most effective it is. I came to it cold, not having known of its existence and was only able to read it a week later; it takes much puzzling out. There are four characters, all identical, and if we can assume, as I will do until persuaded otherwise, that what in Beckett looks identical is identical, they are all the same person. In addition to Bam, Bom, Bim and Bem there is the voice of Bam which comes from a visible, spotlighted microphone on stage at head level.

The clear indication is that what we are seeing is both a memory and a scenario: instructions come from the microphone, the voice of Bam controls what we see, puts the characters through their movements rapidly without words like a film running over its spools at rewind speed, and then starts again, occasionally stopping when Bam is not satisfied and a phrase is improved to add to the force of the theme. Bam wishes to elicit information about *what* was said and *where* it was said. On his instructions each of the Doppelgängers is tortured in turn to obtain the information, but on reporting back after having been "given the works" that they have not been able in spite of the torture to elicit *what* and *where*, they are themselves "given the works" to confess that they have lied and do know what the tortured man had to confess. Ultimately Bam himself fails to get the information from Bem that Bim had confessed to him what Bom had confessed and prepares to be "given the works" himself, either by himself or by the voice that is the nearest reality to the audience.

The play shares many similarities with *Ohio Impromptu*, the identical characters in appearance and dress, the unwinding backwards of events and the stylisation of image and movement in particular. Events are in the past, already caught on the tape that the mind can reel backward and forward, purgatorial in atmosphere, it belongs to the sequence of plays, where memory is equated with a tape or film, that started with *Krapp's Last Tape* and *Play* and that in Beckett's fiction finds its expression in the *Molloy* Trilogy, especially *The Unnamable* and in *How It Is*. It sometimes appears that Beckett sees the universe like a gigantic Dantean computer where every consciousness, living or dead, is constantly running and rerunning the events of life in both directions, a concept close to the theories of J. R. Dunne. The play is about truth, the impossibility of certainty and the distrust of second hand evidence, as unreliable as first hand evidence.

There is of course much more to it than that, and scholars will tease out of What Where once the full implications of what lies behind Bam's voice are thought out. The language, while exercising all the Beckett economy and the stylisation that is part of that economy, is near to the popular vernacular. But one thing is clear: each of these fifteen minute plays is a miniature masterpiece deserving thought and further acquaintance that parallels the extraordinary fictional texts that have appeared since his seventieth birthday, *Company, Ill Seen Ill Said* and *Worstward Ho*. Beckett has never moved far from the world of Dante, but now depicts reality in holographs that, like film, can be shown at will if the magician wills it. Increasingly Shakespearean, Beckett has taken over the role of Prospero, and he now presents literary creation and human creation as metaphors of each other, and the stage, where reality is created and portrayed for the length of time of the performance, a metaphor for life, which he once defined as "the space of a door that opens and shuts" but now sees as the space of a dramatic performance.

There is room for much speculation here for Beckett scholars on the nature of that universal theatre and the playwright who creates it that lies at the core of the current Beckettian perception with all its metaphysical possibilities. In the first cast the always remarkable David Warrilow was partnered by Rand Mitchell, Donald Davis (Director in *Catastrophe* and Bom), Daniel Wirth and Margaret Reed (Assistant in *Catastrophe*). Later Kevin O'Connor joined the cast. The success with a public much greater than the normal public has astonished and delighted Jack Garfein who runs the Harold Clurman Theatre, and he plans another triple bill soon. Due to a delay in publication of the last issues of *JOBS*, this review, written in 1983, although still valid as a review, is now somewhat dated. The successful triple bill went to the 1984 Edinburgh Festival, where it was highly acclaimed as part of a multi-event Beckett season at the Gateway Theatre. The production was also seen at the Jerusalem Festival in June 1985.

A double bill of *Piece of Monologue* and *That Time* followed the success of the triple bill. In spite of the tragic death of Alan Schneider the production has held up very well. Imperceptibly there has been a slight movement towards naturalism. In other Beckett productions mounted by the Clurman company, less attention has been given to the subtleties of line readings, so that, in *Endgame* for example, where stage directions have been carefully observed, there has been a definite falling off in the musical *legato* quality of the text and the big poetic moments are less effective. Big Beckett events are being prepared for 1986 in New York, when Beckett becomes an octogenarian, and it is only hoped that the casting and direction will have the meticulous attention the plays require.

The Autumn theatre season opened in Paris with what amounted to a Samuel Beckett Festival, including three recent short plays—*Berceuse, L'Impromptu d'Ohio,* and *Catastrophe* at the Théâtre du Rond-Point; *La Dernière Bande* at the Poche-Montparnasse; and *Pas Moi* at the Théâtre Essaion. The plays at the Rond-Point, home of the compagnie Renaud-Barrault, were acted by Catherine Sellers, Michael Lonsdale, and Jean-Louis Barrault. The director, Pierre Chabert, has previously worked closely with Samuel Beckett, particularly when he played Krapp in *La Dernière Bande,* under the author's own direction, at the Théâtre d'Orsay in 1975.

He also played Hamm in *Fin de Partie* at the American Centre in Paris in 1981. There was a strong emphasis on the visual image—costumes, props, lighting, attitude and gestures of the actors, the interrelationship of figure, object, and space. Indeed, the visual purity of the images, especially in the first two plays, was a memorable feature of the production. As the curtain opened on *Berceuse,* the light gradually delineated first a face, then the entire view of an old lady in a rocking chair, isolated against the surrounding darkness.

In contrast to the Alan Schneider New York/London production, where Billie Whitelaw's dress was full and elaborately hung with sequins, the tiny figure of Catherine Sellers was enclosed in a close-fitting dress of black pleated silk, reminiscent of the designs of Fortuny in the earlier part of the century. The former gave a more vivid impression of age and decay—Ms. Whitelaw's hair was loose and dishevelled, her face worn, contrasting, like a Miss Haversham, with her stiff and rather fussy gown. Catherine Seller's appearance was more one of faded elegance.

Her face, though deathly pale and shadowed, almost like a mask apart from the anxious dark eyes, was less obviously aged. The image as a whole, in the Paris production, was more refined. Any unnecessary visual detail was eliminated. The narrow vertical lines of the pleated dress emphasised the frailty of the figure, and complemented the lines of the chair, which both imprisoned and embraced her body. The chair was specially designed for the production by the decorateurs—two sculptors, Jean Herbin and Pierre Didelot—so that the speed and depth of the rock could be modulated with considerable sensitivity.

This enabled the rhythm of the chair's movement to follow closely the rhythm of the voice, rising, falling, or stopping momentarily. The recorded voice of Ms. Sellers captured the musicality, and pervasive, incantatory rhythm of the verbal text. It also expressed a softness and a fatigue which contrasted with the apprehension in the large dark eyes, sometimes closed, as she listened to the voice, otherwise staring into void. Her enunciation of the four "Encore's" which punctuate the text conveyed both supplication and dread, suggesting an ambiguity in her attitude to death, desired as a release from her long, agonisingly lonely life, yet also feared.

The voice seemed to be calming the old lady, drawing her, almost enticing her into death, to which she eventually submits, surrendering to the soothing, steady rhythm of voice and rocker. The indivisible unity of figure and chair, the echo between the rhythm of the rocking, and that of the voice, reinforced the poetic intensity, and musical unity of the piece. In the text, though this did not seem to be reflected here in F's attitude on stage, there is a sense of self-reconciliation, or 'recueillement.' Denied any response from the external world, F. (in English W.) eventually turns to herself, to the voice of herself, and to death for comfort. The journey down the stairs is also a descent into the self, almost a descent back into the womb—in the final 'quartet' her image fuses with that of her Mother, who, like her, *'de son plus beau noir vêtue,'* at last sought the arms of the rocker—*'des bras enfin'*.

Towards the and, the light shifted to concentrate on the face, and the haunting rhythm drew us steadily to the final moment, when with a sudden and surprising last burst of energy (like the final effort which gives birth), conveyed in the much harsher line—*'aux gogues la vie,'* F's head slowly fell forward, and after some seconds of silence, the image gradually faded into darkness. In *L'Impromptu d'Ohio,* the lighting (subtle, almost intimate), again gradually brought into view two identically dressed figures, bent over a table. Each face was partially hidden by a hand over the forehead, indeed that of the Listener (Jean-Louis Barrault), behind the table, head lowered, was almost completely obscured.

The light shone downwards, illuminating quite a narrow circle, including the two figures, the open book, on which the light seemed to be concentrated, and a largebrimmed black hat on the table towards the edge of the circle. Michael Lonsdale, reading the final pages of the book, adopted a rather halting, fatigued tone, pronouncing each word with equal, and deliberate emphasis, which evoked the strain of repeated nocturnal readings, and drew our attention to the words which the Reader is trying, sometime with difficulty, to decipher.

However, I felt this monotone, somewhat laboured voice, lost some of the subtlety of Beckett's rhythms, which constantly challenge, and redefine the meaning and suggestivity of the words, creating waves of statement, echo, and re-statement, counterpointing and interweaving sound and meaning, emotional and intellectual response.

The text in fact describes the final stages of a life, identifiable as that of the Listener, through certain motifs common to both stage and text-the long, black coat, the old-fashioned hat. The protagonist attempts to escape the painful memories of a once-shared intimacy. He moves to unknown surroundings, which cannot remind him of the past, thereby, it seems, deserting the '*cher visage*' who warns him in a dream to stay, and promises him comfort, as Christ promised to send his Spirit, the comforter, to his disciples—'*mon ombre te consolera.*'

He is subsequently overcome by solitude, yet in the extremity of his suffering, the promised consolation appears, in the form of the Reader, whether sent by the former loved one, or, as S. E. Gontarski suggests, 'generated from or by Listener himself.' From this point onwards, the text comes to reflect more and more closely the actual stage scene before us, though complete reflection does not occur till the words have ended, and the heads of Listener and Reader are raised in a simultaneous and identical movement, to meet each other's eyes.

Any action or direct speech, apart from the final movement, and the Listener's intermittent taps on the table signalling the Reader to pause, and repeat certain phrases, takes place in the text, suggesting the division between subject and object, self and its existence in space and time, which has been a principal structural pattern in all of Beckett's drama. Here, Listener and voice are no longer alienated (as are Mouth and Auditor in *Pas Moi*), but, as the text tells us, '*ils devinrent comme un seul.*' Their relationship was echoed scenically in the identical dress and pose of the two figures and the Listener's series of slow, but authoritative taps which control the Readers reading.

The growing sense of closeness between them was conveyed visually at one point, when the Listener's hand stayed that of the Reader, raised to find a previous reference, and both hands fell slowly together. The final image of

L'Impromptu d'Ohio came across very strongly onstage. As the text reached its end, announced by the repetition of 'Il no reste rien a dire,' the light narrowed to concentrate on the faces, particularly that of the Listener, now fully revealed, as both hands were lowered, and both heads raised, facing each other in a complete mirror image. The past, with its images of a solitary and suffering life, dissolved into the silence of a timeless present, in which Self and Self, or Self and Comforter (whether Memory, or Creation), or perhaps Life and Death, at last face to face, become indistinguishable.

There was no signal of ending, as when F.'s head dropped forward; instead, the image was held for a few seconds, before fading slowly into darkness. Both of the shorter plays occupied a small area of the stage, the rest remaining in total darkness. *Berceuse* was placed to the audience's left, *L'Impromptu* to the audience's right, the depth of the stage space having been closed off by a screen of black velvet.

This gave a certain softness and richness to the surrounding darkness, which contrasted sharply with the cold, stark, grey walls of the stage, which were revealed for *Catastrophe*, after the interval. The figure of the Metteur-en-scene (Michael Lonsdale) lounged in a chair towards the front of the stage, and was wrapped entirely in a light grey fur coat and hat, contrasting with the slight, whitecoated and upright figure of the Assistante (Catherine Sellers) at his side (on the left of the audience).

The Protagoniste (Jean-Louis Barrault), standing on a pedestal towards the back of the stage, diagonally opposite the Director, was covered, apart from his bare feet, by a coat and hat (large-brimmed, completely hiding his face), of a cold, almost metallic grey. Lonsdale convincingly created a dogmatic, self-satisfied and petulant Director, whose bullying, though menacing in its total lack of sympathy, and sensitivity, inspired laughter and contempt, rather than awe.

This was emphasised by the Assistante, whose fixed smile, and exaggerated gestures of obedience, incongruous with the stark setting, and again provoking laughter, were in fact a form of mockery, and gave way to antagonism, the moment his back was turned. Her brisk movements contrasted both with the slow, rather sensual gestures of the Metteur-en-scene (fingers caressing fur, moustache), and with the statue-like immobility of the Protagoniste.

She was the mediator between these two extremes, and her movements traced lines of antagonism or sympathy, depending on their object. In a moment of respite, when the Director left the stage, she collapsed into the chair (after wiping it vigorously, as if to avoid contamination), looking frail and worn, reminding us that this Assistante was another victim, rather than a collaborator, of the Director. Her sympathy with the Protagoniste was brought out in the gentleness and awe with which she approached and touched him, while adjusting his pose (which she afterwards unconsciously, and momentarily echoed—hands clasped at waist, then higher).

Although the lively gestures and rather smug, indeed comic tone of the Metteur-en-scene at times threatened to distract from, rather than highlight the suffering and silent dignity of the Protagoniste, the contrasts between the three characters, and the web of tensions and relationships between them, across the stage space, heightened the dramatic force of the play, and contrasted with the greater subtlety of the previous plays. After the Director had put the finishing touches to his human 'catastrophe', from his omniscient position off-stage, he ordered the lights to focus on the now denuded figure of the Protagoniste, then on the face alone. Since this is a technique frequently used by Beckett himself in many of his recent plays, and particularly in the preceding two plays in this programme, one had a vivid impression of watching the familiar figure of an essentially vulnerable, suffering human being, not, however, gradually approaching a longed for release in death, but fallen into the hands of this contemptible manipulator, whether director, dictator, or anti-god.

The political dimension of the play was underlined by the Director's phrase '*Fais vite j'ai un comité.*' The play is dedicated to Vaclav Havel, the Czech playwright placed under house arrest by his government for his 'subversive' activity, and writing. The use of the (self-conscious) stage metaphor, also emphasised the director/dictator's control and exploitation not only of the individual, but of the expressive potential and function of Art. Yet the figure of the Protagoniste, humiliated, treated like a window dummy, is not broken. Far from becoming de-humanised, (the Director refers to him in strictly anatomical terms—*'Les jambes. Du tibia.'*)—his essential and unquenchable humanity emerges all the more strongly in the final defiant gesture (executed with great force and dignity by Jean-Louis Barrault), of raising his head amid the clamour of recorded applause.

There were echoes of the soon-to-be-crucified Christ, facing the mocking multitude—though the implied audience of the recording may not be aware of their mockery—they too may be 'manipulated' by the Metteur-en-scene. Indeed the "real" audience hesitated before breaking into applause at the end of the play. A single, central point of light, which in this production, rose to a glow as the rest of the stage was plunged into darkness, seemed to symbolism, or celebrate the stubborn, courageous, and inextinguishable will of the spirit to continue, under the most impossible conditions which society, or life in general may impose. The three plays of the evening were carefully chosen to complement and contrast with each other in tone, and in visual impact. The sensitive lighting played an essential part in the production, and helped, particularly in *Berceuse* and *L'Impromptu d'Ohio,* to capture the visual poetry of Beckett's theatre.

These, undoubtedly, are among the most personal of texts in all of Beckett's output. Closest perhaps in affinity to *Company* is *That Time* (1974/5), the play in which voices emerging from three distinct sound sources are heard by a Listener, whose face alone is visible ten feet above stage level, seen from above, surrounded by darkness. This face of a white haired old man, therefore, is clearly part of a body lying on its back in the dark. That exactly is the situation of the protagonist of the novella *Company* who also is 'on his back in the dark' and listens to a voice or voices recounting fragments from his past life. The close resemblance of these two works, one a piece of narrative prose, the other a stage work, illustrates the fluidity of the boundaries between narrative prose and drama in Beckett's work, all of which, ultimately, can be seen as a series of 'monologues with voices.'

Hence it was less surprising, as might have been expected in view of Beckett's reluctance to transfer works of his from one medium to another, that in the case of *Company* he not only consented to a stage adaptation of the piece, but even actively collaborated with the French actor and director, Pierre Chabert, and the American Beckett scholar and director S. E. Gontarski in turning the prose narrative into a stage piece. The French version of *Compagnie* opened at the Théâtre du Rond-Point (Petite Salle) in Paris on 15 November 1984, the English version [*Company* was originally written in English] under Gontarski's direction, with Alan Mandell in the only part, at the Los Angeles Actors' Theatre (Half-Stage) in February 1985. Essentially the adaptation consists in dividing the text (after certain passages have been cut) into those sections that are spoken by the protagonist live, and those fragments of memory that emerge from several points in the darkness. There are fifteen such passages in all.

The sixteenth voiceover is the final word of the piece. 'Alone.' The main problem facing the director is that of the nature of the image that the protagonist presents to the audience. The protagonist muses about the voice of voices he hears while lying on his back in the dark. The obvious solution would be to repeat the image of *That Time,* namely to show the protagonist in that position, either full length, or merely, as in the earlier play, his head. Gontarski, for obvious reasons, avoids repeating the image. He shows the old man, sitting in a chair—in the act of imagining that situation, following the indication of the first words of *Company*. 'A Voice comes to one in the dark. Imagine.' The protagonist here, therefore, is in the situation of the dramatist in the act of writing a play like *That Time,* re-creating the experience of the supine listener in the dark, recollected in tranquility.

There is, thus, not much scope for design in the piece. A chair on a dark stage. Timian Alsaker, the designer, nevertheless went for a radical solution. Not being able to design the stage, he redesigned the auditorium, breaking up the conventional rows of seats and dotting the chairs in the small auditorium about in an arbitrary arrangement which resulted in nobody actually sitting next to anyone else. In other words: the individual spectators were meant to be as isolated from each other, as alone in the dark, as the protagonist. I personally do not think that this subtle psychological effect was achieved. Thirty people in a small room cannot feel isolated, even if the next chair is not as near as the convention of rows in a theatre demands. But this is a minor point. The lighting, so essential in this piece, for which Alsaker also signs, is superb. Alan Mandell has opened into a bony Beckettlan figure and has become ideal casting for a Beckett protagonist, the haunting image of an old man whose life-long sufferings are etched in the lines of a face of resigned spirituality.

He masters the difficult text with sovereign command of variation and nuance and lends it the gravelly texture of his voice. If anything I found his delivery a little too clear, a shade too loud for the Beckettian voice, which should never rise above a faint murmur. In a passage cut in this adaptation the protagonist speaks of 'words *murmured in his ear*.' But I admit that keeping it so fast and so low might well tax the patience of audiences. (Which, of course, is precisely what Beckett aims at?) Is anything gained by seeing this text performed over merely reading it? Something, I surmise, is gained, something lost. The gain lies in the image, the ease with which the spectator-and listener— can rely on getting the correct phrasing and rhythm inherent in the text and which he himself would have to puzzle out when merely reading it. There is also the gain in the image itself, although here the reader with imagination might come up with more vivid images.

A gain also lies in the relentlessness with which a performance drives towards its fore-ordained conclusion, the compulsion to take the text without interruption, as a whole. And here the performance is a triumph: never, for a moment, does this text, with its almost manic repetition, and continuous returns to the starting point become boring, the tension, the suspense is miraculously maintained from beginning to end—

paradoxically in a piece that has no story to speak of. As so often Beckettand his interpreters in this case—performs the seemingly self-contradictory feat of creating drama of a high order out of material that by all rules of the art should be, by definition, totally undramatic. And so another dramatic piece has been added to the Beckett canon. It is to be hoped that this adaptation which bears the imprimatur of the author himself should be made available as a text for performance by others. Apart from everything else this would put a stop to unauthorised adaptations and performances of *Company* (of which there have already be a number).

Two Arabs wearing knit and cotton caps, open-necked work shirts and baggy pants arrive singly at a construction site, one of the many that dot the landscape of Israel in the 1980s. They have probably been brought from their homes in the occupied lands to what is commonly referred to in Israel as "the slave market"—an area skirting major cities where Arab workers wait to be hired by Israelis for day labour, most often to work on housing projects and settlements in the territories from which the workers come. Behind the pair there is a steel skeleton of the concrete column they will pour that day, and a few cinder blocks on which they occasionally sit or stand. While they wait, the pair talk in Arabic: trading stories, telling jokes, making small talk. Finally, the Israeli foreman—in white shirt, blazer, khaki pants and sunglasses—strides in. He is preceded by his carrier, a poor Arab who is attached to his master by a retractable ruler fastened to his neck and who is carrying his paraphernalia of construction: surveyor's equipment and blueprints, as well as an attaché case and luggage.

With the arrival of the builder, the language of communication shifts from Arabic to Hebrew—his language. He talks to the workers in the slow, labored form one uses with those unfamiliar with a language and they answer him in broken Arabic-accented Hebrew phrases. The carrier, however, in the one set speech he recites, speaks in literary Arabic, a variation of the spoken vernacular form. Aside from this speech and brief verbal exchanges, little happens. The group stands for a period of time, and then the latter pair depart while the original workers remain and wait. There is nothing extraordinary about the general outline of the play. It resembles a number of works written by Jewish and Arab Israeli playwrights during the past decade: plays which condemn the government's handling of Arabs, illustrate the evils of occupation and its effects on the occupier as well as the occupied; mourn the failure of the Zionist dream about the dignity of work and the commitment to self-help; abhor the class distinctions that have emerged in the society, and the material acquisitiveness of the new generation.

The dialogue echoes words and ideas found in modern literature, the media and on the street. When one worker says, "We've lost our rights" the other replies, "We got rid of them." Although the foreman asks the pair what they are doing, "Here? On my land?," he grudgingly admits, "The road is free to all." The pair recoil from his treatment of his carrier—"To treat a man... like that... I think that... no... a human being... no... it's a scandal!"—yet they feel impotent and incapable of intervening, and they are not even certain who is ultimately to blame for the condition. When one asks, "Well? What do we do?" the other answers, "Don't lets do anything. It's safer." Both repeat the hope, "Tomorrow everything will be better," and echo the phrase—the most common expression in modern Hebrew—"Nothing to be done" (*ain ma l'asot*).

The play offers a comment—a painful, familiar comment—on the muddled mess of the Middle East in the 1980s, but it does so through highly unusual means. It never once mentions the combatants, Jews and Arabs; the words "Zion," "Palestine," or "Israel" do not appear. It also offers no solutions to the stark realities it presents, ending as it begins with the workers frozen in place, still waiting. It is not even a contemporary creation nor written by an inhabitant of the region. It was composed in 1948—the year the state of Israel was established—by an Irishman writing in French, a man who had never been to the area but knew instinctively that here "they crucified quick."

The transportation of *Waiting for Godot* to Israel was the

idea of the young, talented Israeli director Ilan Ronen, who had previously won Israel's Producer of the Year award for C. P. Taylor's *Good*. His cast, members of the Haifa Municipal Theatre, reflect the racial mix of the sponsoring city: Makhram Khouri and Youssuf Abu-Warda, who play Vladimir and Estragon, are two leading Arab Israeli actors; Doron Tavori and Ilan Toren, Lucky and Pozzo, are both Israeli Jews (Toron having played Lucky in the 1968 Habimah production of *Godot*). The original conception, described above, was 80 per cent Arabic with the audience, predominantly Hebrew-speaking, required to read the distributed mimeographed translations of the play if they wished to understand the words. This alone was a daring act for the theatre company, replicating for the audience the experience of confronting an unmastered language in their own country—something Arabs face in the nominally bilingual but traditionally Hebrew-speaking society of Israel.

In a second version of the production, which ran after the close of the first—and was perhaps a response to the confusion that the mimeographed form engendered—Viadimir and Estragon speak Hebrew, one in an Ashkenazi or European accent, the other in a Sephardic or Levantine form, and both revert to Arabic when in the presence of the Hebrew-speaking Pozzo. Lucky continues to declaim in literary Arabic, with his monologue reproduced in Hebrew for the audience to read. In this form of the production the emphasis shifts slightly from racial and political to economic and class confrontations among the characters. However, the central image—Pozzo the Jewish master and Lucky the Arab slave— remains undiluted. It is this second version of the play that I saw in a labour union hall in the small town of Nes Tziona, near the centre of Israel, in the summer of 1985, eight months after the original production had opened to wide acclaim.

Following a tradition in Israeli theatre, the Haifa group had traveled there, as they travel to all sections of the country, to bring people outside of urban areas the experience of professional theatre. This audience, comprised of the mixed ethnic working population of the area, received *Godot* unreservedly: they laughed, whispered running comments, sat in rapt albeit pained attention as Lucky spoke in a language few knew, and applauded strongly—not always a gratuitous response of Israeli audiences—as the lights faded on the last tableau. Most important, no one in the sold-out house left, something Beckett audiences in far more sophisticated venues still do; and no one I overheard asked the often parroted question of Shower/Cooker: "What's it meant to mean?" They knew.

The production was a great success; on this point audiences and critics agreed. It made Beckett and *Godot* accessible in ways the five previous major productions in the country had not; it focused on actual situations to which the audience could relate, but it did so without sacrificing the universality of the work. Ronen had posed a question: If characters trade bowler hats for three variations of Arab headdress, if they stand in front of building apparatus instead of a tree, if they speak in two languages, is the play still *Waiting for Godot*? In this production, at least, the answer is "yes." The director and his translator, the bilingual Anton Shamas, did not add a single word to Beckett's original text; they only altered dress and props to indicate how the universal words and actions can fit a particular place and time. They did make excisions, particularly of references to Christian imagery, perhaps since such expressions would be alien to the Semitic characters in the production and the Semitic audiences that viewed them. They did not, however, try to offer commensurate religious references.

The use of the steel skeleton for concrete is particularly effective, since, at the beginning of Act Two when it "grows," it is clear that the expansion breeds further misery, not hope, something the tree/leaf imagery does not always immediately convey to audiences. And even the blend of languages, the most overtly experimental aspect of the production, seems acceptable once it is acknowledge that *Godot* is translated into numerous languages so there is some logic in using two languages simultaneously in a bilingual society. The Israeli *Godot*, however, provides more than an interesting reading of the text; it illustrates one response to the problem facing any director who wishes to produce the play in the'80s: how to relate to a work designated a "classic," how to breathe life into a text that comes trailing countless repetitions, and more countless criticisms and explanations behind it.

A classic can be a dangerous beast in the theatre, Peter Brook argues in *The Empty Space*. Shakespeare productions, for example, can easily become what Brook calls "Deadly Theatre," when slavish repetitions occur, variations are discouraged, the audience is excruciatingly bored, and the scholar alone emerges happy from a routine performance "smiling because nothing has distracted him from trying over and confirming his pet theories to himself, whilst reciting his favourite lines under his breath." No one would wish such a fate for *Godot*. Yet the possibilities are there—and growing—as each now version moves further in time and memory from the original performance. It is already thirtythree years since the first *Godot*, and ten years since Beckett's own direction of the work. Despite first-hand accounts and photographs, video tapes and recordings, the images begin to fade. And perhaps they should, for as Brook reminds theatre people, the meaning that each fresh production must convey "can be checked in each man's own present experience", and there is nothing worse than imitations of imitations "a sound that in turn was a memory of a predecessor's way".

Yet, Brook—and Beckett—recognize the invariable "on the other hand," in this case the submerging of a play in the trendy fashion of the moment, foisted in the name of "present experience." One need only think of the unsuccessful variations of Shakespeare's works—The Tempest on Cape Canaveral, in Brazil, at the shore, on Plymouth Rock, or accompanied by Hard Rock—to recognize the dangers and possible trivializations of modernity. Between slavish reproduction and complete annihilation of the original, some point will have to be sought. It seems to me that in the Israeli production a model may be found: small adjustments made for locale and relationships without any additions to the text, particularizations that enhance not detract from the universality of the work. If the play is performed in Israel, it should follow that the characters can be Jews and Arabs. For it is Vladimir who says, "But at this place, at this moment of time, all mankind is us, whether we like it or not."

All the theatres in the "Circulo" were showing Beckett's plays for over a month. The Festival included a photographic exhibition of Beckett's life through his work, with material provided by the University of Reading— BeckettArchive—and from "Le Centre Georges Pompidou" of Paris. There were also lectures, panel discussions, readings from Beckett's novels, video radio and T.V. shows, together with a bibliographical display of the Beckettian "oeuvre" in English, French and Spanish. The main attraction of the festival was, of course, the theatrical productions. Ten plays, covering almost all periods and styles of Beckett as a dramatist were preformed—the only exception being the theatre of the '70's. The Festival opened with the 1975 "Théâtre D'Orsay" production of *La Derniére Bande*, with Pierre Chabert as Krapp directed by Samuel Beckett, and closed with the "Los Angeles Actors Theater" Production of *Company*, with Alan Mandell as protagonist, directed by Stanley Gontarski.

To show Beckett as a bilingual writer was one of the central aims of this "Muestra," another was to present his most recent plays, that were totally unknown to the Spanish public. This last aim was also achieved by the "Teatros del Circulo" production of *Nana* (*Rockaby*), *Impromptu de Ohio* (*Ohio Impromptu*) and *Catástrofe* (*Catastrophe*), which I translated into Spanish for this occasion."1 These plays were directed by Pierre Chabert and interpreted by Maite Brik, Francisco Vidal and Jose Lifante. Apart from the three short plays, there was another Spanish premiere, the dramatization or the short novel *Primer Amor* (*First Love*), in a production of the "Teatro Fronterizo" of Barcelona, directed by Jose Sanchis Sinisterra and Fernando Grifell, with Luis Miguel Climent as protagonist. The rest of the productions included the two *Acts Without Words, Acto Sin Palabras I y II*, directed and acted by Julio Castronuovo with Miguel Angel Sanchez and Carlos Zabaleta. These two Mimes and *Va y Ven* (*Come and Go*), were also produced by "Teatros del Circulo." The "dramaticule" was directed, in a rather peculiar setting, a church pew, by Angel Facio, with Concha Gregory, Isabel Navarro and Charo Pardo as the three female protagonists. *Qué Hermosos Dias* (*Happy Days*) directed by José Sanchis Sinisterra with Rosa Novell as Winnie and Luis Miguel Climent as Willie, completed the theatrical programme. This last play was a Catalan production—though acted in Spanish in the Festival—which obtained a great success in Barcelona in its Catalan premiere as *Oh Els Bons Dies*! Although I was a member of the organising committee I think it is only fair to acknowledge the quality and professionally of all the productions taking part in the Festival, some of them were really outstanding. This fact has been almost unanimously recognized by public and press, and the "Circulo de Bellas Arles" has to be praised once again for placing art before profit.

According to the printed programme the public performance had been preceded by several dress rehearsals on the campus of the Institute, and at Shanghai Jiaotong University, in December of 1986. Chanqiang Theatre is located on a narrow sidestreet around the corner from the famous landmark Park Hotel on the crowded Nanjing Road East, near the People's Park—formerly the Race course in Shanghai's International Settlement. Before the Communist Revolution, the theater had been known as the Carleton, and its now somewhat seedier appearance belies the fact that it used to be a prestigious Shanghai address in the nineteen thirties. The premiere of this Beckett play in China, therefore, was fraught with a great deal of symbolic significance, beginning with the location of the theatre itself.

The bold heading of the program's title page (illustrated as well in black and white) proclaims the play to be "the representative work of the Theatre of the Absurd," a genre known in Chinese as the *huangdan pai xiju*. The play was directed by Chen Jialin, with music and lyrics by Ouyang Zhanzhi; the text was translated by Shi Xianrong. The translator, Mr. Shi, lives and works in Beijing. A member of the Institute of Western Literature, this veteran translator is a former student of the noted scholar Qian Zhongshu, Vice president of the Chinese Academy of Social Sciences. The cast of the performance included Zhang Baode as Estragon, Li Zhiming as Vladimir, Zhang Ping and Gong Ziaoguang alternating as Lucky (in Chinese, "the Lucky One"), Zheng Rugao as Pozzo, and Peng An-na alternating with Chen Xiayun as the Boy. The cast also included several "dancers".

The stage for the performance was sparsely but effectively set with a stunted willow tree at one end, substantial enough to have a rope thrown across the bough later. The costumes were Western, including the tight boots and the various hats. The entrances and exits for Pozzo, the elaborate gestures with the whip, the bustle with the bags and basket were all staged in the grand manner, which, together with the music and even the appearance of dancers, betrayed an unmistakable affinity to the tradition of the Peking Opera. In this sense the Chinese *Godot*, while presented as a work set in the Western world, was at least partially assimilated into the Chinese cultural orbit. One minor effect was particularly apt: as many scholars realise, in Chinese Gogo and Didi mean "elder brother" and "younger brother" respectively, and the terms are commonly used between friends, according to their ages. This overtone, generally lost on Western audiences, gave a natural closeness to the relationship between Vladimir and Estragon on the Chinese stage. Since the actors were all from the Drama Institute, a training school for actors, most of them looked older than the average college student in an American University, and they played their parts quite professionally.

The performance was lively and spirited, and the audience, consisting chiefly of young, educated college youth, gave it rapt attention throughout, and a warm reception at the curtain. The printed programme offered the following introductory notes to the play: *Dengdai Geduo,* first performed during the fifties in Paris, is now more than thirty years old. The title is now a household word in the West, and the play is required reading for every college student in the humanities in the Western world. This is proof of the play's profound influence, which propelled its author Beckett to the first rank of the world's dramatists. And yet this play is a total stranger to us, since this is its first performance in our country. Why is this play considered the representative work of the Theatre of the Absurd? Because it incorporates all the classic features of this literary genre: there is neither a lively plot nor an attempt at complete characterization; there is neither a clearly delineated topic nor the use of dramatic conflict.

Even the dialogue is often illogical. The one action in the play—"Waiting"—is advanced by a combination of realistic and abstract methods; either by ideas or through the subconscious; by means selfcontained or extended; through life's small incidents or by philosophical reflection; all of this through the circular movement of its simple structure. Thus the play is transformed and expanded until it achieves for "Waiting" a goal that transcends time and space, transcends national boundaries, and even transcends timelessness itself in its artistic effect—in order to reflect mankind's shared emotions.

And the two tramps in the play become mankind's "representatives." The effect so produced shows the great power of pure art and its classic value. This play has had over a thousand performances in the United States. Once, when the author was asked by a director, "Who is the Godot that everyone is waiting for in the play?" the author's reply was that he himself did not know.

We can perhaps offer the following attempt at an answer: "So long as mankind has expectations, an equivalent degree of 'waiting' will exist; so long as that degree of 'waiting' exists, it will be matched by an equal number of 'Godots' in the world.' We hope that the performance of *Dengdai Geduo* will help advance our understanding of the West and, at the same time, provide a new direction for our theatrical enterprise. It is no accident that translated masterpieces of Western drama have been enjoying immense popularity in the People's Republic of China during the past five years or so. The successes scored in Beijing by the gifted translator-*cum*-director-*cum*-actor Ying Ruocheng in his productions of *Measure for Measure* (also translated by Mr. Ying), *Death of a*

Salesman (co-directed with Arthur Miller), and *Amadeus* are still fresh in the minds of Chinese audiences.

The Shakespeare anniversary year alone saw as many as sixteen different productions of Shakespeare's plays in China, translated into various genres, including a Peking-opera style *Othello.* Translations have proved to be a much easier mode of escaping the censors than attempting to produce original scripts on controversial subjects in China—a glum and mute testimony to a lackluster legitimate stage, in spite of the welcome increased activity it has meant for translators. It is all the more ironic that a play as darkly pessimistic as Beckett's *Waiting for Godot* should have been staged in Shanghai during the harshest Winter of Discontent in China since the fail of the their so-called "Gang of Four."

Following widespread student demonstrations in fourteen cities across China in November and December, demanding "freedom" and "democracy," several outstanding scientists and educators, as well as leading journalists such as Liu Binyan and Wang Ruowang, were dismissed from their posts and deprived of their party memberships in January. And in spite of the spirit of hope which permeates the programme notes for the Chinese version of *Waiting for Godot,* no one, including the director and the translator, expects the play to enjoy more than a short run.

Chapter 13

The Prose of Samuel Beckett

There is a moment in Proust's novel when Marcel hears a bird calling through the long afternoon:

Somewhere in one of the tall trees, making a stage in its height, an invisible bird, desperately attempting to make the day seem shorter, was exploring with a long, continuous note the solitude that pressed it on every side, but it received at once so unanimous an answer, so powerful a repercussion of silence and of immobility that, one would have said, it had arrested for all eternity the moment which it had been trying to make pass more quickly.

This 'long, continuous note' of solitude resonates through Samuel Beckett's work since the publication of his trilogy, *Malloy, Malone Dies*, and *The Unnamable*, between 1951 and 1953. With increasing spareness and economy, he has reduced his prose to the point, in *Lessness*, where a few words are entered on the page, then repeated in various orders or identical phrases until their possible meanings have been exhausted. In his plays, we are asked to observe a stage littered with garbage, while an 'instant of recorded vagitus' (in the O.E.D., the word is obsolete, 'a cry, lamentation, or wail') punctuates the sound of breathing, or listen to a disembodied voice hectoring a hooded, silent auditor (*Not I*, 1973). What we are witnessing is the termination of an *oeuvre* designed to die with its author; the trope of immortality, of a work surviving its creator, has been suspended. Beckett would rather dismantle his own fictions than claim their endurance through time.

And yet, despite this dwindling, the French editions of

new texts appearing in their thin, white jackets, Beckett's impulse to make of his work an autonomous tradition resembles in its strategies no one more than Joyce and Proust. Nor is this really surprising, given Beckett's close personal relations with Joyce (some portions of *Finnegans Wake* were transcribed in his own hand, and he collaborated in the French translation of the Anna Livia Plurabelle chapter under Joyce's direction); moreover, his first substantial work had been the monograph on Proust, published in 1930. A year earlier, he had contributed an essay, 'Dante . . . Bruno. Vico . . . Joyce', to the famous collaborative exegesis of *Finnegans Wake,* later collected in *Our Exagmination round His Factification for Incamination of Work in Progress.* In light of his later decision to write in both English and French, composing two separate literatures, the convergence of Joyce and Proust becomes crucial.

With Joyce, Beckett's affinities are more obvious; Hugh Kenner has argued that 'Beckett is the heir of Joyce as Joyce is the heir of Flaubert, each Irishman having perceived a new beginning in the impasse to which his predecessor seemed to have brought the form of fiction'. Joyce, then, in conceiving a work which could recapitulate our experience of consciousness in history, and which could have no possible successor, can be said to have concluded the tradition of the European novel. *Finnegans Wake* subsumes within its borders the international character of Modernism, collective, encyclopedic, multilingual.

Flaubert once expressed the desire to write 'a book about nothing, a book without external support which would sustain itself by the internal power of its style as the earth is suspended in the air'. Beckett later detected this ambition in Joyce, whose 'writing is not *about* something; *it is that something itself*'. And Beckett's own writings in French after 1945 owe a great deal to this legacy of pure style, which achieves its finest expression in Mallarmé. Beckett once said that he wrote in French 'parce qu'en français c'est plus facile d'ecrire sans style'. Such a remark would seem at first to counter the Flaubertian obsession with style, but what Beckett implies here is a writing in which all traces of 'literature' have disappeared, and been replaced with what has now come to be called *écriture*; so that when Roland Barthes draws attention to 'this precarious moment of History in which literary language persists only the better to sing the necessity of its own death', he intends *écriture*, a 'closed system' of discourse, to be the survivor of literary style. In this, Beckett resembles Ponge, whose 'texts' purport to be no more than explorations of the materiality, the viscous texture of language.

How far this all seems from Joyce and Proust, those masters of the sprawling, elaborate Book! Their place in Beckett's later work only becomes evident when we look to the tradition he has appropriated and made his own, a tradition located in what, speaking of Proust, he names 'the necessity of art'. After the war, Beckett returned from the Unoccupied Zone to Paris (active in the Resistance, he had been forced to retreat there), and retired to his room to write the trilogy; for nearly four years, he lived in a manner that can't escape comparison with Proust, spinning a dense web of remembrance in the voices of several related characters, all sharing in the sickliness of Proust's narrator, and in his obsession with reconstructing past events in all their inexorable complexity.

Despite their dereliction, these Molloys, Malones, and Mahoods are no less educated than the Marcel of *A La Recherche du Temps Perdu*. In a reference to the trial of Madame Bovary, Molloy hears 'what the great Gustave heard, the benches cracking in the Court of Assizes', while in *Malone Dies*, the Lambert family (in the French version, Les Louis), recall Balzac's own autobiographical model, Louis Lambert. Nevertheless, Molloy insists, during a difficult moment in his narrative, 'It is not at this late stage of my relation that I intend to give way to literature', and Malone breaks off a lyrical passage to announce: 'To hell with all this fucking scenery'. This is Beckett's declaration that, like Proust, he will surrender to the necessity to write, but will abjure the writing of 'literature'.

Though Beckett refers to Baudelaire only once in all his work (in *Premier Amour*), the motif of illness, the temptation to 'enthrone my infirmities' is everywhere in evidence. Jacques Rivière said once that Proust died because 'he did not know how to open a window'; it is this capitulation to the condition of an invalid that appears in Baudelaire, in Proust, and in the experience of Symbolism.

Baudelaire's direct echo of Poe, 'anywhere out of this world', has its correlative in Beckett's figures, literary enough to long for burial in the *Pére Lachaise,* yet suffering, in a variation of Proust's asthma, from the 'grand apnoea'; in one of the dialogues with Georges Duthuit, Beckett spoke of 'the disquiet of him who lacks an adversary'. And this is the other malady visible in Baudelaire and Proust: the oppressiveness of modern urban life, oppressive because its true character is concealed from all but the most clever of antagonists. Baudelaire's sense of isolation in the crowd, the world he fashioned on the boulevards, appears in Beckett's Malone, observing 'the people who throng the streets' toward evening:

At this hour then erotic craving accounts for the majority of couples. But these are few compared to the solitaries pressing forward through the throng, obstructing the access to places of amusement, bowed over the parapets, propped against vacant walls. Walter Benjamin, in his remarkable study of Baudelaire, *A Lyric Poet in the Era of High Capitalism,* noted that 'It takes a heroic constitution to live Modernism'. Beckett's characters inherit this resistance to the disease of the modern, which so disfigures human relationships. Their sturdiness and endurance belong more to Baudelaire's resourceful *flâneur* than to the later Symbolists, whose aesthetic depended on the exacerbation of nerves.

But how account for Beckett's defection to the French language after *Murphy, Watt,* and the early stories (collected in *More Pricks Than Kicks*)? There were some precedents: the epoch of English Symbolism borrowed its features from the French (Arthur Symons' *The Symbolist Movement in Literature* becomes the central work in this exchange). Wilde wrote *Salomé* first in French. And Ford Madox Ford had translated *The Good Soldier* into French without even consulting his own original text. Beckett's early work, though, is intensely Joycean, consciously Irish, so that the transition to French seems even more dramatic.

His first fictional work, *More Pricks Than Kicks,* the distillation of an earlier, abandoned novel, *Dream of Fair to Middling Women,* reveals both the broad humour and geographical specificity of Joyce. The protagonist of these ten stories, Belacqua Shuah, is a Trinity student, a wanderer through Dublin, and a sort of comic Stephen Dedalus. More than *Ulysses,* the resemblance here is to *Dubliners,* with its rehearsals of Irish dialect (Beckett has also acknowledged the influence of Synge). But there are scattered explicit imitations of the later Joyce: the inclusion of invitations, dates, and letters; archaic or invented words (cenotheca, aliquots, ebriety); foreign languages; passages of music; borrowed names (Purefoy recalls Joyce's Wilhelmina Purefoy in *Ulysses*); deliberate echoes of Swift; and an immense word compounded of English and German that mimes Joyce's hundred-letter thunderclaps in *Finnegans Wake.*

Murphy, his first published novel (1938), was no less Joycean than the stories: landladies reading A.E.'s *Candle of Vision*; versions of the Ithaca chapter in *Ulysses,* where Joyce organised and parodied scientific knowledge in a manner reminiscent of *Bouvard et Pécuchet* (in *Murphy,* Beckett informs us that 'the moon, by a strange coincidence full and at perigee, was 29,000 miles nearer the earth than it had been for four years'); an extravagance of jokes and Irish banter. Beckett's apprenticeship to Joyce was calculated and intense, from 1929, when he came to Paris, until the publication of the trilogy, by which time he was writing exclusively in French.

Even in *Watt* (1942-44), where the weird, repetitive mode that later came to dominate his work was first unveiled, there are obvious Joycean elements: disruption of the text by spaces and musical notation; the long, elaborate sentences incorporating all possible explanations of an event; Watt's odd internal monologues that echo Leopold Bloom's.

The novel, set in the Ireland Beckett remembered from his childhood, is no less localised than Joyce's own Dublin, and his characters talk in loquacious Irish voices not heard again in Beckett's writing until the radio play, *All That Fall*, of 1957.

In these earlier works, Beckett's ambivalence toward Ireland, like Joyce's, was expressed in a close attention to detail, and in the portrait of Irish history as an experience rooted in oppressive politics and religion. Both Joyce and Beckett, in their Paris exile, devoted themselves to the reconstruction of their abandoned nation, the plotting of Dublin streets and landmarks, and both examined their own backgrounds in considerable depth. Beckett's Ireland is more opaque than Joyce's, his explicit references obviously fewer; nevertheless, the same events that excited Yeats and Joyce appear in *Murphy*, even if in a parodic rather than solemn manner.

Where Yeats had applauded, with some reserve, the Easter Rebellion, and commemorated its heroes, and where Joyce had seen in Parnell Ireland's 'Uncrowned King', Beckett satirised the intensity of feeling generated by Ireland's embattled past; Neary, a character in *Murphy*, is observed 'in the General Post Office, contemplating from behind the statue of Cuchulain . . . Suddenly he flung aside his hat, sprang forward, seized the dying hero by the thighs and began to dash his head against his buttocks, such as they are.'

Joyce's hatred of what he has Simon Dedalus call 'an unfortunate priestridden race', of Ireland, 'the sow that eats her own farrow', competed with his loyalties, just as Yeats had both ranted against and celebrated his country, often in a single breath; Beckett, like Yeats a member, not of the Ascendancy, but of the Protestant middleclass, noted once that Protestantism 'had no more depth than an old school tie'. Even so, the portrait of Father Ambrose in *Molloy* reveals a hostility toward those religious institutions (in this case, Catholic) which had made Ireland so moribund.

Adaline Glasheen, in a fine essay on 'Joyce and the Three Ages of Parnell', suggested that Joyce, in his later work, 'had come to see that spiritual sickness is not localised or Irish, but common to all men everywhere'; and it was this insight, evident in the bleak landscape of the trilogy, that led Beckett to universalise the situations he treated, to withdraw from the later work all but a few traces of the more specific Ireland of *Murphy* and the earlier stories, leaving only the distillation of his own mental experience.

Conor Cruise O'Brien has proposed that Irishness 'is not primarily a question of birth or blood or language. It is the condition of being involved in the Irish situation, and usually of being mauled by it.' In this sense, Beckett has drawn from Ireland a number of characteristics that he shares with Synge, the sprawl and wit of Irish speech, with Yeats, a story-telling ability, and with Joyce, among whose cherished traits were 'silence, exile, and cunning'.

When Beckett began writing in French, he continued to exploit some of the more conventional narrative elements of the novel. *Mercier et Camier* (the first work of Beckett's to be composed in French, with the exception of a few poems and the translation of *Murphy*) relates the journey of two characters through some indeterminate landscape. Their dialogues, like those of Bouvard and Pécuchet, are bewildered and abstract; every third chapter offers a 'résumé des deux châpitres précédents' not unlike Flaubert's abbreviated lists of adventures in his two protagonists' lives. Here, too, despite the absence of a specific plot or situation, an episodic development could be discerned, and there was a coherence to their comic meditations:

What have we done to God he said.

We have denied him, said Camier.

You will not make me believe that his rancour goes to these lengths, said Mercier.

And in *Premier Amour*, written the same year, Beckett produced a masterpiece of storytelling. This novella, the last of his works to be told from the vantage of a younger man, belongs more among Beckett's novels in English; like the earliest stories, *Premier Amour* involves a reclusive and somewhat distracted narrator who recalls his unfortunate affair with a woman encountered on the banks of a river. He divulges only that neither of them were French, that he had been evicted from his house following the death of his father and had then moved in with the woman, who supported them by prostitution. The strange affair ends, and he leaves her apartment, having decided that 'l'amour, cela ne se commande pas' (love doesn't depend upon our will).

The direction of Beckett's own life can be detected here; well-educated and more urbane than the later protagonists, the dour speaker admits: 'J'avais lu des romans, en prose et en vers, sous la direction demon tuteur, en anglais, en français, en italien, en allemand.' And elsewhere: 'Oui, je regrette, j'avais de la lecture.' After resigning from Trinity, where he had been an instructor, Beckett spent several years travelling through Europe; his self-imposed exile, like Joyce's, was a condition expressed in figures like Belacqua Shuah and the narrator of *Premier Amour,* who suggests, 'Bricoler, c'est encore une chose possible.'

Lévi-Strauss, in *The Savage Mind,* describes the bricoleur as someone 'adept at performing a large number of diverse tasks', but whose 'universe of instruments is closed . . . the rules of his game are always to make do with "whatever is at hand", that is to say with a set of tools and materials which is always finite'.

In Beckett's case, this finite set is language, which articulates its own borders; it could be conjectured that Beckett had been oppressed by the virtual infinitude of English, with its excessive richness, its diversity of idioms, and so turned to French because it possessed such stringent limits. Joyce's solution, in *Finnegans Wake,* had been to circumvent these limits, invading other languages, inventing words, expanding ordinary grammar until it was capable of embracing several tenses at once. Beckett's, stated in *Premier Amour,* was to become a 'roi sans sujets':

La chose qui m'intéressait moi . . . c'était la supination cérébrale, l'assoupissement de l'idée de moi et de l'idée de ce petit résidu de vétilles empoisonnantes qu'on appelle le non-moi, et même le monde, par paresse.

John Fletcher, in his book on *The Novels of Samuel Beckett,* has provided a close reading of Beckett's French style in its earliest stages, showing how gallicisms had begun to surface in his English prose, and how traces of awkwardness in the

French of the *Nouvelles* (1946) were excised in later editions. What Fletcher's account reveals is the complexity of Beckett's transition from English to French, a transition which resulted in the location and refinement of a voice anxious to hear, 'beyond the fatuous clamour, the silence of which the universe is made'. With the trilogy, Beckett turns to the first-person mode of narrative introduced in *Premier Amour,* and so enters the dense, reductionist world of the later prose.

George Steiner has noted 'Beckett's thinness, his refusal to see in language and literary form adequate realisations of human feeling or society', and it is this conviction that inhabits all his work after 1945, when he wonders, 'What's the matter with my head, I must have left it in Ireland, in a saloon, it must be there still, lying on the bar'; having chosen to compose in French, Beckett abandoned the musical Irish lilt of Joyce and Synge. Nothing of Ireland would remain once the trilogy was complete, unless the 'desolate heaven' of Yeats.

Beckett's narrator in *The Calmative,* collected in *Nouvelles et Textes Pour Rien,* announces, 'we are in a skull'; it is from this hermetic chamber that all the later work issues. The characters in the trilogy share in a condition of impossible solitude, alone, like their author, in rooms where nothing reverberates except Memory, 'the sensation itself, annihilating every spatial and temporal restriction' (from the monograph on Proust). However opaque their situation, Molloy, Malone, Mahood, even the Unnamable, are storytellers, aware of each other and of their place in Beckett's *oeuvre*: 'a gallery of moribunds. Murphy, Watt, Mercier, and all the others'. (Like Balzac's, Beckett's characters appear over and over in the novels, a troupe whose identities are assumed to be well known.)

When Jacques Moran retires to his desk to write a report on Molloy, he begins: 'It is midnight. The rain is beating on the windows.' In the novel's last paragraph, Moran is referred to in the third person, while another voice concludes: 'Then I went back into the house and wrote, It is midnight. The rain is beating on the windows. It was not midnight. It was not raining.' This disclosure dissolves the fiction of the entire novel, just as the last pages of *Malone Dies*, where several inmates of a mental institution are murdered by a madman named Lemuel (Swift is a constant presence in Beckett's work), end in the breakdown of language:

never there he will never
never anything
there
any more

In the same way, Molloy finds it impossible to render his experience coherent: 'It seemed to me that all language was an excess of language.' Hesitant to elucidate what appears impenetrable, the *texture* of a world in which contingencies impose their will, Beckett verifies Wittgenstein's claim: '*Nothing* is lost if one does not seek to say the unsayable. Instead, that which cannot be spoken is —unspeakably — *contained* in that which is said!' The 'Unnamable' of Beckett's novel is a protagonist, but also a felt condition, the expression of necessity: 'Having nothing to say, no words but the words of others, I have to speak. No one compels me to, there is no one, it's an accident, a fact.' Inevitably, the identical nature of accident and fact is what determines Beckett's vantage, from which the violation of Wittgenstein's axiom would appear to be so dangerous; to state what is 'unsayable' is to invent reality rather than elicit its character.

There is a crucial passage in *Malone Dies* where Beckett notes the manner in which the Saposcats, a frail married couple, communicate: 'They had no conversation properly speaking. They made use of the spoken word in much the same way as the guard of a train makes use of his flags, or of his lantern.' Such a metaphor underlies the whole enterprise of structural linguistics and semiology; in particular, Saussure's map of language as a system of signs, where the signifier, or expressive lexicon, mediates the signified, in Roland Barthes' words, a mental representation' of the thing expressed. So that when Beckett complains there is 'nothing to signify', it should be clear that he will no longer operate within the realm of ordinary linguistic discourse. Inscribed in Beckett's trilogy is an obstinate refusal to mean; signs are to be self-referential, their employment no more ambiguous, no less arbitrary than a train-signal.

And yet, there still exist in these novels remnants of place and exact locale; Molloy's Bally is Beckett's Ireland, while Father Ambrose, who dispenses Communion to Moran, possesses the provincial temperament of Joyce's priests. The Unnamable's cadence of speech echoes the vehemence of Swift; on occasion traces of a baroque and formal prose remain, vestiges of Ruskin or Sir Thomas Browne left standing in the ruins of English literature. *The Textes Pour Rien* which follow the trilogy reveal Beckett's increased impatience with language, and his renunciation of those formal properties which once represented the novel. Writing has become, literally, 'wordshit' (in the French version, *fatras*, a somewhat milder epithet); the writer's apprenticeship to words is shown to be a chronicle of lost nerve:

Words, mine was never more than that, than this pell-mell babel of silence and words, my viewless form described as ended, or to come, or still in progress, depending on the words, the moments, long may it last in that singular way.

What Beckett struggles to situate after the trilogy is 'a new no', since, were the voice to cease quite at last, the old ceasing voice, it would not be true'. Steiner has often contended that silence is the central motif of European Modernism, and will summon Webern, Hofmansthai, and Hermann Broch as witnesses to the devastation that has ended in what he calls 'post-culture': 'a strain of barbarism, of profound disillusion with literacy' ushered in by the spectacle of the Nazi Holocaust and hastened by mass culture. Beckett's disposition, despite the near-inarticulate, the diminished tonalities of his work over the last two decades, has been to counter this impulse toward silence.

The 'new no' that becomes clarified in the later texts corresponds to Adorno's gloss: 'To Beckett, as to the Gnostics, the created world is radically evil, and its negation is the chance of another world that is not yet' (*Negative Dialectics*). Ironically enough, then, it's possible to consider the shreds of discourse, the rude, unfinished soliloquys that are Beckett's tactic now, utopian, in that writing promises a way out of the impasse created by modern life, which is, after all, a 'concentration camp' (in Adorno's view). And this is what occupies the disembodied voices of *From an Abandoned Work, Enough, Ping, Imagination Dead Imagine, Lessness,* and *The Lost Ones*: the activity of escape.

Even the thin appearance of these works implies the transience of a condition which poses no hope of respite in this world; there is nothing to be done except survive, always with Kafka's admonition in mind, that 'There is Infinite Hope, but not for us'. These texts disclose the dwindling store of experience that can still be validated and made other than random. Literature is discontinuous, a set of images that exist only to be repudiated. *From an Abandoned Work* (1958) illustrates this tendency: a figure wanders over some adumbrated landscape, falling, struggling up, then pushing on. During this ordeal, he recalls his parents, his education, his eventual dereliction, and a number of images which possess a stubborn importance: the colour white, a white horse, a synaesthetic white 'sound'; 'all has gone but mother in the window, the violence, rage and rain'. The voice still manages to achieve moments of lyrical utterance, though, before lapsing into repetition.

The thirteen pages of *From an Abandoned Work* are all that remain of a novel initiated in 1955 and, in a literal sense, abandoned later on. What Hugh Kenner calls the 'complex hermetic miseries' of this text elaborate a theme that has no resolution. Like Ping, a four-page fragment collected twelve years later in *No's Knife* (the title is drawn from the thirteenth 'text for nothing', where Beckett hears 'the screaming silence of no's knife in yes's wound'), *From an Abandoned Work* subscribes to Valéry's theory that a work is never completed, only abandoned in the midst of its composition. In a preface to the 1967 edition, the editors note: '*Ping* is all that is left of a novel that Mr. Beckett started on in late 1965.' It seems reasonable to say, then, that the texts after 1950 encounter a problem not entirely deliberate; since their development is entropic, tending toward a reduced state of consciousness, these works would appear to stipulate their own eventual disappearance.

The dissolution of grammar, the reduction of language to mere sound notation, places Beckett's writing within the domain of contemporary criticism in France, where discussion no longer approaches an imaginative work as literature, but as *écriture*. The text has become an example, a literary artifact encircled by hermeneutics. Its intent is to provide a point of departure for speculation about linguistics, critique *de conscience*, and phenomenology.

The consequence of such practices is, of course, that literature forfeits its own interpretive capacities; where once it acted as a lens through which the social world could be magnified or distorted by the writer's own sensibility, now the work of art imitates theories of criticism, serving as a pretext for their otherwise unfocused energies. This explains why the progressive diminution of Beckett's work has been accompanied by the most elaborate criticism ever devoted to a contemporary (Kenner concludes his discussion of *Come and Go*, a miniature 'dramaticule', with the observation that he has written 'almost three times as many words as the text contains'), and why it requires the technical, immense apparatus of contemporary French criticism to support its lean structure.

Another feature of such enterprises is their claim to science; what are called in France *les sciences humaines* have increasingly taken over the procedures of science. Structuralism in linguistics, anthropology, and psychoanalysis tends to construct exact and technical models, as if to refute any suspicion that such disciplines are still speculative or subjective. With science and its technological resources threatening to render imagination tautological (Adorno identifies in Beckett s *End Game* the notion that 'there really is not so much to be feared any more'), the only choice available to the writer who wishes to record this impingement of the actual upon the imagined is to appropriate science as a metaphor. So Beckett has erased from his texts those very features of literature which once made it capable of transcendence: fictions; imaginative re-creations of history; invented lives.

His later texts plot a world circumscribed by mathematics. A remark he made once about the painter Jack Yeats informs his own work: 'He brings light, as only the great dare to bring light, to the issueless predicament of existence, reduces the dark where there might have been, mathematically at least, a door.' To locate this door demands the rigour of mathematics, and Beckett directs us, in *Imagination Dead Imagine*, to 'omit islands, waters, azure, verdure': in other words, all that represents the world in a figurative manner. Rather, we discover ourselves in a rotunda, 'Diameter three feet, three feet from ground to summit of the vault. Two diameters at right angles AB CD divide the white ground into two semicircles ACB BDA.'

And *The Lost Ones* (*Le Dépeupleur*, 1970) inhabit a cylinder fifty meters round and eighteen high, from which escape seems possible, though none of the two hundred 'bodies' ever achieve it. *Enough* (1965) is Beckett's last attempt to report even the semblance of a story, though the discourse is entirely mathematical, expressed in what Kenner calls 'geometrical visualisations'; the narrative, told in the first person, relates the prolonged journey of a couple whose ages are unspecified, and the desertion of the other. Obsessive calculations of the distance travelled, 'Whole ternary numbers in this way to the third power sometimes in downpours of rain', dominate his recollections.

Lessness, Beckett's most recent published prose, announced a further diminution of landscape; the transition between 'subject object subject object' noted in *How It Is* has its counterpart in serial music, with its total organisation of the tone row.

In the twenty-four paragraphs of *Lessness*, each sentence is repeated once, and the sixty sentences that compose the work are divided in tens, within which each set features a recurrent word or phrase. There is no longer any question of episode or even voice; *Ping* has no verbs, and is orchestrated with an equivalent of rests: 'ping silence ping over'. Where, in *How It*

Is, the absence of punctuation allows us to arrange the phrases to form variant readings, the later texts refuse even this modest anarchy, and insist on the suppression of randomness.

It could be said that Beckett has worked out the consequences of Modernism, producing the companion to Rauschenberg's white canvases. To wish that he had continued to write in the verbal, anecdotal tradition of Irish literature, or embroidered Proust, would be nostalgic; both *Finnegans Wake* and *A La Recherche du Temps Perdu* were the last comprehensive works in their respective literatures, when the totality of lived experience could be deposited in a book.

Mallarmé had conceived a similar project, proposing that *Tout, au monde, existe pour aboutir à un livre*. Beckett's recent work constitutes the residuum of this Livre. There were moments, though, when I read these texts with the hope that, like Borges' Funes the Memorious, who devised a system in which all numbers were given special titles, he would provide us, not simply with ciphers, but with names to revive and enhance their value.

Bibliography

John Fletcher, *Samuel Beckett's Art*, London: Chatto and Windus, 1967.

Ruby Cohn, *A Casebook on 'Waiting for Godot'*, New York: Grove Press, 1967.

Ronald Hayman, *Samuel Beckett*, London: Heinemann, 1968.

Michael Robinson, *The Long Sonata of the Dead: A study of Samuel Beckett*, London: Rupert Hart-Davis, 1970.

Raymond Federman and John Fletcher, *Samuel Beckett: His Work and His Critics*, Berkley (CA): University of California Press, 1970

Melvin J. Friedman (ed) *Samuel Beckett Now: Critical Approaches to his Novels, Poetry, and Plays*, Chicago: University of Chicago Press, 1970.

Francis Doherty, *Samuel Beckett*, London: Hutchinson, 1971.

Colin Duckworth, *Angels of Darkness: Dramatic Effect in Beckett with Special Reference to Ionesco*, New York: Barnes and Noble, 1972.

John Fletcher, *Beckett: A Study of his Plays*, New York: Hill and Wang, 1972.

Brian Finney, *'How It Is': A Study of Samuel Beckett's Later Fiction*, London: Covent Garden Press, 1972.

Al Alvarez, *Samuel Beckett*, New York: Viking, 1973.

Ruby Cohn, *Back to Beckett*, Princeton: Princeton University Press, 1973.

Hugh Kenner, *A Reader's Guide to Samuel Beckett*, 1973.

H. Porter Abbott, *The Fiction of Samuel Beckett*, Los Angeles: University of California Press, 1973.

Ruby Cohn (ed), *Samuel Beckett: A Collection of Criticism*, New York: McGraw-Hill, 1975.

Hannah-Case Copeland, *Art and the Artist in the works of Samuel Beckett*, Paris: Mouton, 1975.

James Eliopulos, *Samuel Beckett's Dramatic Language*, The Hague: Mouton, 1975.

Katherine Worth (ed), *Beckett the Shape Changer*, London: Routledge, 1975.

John Pilling, *Samuel Beckett*, 1976.

S.E. Gontarski, *Beckett's 'Happy Days': A Manuscript Study*, Columbus: Ohio State University Press, 1977.

Beryl Fletcher *et al*, *A Student's Guide to The Plays of Samuel Beckett*, London: Faber and Faber, 1978.

James Knowlson and John Pilling, *Frescoes of the Skull: The Later Prose and Drama of Samuel Beckett*, 1979.

Robin J. Davis, *Samuel Beckett: Checklist and Index of his Published Works*, Stirling: The Library: University of Stirling, 1979.
